THE WORLD AIRCRAFT INDUSTRY

THE WORLD AIRCRAFT INDUSTRY

DANIEL TODD and JAMIE SIMPSON

CROOM HELM
London & Sydney
AUBURN HOUSE PUBLISHING COMPANY
Dover, Massachusetts

© 1986 Daniel Todd and Jamie Simpson
Croom Helm Ltd, Provident House, Burrell Row,
Beckenham, Kent BR3 1AT
Croom Helm Australia Pty Ltd, Suite 4, 6th Floor,
64-76 Kippax Street, Surry Hills, NSW 2010, Australia

British Library Cataloguing in Publication Data

Todd, Daniel
    The world aircraft industry.
    1. Aircraft industry
    I. Title II. Simpson, Jamie
    338.7'62913   HD9711.A2

    ISBN 0-7099-2486-0

© 1986 Todd, Daniel,
Auburn House Publishing Company,
14 Dedham Street, Dover,
Massachusetts 02030

Library of Congress Cataloging in Publication Data

Todd, Daniel.
    The world aircraft industry.
    Includes bibliographical references.
    1. Aircraft industry. I. Simpson, Jane. II. Title.
HD9711.A2T63   1986   338.4'762913334   85-26751
ISBN 0-86569-141-X

·1986 Todd, Daniel, Auburn House Publishing Company,
14, Dedham Street, Dover, Massachusetts 02030

Printed and bound in Great Britain
by Billing & Sons Limited, Worcester.

CONTENTS

TABLES

The World Aircraft Industry

FIGURES

ACKNOWLEDGEMENTS

The authors wish to thank the University of Manitoba Research Grants Committee for backing their preliminary interest in the area of aerospace and its implications for national and regional development. This book is an outgrowth of those first cursory explorations and has benefited from the discussions held with industry and government representatives which were made possible through the original project.

The second of us, Simpson, wishes to express his gratitude to his family and Tara. The two of us are indebted to Marjorie Halmarson for her able draughtsmanship.

Chapter One

OVERVIEW OF THE INDUSTRY

In everyday usage the aircraft industry is generally
lumped with the 'aerospace' sector. A loose coinage,
aerospace embraces aeroengines, avionics (aviation
electronics), missiles, and space vehicles in addition to the manufacture of aircraft. Indeed, the aircraft industry in its present form is really focused
on the airframe producers, that is to say, the manufacturers of aircraft fuselages and wings who also
undertake the installation of power plants and all
the other components and systems, manufactured elsewhere, but brought to the airframe plant for final
assembly. The aircraft industry is in truth a part-
fabricator, part-assembly operation which constitutes
perhaps the most visible aspect of the much more
amorphous aerospace sector.
    It is worth stressing, however, that the air-
craft industry is not necessarily the most important
part of the aerospace sector notwithstanding its
obvious pivotal role. In Canada's case, for example,
it is aeroengines and avionics (navigation and flight
systems and aircraft flight simulators; to name but
two) which are looked upon to counter the country's
balance of payments deficit in finished aircraft.[1]
Between one quarter and one third of Britain's entire
aerospace exports are aircraft parts and subsystems
and it is easy to make a case for the view that it is
this component of the aerospace sector which accords
the UK its greatest comparative advantage.[2] Not only
does it underwrite the airframe industry, but it
enables Britain to enjoy a level of aerospace infras-
tructure not available to other European nations.
Arguably, UK components producers have displayed the
greatest success of any foreign aerospace enterprises
in penetrating the vital US market: Lucas Aerospace,
to name but one example, has a production plant in
New Jersey geared to the provision of electrical systems for US Army helicopters.[3] In truth, the bulk of

1

the aerospace industry falls into the parts, systems, or components category; leaving only a handful of airframe or aeroengine manufacturers (Figure 1.1). Yet, when the diverse range of products of these components or so-called Tier II firms is contemplated – aircraft instruments, supplies and accessories, avionics, communications equipment, computer systems, gears and transmissions, landing gear, navigation systems, satellites, welding and metal finishing and so on – it is evident why aerospace is an equivocal grouping among the set of industrial categories. Clearly, several of the suppliers in question manufacture products that are not unique to the aircraft and missiles sector; thus the obvious query arises as to how far they are truly aerospace enterprises in contrast to, say, telecommunications or vehicles enterprises. Their common focus is, of course, the airframe industry (part of the so-called Tier I of aerospace) to which they supply at least some of their production. In the same vein, the term 'aerospace' is sufficiently broad to cover firms whose prime interest is aircraft overhaul and repair (the Tier III operations). Likewise, these firms are ultimately dependent upon the airframe and aeroengine manufacturers though at one step further removed than the components producers. They are, in short, best viewed as the 'service' aspect of the aerospace sector.

The aim of this book is to concentrate attention on the airframe producers precisely because they are the core of the aerospace sector. Aeroengines are delivered to the plant of the airframe firm for installation, as are the parts emanating from the Tier II enterprises. The only Tier I operation independent of the airframe assembly outcome is that denoted in Figure 1.1 as the Missiles and Space Vehicles group and, arguably, this activity owes as much for its genesis to the automotive and ordnance industries as it does to the aircraft industry.[4] It receives attention in this book only in as much as it comes to bear on the organisation of aircraft enterprises. By the same token, aeroengine firms and Tier II and Tier III operations are the object of peripheral treatment except where they have a direct bearing on the actions of airframe producers. It is hoped, in consequence, to provide an understanding of the activities of the aircraft industry without clouding the issue with concerns which are more germane to electrical or mechanical engineering sectors. Before singling out the airframe producers, however, it is important to review the global distribution of the aerospace sector; the context within which the

Figure 1.1 :   The Aerospace Sector

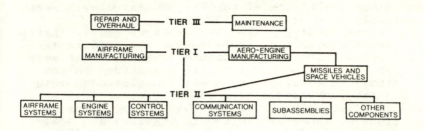

manufacturers of aircraft must function.

GLOBAL DISTRIBUTION

The Advanced-Industrial Countries

By far the largest of the world's aerospace industries, the US industry, employed 1.2 million people
(at the end of 1980), utilised 1,150 establishments,
and accounted for sales worth $74.7 billion (in
1983). It was responsible for 2.2 per cent of the
country's GNP and was consistently the largest manufacturing employer since data were first reported on
an aerospace basis in 1959.[5] The industry was a
'star' among American industries on several counts,
including its contribution to exports, research and
development (R & D), and, not least, its record of
accelerating growth. On the first count, aerospace
displayed a massive surplus in the balance of payments: in 1980, for example, US aerospace exports
amounted to $11.7 billion whereas imports were placed
at $1.6 billion; while by 1983 the balance of trade
stood at $12.7 billion or the best of any industry.
An aerospace firm, Boeing, has the highest exports to
total sales ratio (43.3 per cent) of the top 50 US
exporting companies in all industries.[6] Secondly, the
Aerospace Industries Association estimated that the
industry's investment in R & D equalled 23.7 per cent
of its sales, a figure far larger than the electrical
and electronics industry, the next largest investor
with a value equivalent to 7.3 per cent of sales.[7]
Thirdly, the industry's sales have been growing
steadily, increasing by 11.5 per cent between 1982
and 1983 alone, and achieving an annual growth rate

of 3.5 per cent throughout much of the 1970s. Such growth has translated into job creation with the industry employing more people in 1980 than it had done since the height of the Vietnam War eleven years previously.

Interestingly, little over half of the 1.21 million aerospace workers in 1981 were employed in airframe and aeroengine manufacture: the remainder were occupied in Tier II and Tier III operations on the one hand, and missiles and space vehicles manufacture on the other. Consequently, complete aircraft accounted for sales levels of about three times the magnitude of those attributed to missiles and space. A breakdown of US aerospace export sales for 1979 (Table 1.1) underscores the importance of aircraft production in American international trade relative to the contributions made by the other constituents of the aerospace sector. Moreover, that table indicates the pre-eminence of civil aircraft exports within the complete aircraft category. American dominance of world jetliner markets through the products of Boeing, McDonnell-Douglas(MD) and Lockheed is the major factor on this score. One estimate implied that of 259,640 workers directly employed in commercial aircraft manufacture, no less than 104,000 were working on export orders and, what is more, every 100 of those jobs was responsible for creating 163 in other manufacturing and services.[8] Only in recent years has the US emphasis on civil aircraft exports been challenged by concerted efforts to sell military aircraft, for, traditionally, the lion's share of combat machines has been earmarked for the US armed forces. Yet, after the mid-1970s, the US Government actively supported attempts by American aircraft firms to sell combat aircraft abroad in anticipation of sizeable benefits. It was suggested, for example, that if General Dynamics could supply, in the form of the F-16 , some 2,000 of the 'Free World's' requirement for 5,000 fighters, the USA would benefit to the tune of 900,000 jobs, $9 billion in balance-of-payments receipts, $6 billion in tax receipts, and would recover $470 million of its R & D expenditures.[9]

The importance of export sales from the aerospace sector has not been lost on the countries of the EEC; which together rival the Soviet bloc as the second concentration of global aerospace activity. In 1975 the EEC accounted for $8.25 billion of the Western World's $35.3 billion in comparison to the $24.04 billion contributed by the USA (Table 1.2). This 23 per cent share of the non-communist market was double the EEC penetration of the market of 1960: indication enough of the enhanced competitiveness of European

Overview Of The Industry

Table 1.1 :   US Aerospace Exports 1979

Markets	Civil ($ million)	Military ($ million)
Transport aircraft	4,998	–
Light aircraft	650	–
Helicopter	207	–
Other	322	–
Combat aircraft	–	838
Total complete aircraft	6,177	838
Aeroengines	375	74
Aircraft and engine parts	3,220	492
Missiles and parts	–	571
Total	9,772	1,975

Source: Derived from Flight International, 7 February 1981.

aerospace. Indeed, European firms had acquired a one-third share of the world market for combat aircraft and helicopters along with a 32 per cent share of the market for civil light-turbine aeroplanes. However, they had scarcely dented the US hold on jetliner sales, accounting for only nine per cent of the market. Enjoined to make good the discrepancy, the EEC has devoted much collaborative effort to the Airbus family of jetliners. Initial success with the A300 and A310 airliners induced the Europeans to launch the A320 Airbus in 1984. Likely to cost over £2 billion, the UK Government was prepared to add £250 million to the £200 million-plus allocated to the project by BAe, while the French Government, for its part, was prepared to advance £430 million and the West German Government was forthcoming with £395 million.[10] Clearly, the virtual free-hand enjoyed by the Americans in jetliner markets for so long is now at an end.

In terms of individual EEC industries, the onset of the 1960s witnessed the eclipse of the UK by France in aerospace sales (Table 1.2). In 1961 French aerospace exports exceeded those of Britain for the first time: the result of sales of Mirage fighters, Caravelle jetliners, Alouette helicopters and Nord

missiles. At that time, the 85,000 manpower of the
French industry was comprised of 48,400 airframe
workers, 16,400 aeroengine workers, and 20,200 in
other lines.[11] Twenty years later, the French aerospace industry amounted to 150 firms employing
113,000 workers with export sales in excess of £3.3
billion. Composition of 1983 export sales was: complete aircraft (52.9 per cent), helicopters (7.2 per
cent), aeroengines (18.1 per cent), missiles (3.3 per
cent), space (2.7 per cent) and avionics and parts
(15.8 per cent).[12] About 36 per cent of French aerospace exports derived from collaborative projects
mostly with other EEC partners.[13] The largest single
European aerospace manufacturer in terms of turnover
(recording over FFr 13 billion in 1980), Aérospatiale, is a state-owned enterprise employing almost
40,000 which concentrates on airliner, helicopter and
missile production. Conversely, the other major
French airframe producer, Dassault, concentrates most
of its efforts on fighters (the Mirage family), military jet trainers (Alpha Jet) and business jets (Falcon series); and used to be regarded as a classic
example of the effectiveness of the private owner-
designer model in aircraft manufacture.

Employing a larger workforce than the French
(Table 1.3), the aerospace industry in the UK is dominated by the partially state-owned BAe (itself
employing 77,500 in 1983). Organised into aircraft
and missile divisions, BAe assigns particular aeroplane types to specific plants;namely, War-
ton(Preston) for Tornado MRCA and Jaguar fighter-
bombers, Prestwick for Jetstream light turboprop
airliners, Manchester for the BAe 748 turboprop
transport and its ATP successor, Chester for BAe 125
bizjets and Airbus wings, Kingston for Harrier and
Hawk military jets, and Hatfield for the BAe 146 airliner. The enterprise increased its sales by 24 per
cent between 1981 and 1982 to record a figure of just
over £2 billion. About 80 per cent of the firm's
sales were destined for military customers. The only
other UK airframe producers of importance are Shorts
of Belfast, builders of small turboprop transports,
Westland at Yeovil which concentrates entirely on
helicopter manufacture, and PBN on the Isle of Wight,
responsible for the Islander type of light transport.

The third EEC aerospace industry, that of West
Germany, is substantially smaller than the industries
in France and Britain (Table 1.3). In 1982 it
employed about 76,000; of which 26,000 were working
for the MBB enterprise. Gross sales in 1980 stood at
$4.5 billion, of which no less than $1.6 billion was
associated with the Tornado MRCA airframe programme

Table 1.2 :   European and Western World Aerospace
Sales, 1960 and 1975

Country	1960 ($billion)	% of West (rounded)	1975 ($billion)	% of West (rounded)
UK	1.43	7.8	3.55	10.1
France	0.48	2.6	3.61	10.2
West Germany	0.10	0.5	1.43	4.1
Netherlands	0.05	0.3	0.26	0.7
Belgium	0.01	0.0	0.10	0.3
Italy	0.07	0.4	0.59	1.7
EEC total[1]	2.02	11.0	8.25	23.4
Other European	0.05	0.3	0.62	1.8
USA	15.77	85.7	24.04	68.1
Canada	0.40	2.2	0.81	2.3
Japan	0.08	0.4	0.76	2.2
Other	0.10	0.5	0.80	2.3
Western World	18.40		35.30	

Note: 1. Less EEC intra-industry transactions
Source: Aviation Week & Space Technology, 6 June 1977, p.163.

Table 1.3 :   European Aerospace Turnover and Employment

Country	Turnover[1] (ECU millions)	% Change 1970-78	Employment[2] ('000)
France	3482	63	103
UK	3211	45	215
West Germany	1284	-1	56
Italy	523	65	36
Total EEC	8802	41	421
USA	20661	-17	967

Notes: 1. European currency units for 1978 pegged to 1975 rates
        2. 1978 Figures
Source: EEC, The European Aerospace Industry, Brussels 1980.

jointly conducted with the British and Italians, and
a further $450 million stemmed from engine sales
again largely deriving from the MRCA venture.[14] In
fact, the West German aircraft effort was inordinately dependent upon international programmes with
the Tornado (42.5 per cent share) and Airbus
A300/A310 (37.5 per cent share) projects assuming
greatest significance. During 1984–5 the industry
will select a follow-on venture for the Tornado in
order to keep itself occupied into the 1990s: the
five-nation EFA combat aircraft has been touted for
this purpose.[15] The second sizeable West German aircraft manufacturer, Dornier has produced a successful
series of utility transports (models 28, 128 and
228).

Unlike the other EEC producers, Italy has clung
to licence-production of foreign (mainly US) aircraft
designs for the bulk of its aerospace activity. Agusta, for example, builds most of the Bell- Helicopter-Textron models at Cascina Costa and sells them to
areas of the world (primarily the Middle East and
Africa) in which the American licensor is somewhat
unwelcome. While advantageous in so far as it reduces
development costs, such practices require the Italian
enterprise to import from the USA something in the
order of 50 per cent of the value of each helicopter
made.[16] As with Italian industry in general, the
aerospace industry was heavily concentrated in the
North of the country or around Rome. Since 1970, however, the two firms under state operation – Aeritalia
and Agusta – have followed (at government instigation) a policy of expansion in the South. In no
uncertain terms, the Italian Government has attempted
to link the aerospace sector into its strategy for
Southern regional development.

Other European aircraft industries of significance – both inside and outside of the EEC – include
those of Sweden, Spain and Yugoslavia. The first is
particularly noteworthy in light of Sweden's determination to maintain an independent defence-industrial
base which includes a capacity to design and manufacture state-of-the-art combat aircraft. As a result,
Saab-Scania has produced, since World War II, a
series of fighter aircraft (types 29, 32, 35 and 37)
equal to contemporary aircraft emanating from the
great powers. Its technological expertise is currently being exercised in two directions: formulation
of an MRCA to serve as Sweden's next-generation military aeroplane (known as the JAS 39 project) and co-
production with Fairchild of the USA of a light turboprop airliner (the Saab-Fairchild 340). For these
ends, major investments have been underway at the

aerospace complex in Linkoping, including the
erection of a new 270,000m^2 factory for airliner
assembly and a carbon-fibre production facility for
manufacturing the composite materials needed in the
JAS programme.[17] The Netherlands, like Sweden, is
keen on making its presence felt in the small airliner market. Its Fokker firm has built an enviable
reputation in this field with the F-27 and F-28 models. Unable to internalise production of engines and
parts, Fokker has relied on sub-contractors elsewhere
in Europe; the F-28, for example, is about 60 per
cent British supplied, receiving its engines from
Rolls-Royce(R-R) and its wing sections from Shorts.
Final assembly of the F-28 at Schiphol also requires
delivery of fuselage sections, engine nacelles and
empennage from MBB of West Germany.[18] The Spanish
aircraft industry, in similar fashion to Sweden and
the Netherlands, is centred on a single major enterprise; in this case CASA. This state enterprise
acquires 'know-how' through offset agreements with
foreign manufacturers which allows for part-manufac-
ture and assembly in Spain of foreign military aircraft designs (e.g. MD F-18, Northrop F-5, Dassault
Mirage, MBB BO105). It also undertakes a considera-
ble amount of subcontract manufacture for foreign
firms: its Getafe plant building horizontal stabilisers and passenger doors for the A300/A310 Airbus
while similar fixtures are made for Boeing 727 and MD
DC-9 and DC-10 aircraft. Its most recent venture, the
CN-235 light transport, is a joint venture with
Indonesia. In 1981 the firm enjoyed sales of £132
million of which £86 million was attributed to
exports.[19] Yugoslavia also boasts a state aircraft
enterprise - Soko - which again manages to produce
its own designs despite major efforts devoted by the
country to the procurement of foreign (Soviet in this
instance) combat aircraft. Employing 3,000 at four
factories (the largest of which are Mostar and Kra-
guj), Soko has produced the Galeb and Super Galeb
trainer and Jastreb fighter equipped with British
engines, wheels, ejection seats and avionics. It is
currently co-operating with Romania in the production
of an indigenous new-generation fighter.[20]
        Other integral parts of the AIC aerospace sector
are to be found in Canada, Japan and Australia.
While producing its own aircraft designs in two
state-owned firms, Canada depends on the US aircraft
industry for much of its aerospace business, supplying to that country a host of parts and components
ranging downwards from airliner wings. Australia,
likewise, participates in US offset work, although to
a much smaller extent than Canada. The policy of the

Australian Government is to obtain 30 per cent of the
value of foreign aircraft acquisitions for its own
aerospace industry. That industry, in turn, employs
about 6,000 workers centred on three firms: state-
owned Government Aircraft Factories, and privately-
owned HDH and Commonwealth Aircraft Corporation. Only
the first has an indigenous design in the STOL
Nomad.[21] While only a little larger than the Canadian
industry, Japanese aerospace displays much more ambi-
tion. Under the auspices of MITI, investment has
been made available for several long-term projects
aimed at turning Japan into a major player in aerospace. These include the YX modification of the 767
airliner with Boeing, the YXX 150-seat airliner, and
the RJ500 fanjet in co-operation with R-R.[22] Furthermore, Japan has been much more adventurous in supporting large, domestically-designed aircraft programmes; no doubt a legacy of its pre-1945 Imperial
stature. The Nihon Aeroplane Manufacturing Company -
a combination of several firms brought together by
MITI - not only engineered Japan's first turboprop
airliner (the YS-11), but also produced one of the
world's few military jet transport aircraft (the
C-1).[23] By the early 1980s, 25,000 workers were
employed in Japanese aerospace; engaged, in the main,
in the aircraft divisions of the major conglomerates;
namely: MHI (at Nagoya), Kawasaki (Gifu) and Fuji
(Utsunomiya); with IHI (Tanashi) concentrating on
aeroengine production. While largely occupied manufacturing US combat types under licence, these firms
also produce aircraft to their own designs (e.g.
Mitsubishi T-2/F-1/MU-2, Kawasaki XT-4, Fuji
T-1/T-3). The most recent Japanese conglomerate to
take an interest in aerospace, Mitsui, has agreed to
produce the Bell 214ST helicopter in Japan with the
aid of its US designer, Bell-Helicopter-Textron.[24]

The Communist Bloc
Rivalling the USA in the scale of its aerospace
activities, the USSR is reputed to produce 1,800 aircraft per year.[25] The Soviet industry is overwhelmingly geared to defence production: even civil aviation coming under the rubric of the state's defence
posture (with, for example, the state airline Aeroflot being commanded by an Air Force General and having its airliners earmarked as a reserve military
air-portable service). American estimates suggest
that the USSR manufactured 6,100 tactical warplanes
between 1974 and 1982, double the US total, and completed a further 680 such aircraft in 1983-4.[26] The
workforce employed to produce this effort is unknown,

partly because of the secretive attitude of Soviet
aerospace officials and partly because of the Soviet
practice of undertaking diversified manufacturing in
what are ostensibly aircraft plants. In order to
maintain defence-production capability at a high
level, military output has been linked with compatible civilian production (e.g. the manufacture of
tanks and railway rolling stock in the same factory)
with the result that special plant is not underused
and workers skills are continually being honed.[27]
Thus the Kiev factory formerly tasked with building
An-24 transports also makes camping trailers, kitchen-
ware and agricultural implements; the Kharkov plant
responsible for Tu-134 jetliners also turns its
attention to sporting goods and baby carriages; while
the aeroengine factories at Zaporozhye and Perm
produce marine and industrial engines as well.[28]
    Given the overall direction of economic activity
by the state, the Soviet aerospace sector differs
fundamentally from its Western counterparts in sepa-
rating design from production. The former is the
bailiwick of various bureaux which specialise in particular aircraft classes - fighter, bomber, transport, helicopter - and respond to specifications
handed down by military planners. The foremost airframe design bureaux are Tupolev, Antonov, Yakovlev,
Ilyushin and MIG (Migoyan-Gurevich). Tupolev is
renowned for its bomber and jet transport designs,
Antonov for its transports, Ilyushin for its attack
aircraft and the other two for their fighter aircraft. In addition, Mil is entrusted with helicopter
design. Successful testing of the resultant designs
leads to the allocation of the necessary production
facilities by the Ministry of Aircraft Production.
Operating about 40 Tier I plants, the Ministry dele-
gates five of these for fighter production, nine for
bombers and large transports (including airliners),
ten for helicopters and light aircraft, and another
ten for aeroengine production.[29] To all intents and
purposes, the aircraft plants can be divided into a
Western group and an Eastern group. The former occurs
in the traditional industrial heartland of the USSR
and, by and large, dates from Stalin's first and second Five-Year Plan initiatives (1928-32 and 1933-5
respectively). Located at Riga, Leningrad, Moscow,
Taganrog, Rybinsk, Voronezh, Zaporozhye, Kharkov,
Gorki, Saratov and Kazan; these facilities suffered
extensive damage in World War II. Since rebuilt and
enlarged, they continue as a vital component of the
Soviet aerospace sector; Voronezh, for instance, formerly building the An-10 turboprop freighter and the
less-than-successful Tu-144 SST whereas Saratov was

reputed to produce one Yak-40 feederliner every second day.[30] Supplemented by the Eastern group as an emergency war measure, the plants beyond the Urals at Irkutsk, Semenovka, Tomsk, Novosibirsk, Sverdlovsk, Tashkent, Khabarovsk and Kuznetsk have assumed increasing importance in postwar years.[31] The process of geographic dispersion of the industry has not ceased; for factories have been established at Kuibischev, Tiflis, Ascha and other sites in the periphery of the USSR. A latecomer was the An-24 transport-aircraft factory at Ulan-Ude in southern Siberia created in the 1960s.[32]

Although mainly concerned to supply the aviation needs of Soviet and Warsaw Pact forces and airlines, the Soviet aircraft industry has emphasised exports to other countries in recent years. Undertaken both to acquire foreign currency earnings (especially from OPEC states) and bolster Soviet influence abroad, the sale of aircraft also alleviates the R & D and production costs burden shouldered by the USSR aerospace sector. Hard currency payments have been received from Iraq, Libya and Algeria in return for the best-selling Mig-21 fighter.[33] It has been estimated that 27 per cent of the Soviet Union's total output of combat aircraft was exported in the years 1967-73; 29 per cent during 1974-8, and a sharply increased 41 per cent for the 1977-80 period.[34] Soviet aircraft are comparatively cheap by virtue of their relative simplicity in contrast to most Western equipment and this has been a principal factor in their export success.

The aircraft industries in the Warsaw Pact states are virtual satellites of the Soviet aerospace sector. For the most part, they produce copies of aircraft designed in the USSR and their contributions to the aggregate Warsaw Pact armoury are quite substantial. The Czech Aero Trust, for instance, produced about three Mig-21 fighters each month and, at its peak during the Korean War, was capable of making three Mig-15s per day. Indeed, the East European aircraft industries are so integrated into the Soviet aerospace sector that they have been allowed to produce specific aircraft types not only for their own air requirements but in order to fulfil Soviet needs too. The Polish PZL works, for example, is authorised to manufacture general-aviation aircraft for the alliance and also utility helicopters such as the Mi-2 (Okecie and Mielec turning out a prodigious number of agricultural aircraft). The Czechs, in turn, employ much of their 28,000 strong aerospace workforce on the production of jet trainers for Pact air forces at Vodochody and Kunovice.. The initial

model, the L-29, had a production run of over 3,000
aircraft and was replaced on the production lines
after 1974 by the L-39. Only the Romanian aircraft
industry functions independently of Soviet directives
and it has flourished as a consequence of joint ventures with Yugoslavia and Britain. While relatively
small, the industry in Romania has managed to produce
a derivative of the BAe 111 jetliner and a R-R Viper
powered jet strike-fighter.

China is, of course, an autonomous member of the
communist bloc and has gone its own way since 1960 in
aerospace as in everything else. Nevertheless, its
aircraft industry is still wedded to Soviet technology in terms of aeroplane design and production methods.[35] The Xian factory in Shensi Province, for example, manufactures modifications of the An-24
transport (called the Y-7) and the Tu-16 bomber (the
H-6 in Chinese designation), while Hanzhong builds
the An-12 tactical transport (as the Y-8). In a similar manner, the main Shenyang aerospace complex produces the F-6, a derivative of the Mig-19 fighter
(also built at Tianjin); while Nanchang is tasked
with producing an attack version of this aircraft
known as the A-5.[36] All these types are powered by
Soviet-designed Tumansky engines. It is only since
the late 1970s that China has been able to break away
from Soviet influence in its aircraft designs. In
large measure, this new freedom arose out of agreements with Western aerospace firms for the transfer
of technology. Aeroengine builder R-R was a prominent player in this process, allowing the Chinese to
licence-build the Spey turbine at a specially-built
plant at Hsian.[37] Other UK companies provided back-up
facilities.[38] By 1980, China was able to fly its own
jetliner, the Y-10, (looking remarkably like a Boeing
707) from the Shanghai aircraft factory equipped with
US JT3D-7 engines and was intent on flying a new
fighter - the Shenyang J-8 - powered by Spey turbofans. The industry had even been co-opted into the US
airliner programme; providing simple machine parts
for Boeing's 737 and 747 models and landing gears for
MD's super 80.[39] The latter type is to be assembled
in China by the Shanghai Aircraft Industrial Corporation to meet the needs of the country's airline. It
will join another US type, the Bell 412 helicopter,
in being assembled domestically (at Harbin in this
instance). Chinese factories operate as self-suffi-
cient entities, containing engine works, ejection
seat plants and landing-gear assembly operations
within the one complex. Such integrated production is
necessary owing to the absence of Tier II and Tier
III enterprises in the country: a state of affairs

that China shares with other NICs.

The Newly-Industrialising Countries

The aircraft industry is promoted in NICs for two
reasons: in order to further export-led manufacturing
expansion in the first place, and to safeguard the
supply of military hardware in the second. The former
ploy is best exemplified by Brazil and Indonesia and,
from the socialist camp, Romania. Those national
industries are the subject of scrutiny elsewhere in
this book (Chapter 8) and, therefore, will not be
dwelt upon here. Most NICs, however, engage in aircraft manufacture for the second reason. Table 1.4
indicates the range of nations falling into this category. All of those countries persist in aircraft
manufacture notwithstanding excessive costs and often
inefficient production methods because national
security concerns are paramount. Dependence on foreign suppliers carries with it an element of vulner-
ability to embargoes of spare parts. Israel, for
example, opted to develop its own fighter aircraft
after 1967 when France slapped a ban on the export of
weapons to the Middle Eastern adversaries. The first
effort of IAI at Lod Airport resulted in the Nesher
in 1969; a virtual copy of the French Mirage. Subsequent marrying of a modified Mirage airframe and a
US J79 engine resulted in the Kfir flying in 1974.
Complementing the fighter programme was the Arava
STOL transport (first flight in 1969) and the Westwind executive jet (developed from a US design).
Currently, IAI is working on a new-generation
fighter, the Lavi, with the aid of US funds, components and engines.[40] Under the wing of the Defence
Ministry, IAI mostly produces for the military market
(77 per cent of its output) and employs about 18,000
workers. It is supplemented by over one hundred parts
and avionics firms and has a subsidiary - MBT Weapon
Systems - devoted to the production of the locally-
designed Gabriel missile.[41] South Africa, for comparable reasons, has attempted to become self-suffi-
cient in warplane provision. Its Atlas Aircraft
Company, a branch of the state Armaments Development
and Production Corporation, has built Mirage fighters
and Impala attack aircraft under licence from France
and Italy respectively and has a workforce of about
3,500.
   While not prone to embargoes to the same degree
as Israel and South Africa, the largest Arab nation -
Egypt - has attempted over the years to establish a
warplanes industry for similar pressing national
security reasons. In the 1950s inspiration for the

Table 1.4 : Aircraft Capability of NICs (Licence
Production or Indigenous Design)

Country	Jet Fighter Production	Helicopter	Jet Trainers or Light Attack Aircraft
Turkey	licence		
Argentina	–	licence	indigenous
Brazil	joint design with Italy	licence	licence
Chile	–	–	licence
Peru.	–	–	licence
Venezuela	–	licence	–
Nigeria	–	licence	–
South Africa	licence	licence	licence
Egypt	licence	licence	licence
Iran	–	licence	–
Israel	indigenous	licence	licence
India	indigenous	licence	indigenous
Indonesia	–	licence	–
North Korea	licence	–	–
South Korea	licence	licence	–
Pakistan	–	licence	–
Philippines	–	licence	–
Taiwan	licence	licence	indigenous

Source: Partly Derived from N.Ball and M.Leitenberg (eds).
The Structure of the Defense Industry, Table 10.1,
pp. 314-15.

Egyptian industry came from German and Austrian expa-
triate designers: the unsuccessful Ha-300 delta-
winged fighter was the brainchild of Willi Messerschmitt while its turbojets were designed by Prof.
Brandner. However, by the mid-1970s the aircraft
plants at Helwan and Heliopolis were largely denuded
of new construction.[42] It was only after the rapprochement with the West that the Egyptian industry
was retooled; albeit to assemble aircraft and parts
designed elsewhere. Starting with small assemblies
for the Dassault Falcon 50 executive jet and Aérospatiale Puma and Gazelle helicopters, Helwan gradu-
ated to assembling the latter type as well as the

Franco-German Alpha Jet and is about to produce the
Brazilian-designed Tucano turboprop trainer.[43] About
7,300 people are employed by the Arab Organisation
for Industrialisation in airframe and aeroengine work
at Helwan and this centre will begin to assemble the
Mirage 2000 - the most complex of Dassault's family
of fighters - by the end of 1986.[44]

The largest NIC aircraft industry is that of
India. Under the auspices of state enterprise HAL,
about 40,000 workers are devoted to meeting the country's huge military aviation needs. Most of this
effort is, in conformity with other NICs, aimed at
licence-production.[45] The sophisticated Anglo-French
Jaguar fighter-bomber is, for example, produced at
Bangalore along with its Adour engine. An associated
avionics plant for the aircraft's navigational and
attack systems has been established at Korwa in Uttar
Pradesh.[46] To display even-handedness, as it were,
the latest Soviet technology has been adopted in the
form of licence-production of the Mig-21/27: the
airframe emanating from Nasik, the engine from Kora-
put and the avionics from Balanagar. Military transports (initially BAe 748 and now Dornier 228) are the
province of the Kanpur plant. Similar defence-ori-
ented production is underway in Taiwan and South
Korea. Established in 1969 at Taichung (with an
engine factory at Kang Shan), the Aero Industry
Development Centre is a spin-off of the Nationalist
Chinese Air Force. In the succeeding years it produced American types under licence: the PL-1 trainer,
the UH-1H helicopter and the F-5E fighter. Beginning
in 1973 it also initiated indigenous projects: the
T-CH-1 turboprop trainer followed by the XC-2 twin-
turboprop transport. From 1980, Taiwan was persever-
ing with the XAT-3 jet trainer assisted by the US
Northrop Corporation.[47] South Korea, for its part,
was assembling Northrop F-5 fighters at the Pusan
factory of Korean Air Lines.[48] Other Asian nations
undertaking aircraft construction include Singapore,
Turkey, Iran, Pakistan, Thailand, the Philippines
and, above all, Indonesia. The last is rather
unusual for NICs in as much as the impetus for establishing an aircraft industry derives from civil
rather than military objectives: indeed, aerospace is
regarded as an integral part of Indonesia's national
development programme (and as such, is subject to
scrutiny in Chapter 8).

Latin America is the remaining venue for NICs
with significant aerospace industries and its leading
representative, by far, is Brazil. The Embraer company maintains initiatives in military and civil
transport aircraft and co-operates with Italy in the

development of the AM-X light ground-attack fighter.
Brazil shares with Indonesia and Romania the central
role accorded aerospace by the state in furthering
national development and, like them, is reserved for
detailed treatment later. Much more conventional in
its military mould is the industry in Argentina.
There, the military aircraft factory(FMA) at Cordoba
concentrates on the locally-designed Pucara twin-turboprop ground-attack aircraft and the IA63 jet
trainer: confining its civil involvement to the
licence-production of US Cessna light aeroplanes and
agricultural aircraft. Rivalry with Argentina renders
it imperative for Chile to develop a military aerospace capability as well. Consequently, Indaer is
building the Pillan primary trainer designed for it
by the US Piper company and is also assembling the
C-101 attack trainer under licence from CASA of
Spain. Peru, likewise, professed an intention to manufacture light jet trainers/attack aircraft under
licence, but in this case relying on Aermacchi
(of Italy) for its MB.339. For that purpose, a $5
million complex at Collique, north of Lima, was commenced in the early 1980s, and was equipped with
tools and machinery by Aermacchi worth a further $10
million. A modest 350 are employed in this enterprise
which is currently stalled owing to the country's
debt crisis.[49]

SUMMARY

The aerospace sector, to which the aircraft industry
remains central, plays a leading role in the economies of the West, the communist bloc, and increasingly in the industrialisation strategies of NICs.
Such a role derives, in the first place, from the
fact that the sector can act as a major employer of
manufacturing labour - in the USA it has traditionally vied with motor vehicles as the single largest
source of manufacturing employment. Secondly, it is
one of the few sectors in AICs which has continued to
prosper as an export-earner. The USA, France, Britain, and now the USSR too, have all recognised the
sector's importance in easing their balance of payments difficulties. Of course, the export aspect of
aerospace serves as a useful supplement to the sector's production activity aimed at fulfilling domestic markets, and the whole issue of demand for aircraft is dealt with in Chapters 3 and 4. Before
arriving at that juncture, however, it is necessary
to outline the evolution of the industry - the subject of the next chapter - and in particular the

inextricable connection between demand and technical change. Operating in tandem, those factors amount to a rationale for the emergence of aircraft enterprises and account for their subsequent expansion or contraction: the essence of Chapter 6.

The production patterns of the aircraft industry vary according to the source of demand: markets for civil aircraft (as explained in Chapter 3) behave in a markedly different manner from those regulating demand for warplanes (Chapter 4). In both instances, though, the state is a principal agent. What is more, the state also influences the location of aircraft plants (as elaborated upon in Chapter 5), provides the bulk of the R & D funds necessary to maintain the industry's technological progress (Chapter 6), and frequently offers an alternative form of business organisation to that available from private enterprise (Chapter 7). Finally, in recognising the development prospects of aerospace, the state often deliberately fosters it as an instrument of national and industrial expansion (Chapter 8). The remainder of this book examines the close interaction between aircraft enterprises, the state, and technological change under the broad rubric just outlined. A concluding chapter attempts to integrate the consequences of this interaction as it comes to bear on the world aircraft industry.

NOTES AND REFERENCES

1. AW & ST, 27 October 1980, p.59.
2. AW & ST,1 September 1980, p.83.
3. Ibid, p.284.
4. G. R. Simonson, 'Missile and Creative Destruction in the American Aircraft Industry,1956-61', Business History Review, 38 (1964), pp.302-314.
5. AW & ST, 26 December 1983, p.18.
6. Fortune, 6 August 1984, p.65.
7. AW & ST, 6 October 1980, p.18.
8. AW & ST, 30 August 1971, p.14.
9. AW & ST, 4 August 1975, p.7.
10. FI, 5 May 1984, p.1216.
11. FI, 15 March 1962, p.396.
12. FI, 7 April 1984, p.941.
13. FI, 5 December 1981, p.1686.
14. AW & ST, 19 October 1981, p.26.
15. FI, 19 May 1984, p.1327.
16. AW & ST, 1 February 1971, p.48.
17. AW & ST, 14 September 1981, p.141.
18. AW & ST, 27 April 1970, pp.99-100.

19. FI, 20 February 1982, p.416.

20. AW & ST, 2 June 1969, pp.207-212.

21. AW & ST, 23 November 1981, p.51. Note, all three firms are currently co-operating on the AAC (Australian Aircraft Consortium) trainer for the country's air force.

22. FI, 10 October 1981, p.1065.

23. Organised by MITI, Nihon was a joint venture of Mitsubishi, Kawasaki and Fuji, set up in 1959 and capitalised for $34 million. It produced 182 YS-11 airliners and was responsible for the design of the C-1 jet transports before liquidation in 1982.

24. AW & ST, 20 October 1980, p.33.

25. M. J. Armitage and R. A. Mason, Air Power in the Nuclear Age, (University of Illinois Press, Urbana, 1983), p.140.

26. Secretary of Defense Weinberger's figures quoted in FI, 12 February 1983, p.378.

27. F. M. Fabian, 'The Soviet Industrial Base' in L. D. Olvey, H. A. Leonard and B. E. Arlinghaus, Industrial Capacity and Defense Planning, (D. C. Heath, Lexington, 1983), pp.65-9.

28. AW & ST, 2 July 1973, p.28.

29. A. Boyd, The Soviet Air Force since 1918, (MacDonalds and Jane's, London, 1977), p.277.

30. AW & ST, 2 July 1973, p.7 and p.55.

31. Asher Lee, The Soviet Air Force, (Harper & Brothers, New York, 1950), p.84.

32. AW & ST, 9 March 1970, p.47.

33. David Holloway, 'The Soviet Union' in N. Ball and M. Leitenberg (eds.), The Structure of the Defense Industry, (St Martin's Press, New York, 1983), p.70.

34. Ibid, pp.70-1.

35. AW & ST, 11 May 1981, p.64.

36. AW & ST, 15 June 1981, p.63.

37. AW & ST, 19 January 1976, p.19.

38. To be specific: Lucas Aerospace (jet pipes,fuel control systems, pressure controllers etc.), Plessey Aerospace (gas turbine starters, engine pumps) and Dowty (afterburning fuel control systems). See AW & ST, 12 July 1976, p.16.

39. AW & ST, 22 June 1981, p.36.

40. AW & ST, 18 June 1984, p.15.

41. FI, 3 April 1975, pp.562-4.

42. FI, 13 March 1975, p.417.

43. AW & ST, 18 January 1982, p.61 and Air Pictorial, March 1984, p.84.

44. FI, 26 May 1984, p.1411.

45. India also has persevered with indigenous designs. Perhaps its most successful are the Kiran jet trainer and the Ajeet lightweight fighter (itself

a progressive development of the British Gnat aircraft).

46. FI, 18 December 1982, pp.1771-2.
47. Air Pictorial, May 1982, p.196.
48. AW & ST, 24 November 1980, p.27.
49. FI, 6 March 1982, p.530 and 2 October 1982,
p.1028.

Chapter Two

EMERGENCE AND EVOLUTION

As a creature of technology, the aircraft industry
is, in consequence, very sensitive to technical
change. Its rapid evolution in this century has
stemmed from recognition of the versatility of aircraft as weapons of war and vehicles for promoting
rapid transportation of passengers and cargo. Yet,
while the aircraft industry flourished as a result of
those redeeming qualities, it transformed itself by
way of continual technical progress and innovation
into the medium capable of fulfilling the elevated
views of its usefulness held by military and civilian
organisations alike. In all likelihood, of course,
the relationship between customer demand and technical progress is an interactive one; that is to say,
innovation probably owes as much to customer stimulus
as customer enthusiasm responds to technical performance. In other words, the evolution of the aircraft
industry was rendered possible by a combination of
technology-push innovations and demand-pull innovations. The former refers to innovations which influence subsequent activities: both in terms of the complexion of the industry and the conditions of the
market. The latter, however, arises whenever the
particular requirements of the market - the military
or civil aviators - are met by new technology.[1]
    The prime object of this chapter is to outline
the evolution of the aircraft industry in light of
the scope for expansion accorded it by technical
developments on the one hand and the needs of its
customers on the other. In reality, separation of
technical change and market emergence is somewhat
artificial and is only maintained initially to enable
the salient steps in the industry's growth to be set
down. For the latter part of the chapter, the interaction between technical change and markets is
explicitly recognised and addressed from the point-
of-view of a conceptual stance denoted as the

'wave-cycle' model. The position taken by the model,
and adopted wholesale in this book, is that aircraft
production is regulated, by and large, by the state
and, correspondingly, owes little to orthodox market
mechanisms. Before addressing such issues, however,
it is necessary to briefly outline the sequence of
technical developments experienced by the industry in
the first place, and to elicit how the markets for
aircraft evolved in the second.

EVOLUTIONARY HIGHLIGHTS

The story of the pioneering innovations in aeronautics has been told and retold elsewhere and need not
concern us because it occupies an era prior to the
emergence of a 'proper' aircraft industry.[2] The
industry really came into its own during World War I
when it blossomed to fulfil military needs. Hindered
more than anything else by barriers in aeroengine
design (e.g. most British designs in the beginning
relied on the French Gnome seven-cylinder rotary
engine), the industry was transformed in the space of
four years from a crafts-oriented workshop operation
into a manufacturing process geared to mass-production. With the exception of France, the monoplane
was eschewed in favour of the biplane: a type of aircraft that was stronger, lighter and more manoeuvra-
ble than its single-wing counterpart. The universal
use of wood in airframe construction allowed for the
infusion into the industry of a host of furniture
makers either as sub-contractors or as full-fledged
aircraft manufacturers. Such enterprises were adept
at producing the wooden box-like structures coated
with fabric, while automobile engineers were co-opted
into manufacturing the rotary and radial aeroengines
which had to be mated to the airframes. By 1918, a
state-of-the-art fighter - the Fokker D.VII - was
powered by a 160hp Mercedes six-cylinder water-cooled
radial engine and weighed 670kg empty. Measuring
6.95m in length with a wingspan of 8.9m, this machine
was capable of 189km/h maximum speed. By way of contrast, the world's first strategic bomber, the Handley Page V/1500, was powered by four 375hp R-R Eagle
engines, weighed 7,352kg empty, was 18.89m long with
a span of 38.4m, and was able to achieve 156km/h.[3]
     There was little challenge in the 1920s to the
supremacy of the biplane. However, the first aircraft to have a modern-style retractable undercarriage
appeared as early as 1920 (the Dayton-Wright RB
racer); although this innovation was slow in gaining
acceptance. The principal change arose in respect to

aircraft materials with wood steadily losing out to
metal. In 1924 the UK Air Ministry, for example,
ordered three experimental fighters; two of which had
steel fuselages and wooden wings while the third was
of all-steel construction.[4] By the end of the decade,
the first all-metal transport (Boeing's Monomail) had
materialised and was the precursor to a series of
airliners in the early 1930s (Boeing 247, Lockheed
10, Douglas Commercial). Metal construction allied
with the slim, liquid-cooled in-line engine was the
epitome of aircraft design in the late 1920s.

The monoplane came into its own as the 1930s
unfolded. Its acceptance entailed adoption of a host
of associated novel features: retractable undercarriage, take-off and landing flaps, variable-pitch
propeller and cockpit canopy. Representative of the
all-metal, stressed-skin, low-wing monoplane was the
Curtiss Hawk fighter of 1935. Equipped with a
1,050hp P & W Twin Wasp radial engine, the Hawk was
capable of achieving 488km/h and weighed 2,060kg
empty. Originating in the same year, the Douglas
DC-3 airliner embodied most of the technical advances
then extant.

> It had a robust structure of newly developed
> high-tensile aluminium alloy for long life and
> ease of maintenance; a fatigue-resistant multi-
> spar wing with split flaps... enabling the wing
> loading to be increased and resulting in a more
> efficient structure; two reliable supercharged
> air-cooled engines...; variable-pitch, feath-
> ering, three-blade, metal propellers with gover-
> nors to keep them running at a constant, pre-set
> speed; and a retractable undercarriage with toe-
> operated hydraulic wheel blades.[5]

Nor was crew and passenger comfort neglected, for,
the DC-3 boasted an autopilot and air-conditioning
combined with noise-reduction. This impressive aircraft was able to carry two dozen passengers for up
to 3,420km at a maximum speed of 370km/h.

World War II witnessed the ultimate development
of the piston-engined monoplane and also ushered in
jet-propulsion. Single-engined piston machines were
developed in terms of toughness, speed, range and
firepower. The P-51D Mustang, for example, had a
combat range of 1,529km; the P-47D Thunderbolt was
capable of carrying 1,134kg of bombs as well as pack-
ing eight 0.5in machine guns; whereas the Yak-9U
could reach 700km/h, range up to 890km, and carry one
20mm cannon and two machine guns. The war also led
to great strides in four-engined aircraft; perhaps

23

best represented by the Boeing B-29. This strategic
bomber had a tricycle undercarriage and pressurised
cabin, and was able to carry 4,540kg of bombs for
5,230km. Developments in four-engined transports,
the DC-4 and Lockheed Constellation in particular,
set the standard for postwar commercial aviation.
German and British jet-engine technology, formulated
during the war, was instrumental in creating the best
of the new generation fighter aircraft: represented
by the US F-86 Sabre and the Soviet Mig-15. The former was the first to make use of German swept-wing
technology and was, equally, the first production
supersonic fighter. The latter, powered by a derivative of a R-R turbine, was so successful that about
8,000 were constructed in the USSR and extra sizeable
runs emanated from Mielec (Poland), Vodochody
(Prague, Czechoslovakia) and Shenyang (China). A
comparison of the rapid progress in fighters and
bombers after the war is discernible from Table 2.1.

It is evident, therein, that speed of aircraft
climaxed in the early 1960s and that developments
over the past twenty years have been less in terms of
boosting speed and more in terms of enhancing the
survivability of aircraft under combat conditions.
One innovation flowing directly from this concern was
the VTOL fighter (e.g. BAe Harrier) which dispensed
with the need for the very long runways required by
conventional high-performance aircraft. Advances in
jet engine design by the early 1960s made possible
the installation of sufficient power in an airframe
to exceed the total weight and allow for vertical
thrust. Another innovation was variable-geometry, or
the ability to alter the configuration of the aircraft's wings to optimise missions of varying speed
and altitude (e.g. the F-111, Mig-23, Panavia Tornado) and thereby produce a machine truly capable of
multiple roles. Combat-aircraft developments were
instrumental in fostering changes in materials too.
The first aircraft built extensively of titanium was
the North American F-100 fighter of 1953; whereas the
same company's (albeit under different corporate
guise) B-1 bomber was a pioneer in the use of composite materials in the early 1970s.

Since World War II two other important aeronautical breakthroughs have created the helicopter and
the jetliner. The former had materialised during the
war in experimental form (e.g. the Sikorsky R-4), but
it was only through the Korean War that the helicopter's suitability for casualty evacuation and search
and rescue was demonstrated. In 1955 the turboshaft
engine was first used in a helicopter (the Alouette
II) pointing the way towards designs with much

Table 2.1 :   Post War Developments in Combat Aircraft

Year	Jet Fighters (maximum speed/range)	Bombers (maximum speed/range)
1944	Gloster Meteor (UK) (737 Km/h;2156Km)	
1948	North American F-86A(US) (1091 Km/h;745Km)	Boeing B-50A(US) (640Km/h;7886Km)
1950		Boeing B-47A(US) (980Km/h;5794Km)
1953	Hawker Hunter(UK) (1142Km/h;788Km)	
1955		Boeing B-52A(US) (1014Km/h;9978Km)
1956		Tu-20(USSR) (870Km/h;12,550Km)
1958	Su-7B(USSR) (1700Km/h;459Km)	
1960	SAAB-35 Draken(Sweden) (1487Km/h;636Km)	
1961	Dassault Mirage 111(France) (2349Km/h;1199Km)	
1962	McDonnell F-4(US) (2549Km/h;1056Km)	
1965		Tu-22(USSR) (1480Km/h;2252Km)
1968		F-111A(US) (2655Km/h;2413Km)
1971	Mig-23(USSR) (2445Km/h;1126Km)	
1974		Tu-26(USSR) (2655Km/h;11,496Km)
1975	MD F-15A(US) (2655Km/h;1930Km)	
1976		Panavia Tornado(European) (2574Km/h;1207Km)
1984		Rockwell B-1(US) (2124Km/h;9815Km)

Source: Compiled from information in C. Cook and J.Stevenson, The Atlas of Modern Warfare, (Weidenfeld and Nicolson, London 1978).

greater power-to-weight ratios than was forthcoming with the piston engine. Today, twin-turbine helicopters act as useful airlift vehicles not only for military tactical support but also in such civil operations as oilrig replenishment and intracity passenger transit. The jetliner, meanwhile, stemmed from experiments underway in the early 1950s in both the UK and USA (resulting in such first-generation machines as the DH Comet, Boeing 707 and Douglas DC-8). At one fell swoop, jet transports made trans-atlantic travel brief and comfortable and, subse-quently, in the era of wide-bodied transports, made cheap long-haul travel much more widely available than hitherto.

Market Evolution
As intimated, the aircraft industry came into its own as a result of the demands of war. In World War I production figures were quite astounding for a nas-cent industry: Britain built 52,440 airframes, France 51,000, Germany 48,000; while Italy managed 6,488 in 1918 alone.[6] The USA and Russia were plagued by a variety of production difficulties: the former, given its late entry into the conflict, was deficient in aircraft design and had to rely inordinately upon licence-production of French and British machines. Nevertheless, it did make 13,111 machines between 6 April 1917 and 1 November 1919.[7] Russia was equally dependent on the Allies for assistance in aircraft production, although it was directed mainly at making up deficiencies in aeroengine capacity. The Tsarist state was only able to provide about 2,200 aircraft from its own resources in the years 1914–17.[8]

   The cessation of hostilities cut the burgeoning industry in the bud and inaugurated a pattern of 'boom' and 'bust' which was to plague the aircraft industry hereafter. As elicited from Table 2.2, orders for British aircraft placed in the final year of war were slashed by half. To make matters worse, the brunt of the cancellations fell on machines newly entering production (e.g. the DH 10, Vimy, and the various late-model Sopwith designs).[9] The few types kept in production in the aftermath of war were ordered in minute batches. Orders for the Bristol F2B, for example, were placed in 1920, 1924, 1925 and 1926; but totalled only 379 aircraft in marked con-trast to the 1,403 built in 1918–19 (not to mention the 1,747 cancelled at that time). Throughout the succeeding fifteen years new combat designs were ordered in penny-packet numbers and it was only with the rearmament schemes commencing in 1934 that pro-duction runs for military aircraft began to return to sizeable proportions. The DH Tiger Moth aptly illus-trates the effect of rearmament. Conceived to fit a 1931 Air Ministry specification for a trainer, it was initially ordered in numbers of 35, 50, two and two;

but after the expansion schemes were effected, 30
civil machines were bought directly off the production line and fresh orders were placed for 50, 400,
300 and a further 400 prior to the start of World War
II (which manifest itself through an immediate contract for 2,000 of these aircraft).

World War II was a replay of the pattern of the
earlier war in terms of expansion of aircraft production: although now the totals were truly astronomi-
cal. The USSR made 137,271 aircraft between January
1941 and June 1945, the USA turned out about 300,000
machines (96,318 in 1944 alone), while the UK built
in excess of 119,000 aircraft from 1940 to 1946
(29,220 of them in 1944). Germany was able, throughout 1944, to produce on average 2,811 aircraft each
month. Production runs of tried-and-true designs
were phenomenal: the Ilyushin Il-2 was built at a
rate of 1,200 per month and total output exceeded
35,000 whereas the Messerschmitt Bf-109 was built in
numbers exceeding 33,000. However, with the ending
of hostilities orders were slashed across the board:
the P-47 Thunderbolt, for example, had 10,154 units
deleted after contracts for 15,683 had been completed.[10] Again, as with the earlier postwar episode,
production contracts for new designs were largely
abandoned and those for existing designs were sharply
curtailed. Table 2.3 is eclectic in as much as it
highlights a number of aircraft designs ordered into
production in 1943 by the UK Government and traces
the wartime output, end-of-war production termination, and postwar trickle of output for the types in
question. Conforming to the standard strategic
bomber format, the Lincoln was a progressive development of the Avro Lancaster and was ordered into
large-scale production only to have the body of that
programme dropped in 1945. The dribble of postwar
output was merely to serve as replacements for attri-
tion suffered by the peacetime air force. The Hornet
case is comparable, although postwar naval requirements required a relatively significant production
run. A new variant of the Spitfire/Seafire scarcely
saw the light of day, however, with production plans
being largely shelved: instead resources were redirected to producing new-technology jet fighters (Vampire and Meteor) which, consequently, escaped end-of-
war cutbacks. Finally, the Brigand bomber also
avoided cancellations but its overall production was
very modest indeed compared to its immediate pred-
ecessor, the Beaufighter, of which almost 6,000 were
built.

Limited production runs have been the order of
the day for Western combat aircraft since World War

Table 2.2 :   Impact of the Vanishing of Military Demand

Type	Number built	Number cancelled	%completed of total order
Airco DH4	251	0	100
DH6	100	0	100
DH9/9A	2163	1057	67
DH10/10A	237	454	34
AW[1] FK8	484	112	81
Avro 504K	2779	871	76
Bristol F2B	1403	1747	45
HP[2] O/400	139	130	52
V/1500	33	120	22
Martinsyde Buzzard	273	1286	18
Nieuport Nighthawk	41	109	27
RAF[3] FE2b	0	550	0
RE8	350	100	78
SE5A	1051	374	74
Sopwith Camel	1495	348	81
Snipe	647	2171	23
Salmander	124	1276	9
Dolphin	170	180	49
Cuckoo	0	50	0
Dragon	4	296	1
Vickers Vimy	199	899	18
Total	11,943	12,130	50

Notes: 1. AW = Armstrong Whitworth
       2. HP = Handley Page
       3. RAF= Royal Aircraft Factory

Source: Compiled from information in B. Robertson, British
        Military Aircraft Serials, (Patrick Stephens,
        Cambridge, 1979).

II.   Unusual expansion arises only during hostilities
or quasi-hostilities (chilly episodes in the Cold
War).   Thus, US aircraft production was greatly
boosted during the Korean War following a period of
quiescent military demand.   Rae notes that two civil
lightplane manufacturers – Beech and Cessna – had
been engrossed in overhaul and the making of furniture and farm machinery in lieu of aircraft construction when the outbreak of war in 1950 immediately
electrified their production divisions: Cessna, for

Table 2.3 : Transition From Wartime Production

Type	End-of-war completions	End-of-war cancellations	Postwar output
Lincoln			
4-engine bomber	507	2220	21
Seafire(45-47)			
piston fighter	0	735	76
Hornet			
2-engine fighter	35	495	209
Vampire(1-3)			
jet fighter	200	0	121
Meteor(4)			
jet fighter	100	0	316
Brigand			
2-engine bomber	80	0	56

Source: Compiled from information in B. Robertson, British
       Military Aircraft Serials, (Patrick Stephens,
       Cambridge, 1979).

example, receiving a contract for 400 army liaison
planes.[11] The brevity and general containment of such
postwar 'emergencies' is evinced through the size of
contracts: the USA building only 7,000 aircraft in
1952 at the height of the Korean War whereas it was
forthcoming with 96,000 at the height of World War
II. The British likewise have failed to come close
to wartime production figures with the Falklands conflict, for instance, resulting in the purchase of 15
US F-4 fighters and orders for smaller numbers of Sea
Harriers and helicopters as replacements for combat
losses. All told, UK production of combat aircraft
in 1983 scarcely mustered 100 machines.[12]
    Commercial aviation, represented by the air-
lines, came to the fore after World War I. Its gestation period was long and difficult, however, partly
because of the inadequacy of current aircraft and
partly owing to the parlous economic conditions then
prevailing which acted to impede market expansion.
The first airline fares were so uncompetitive in comparison with other modes of transport that all UK
airline companies had been forced out of business by
1921.[13] Inadequate equipment - mainly converted bombers - merely compounded the uncompetitiveness. They
were not designed with either passenger comfort or
fuel economy in mind, and, further, imposed high

servicing costs upon their operators. Table 2.4 indicates the progress made in airliner development from the sorrowful machines of the 1920s through the tailor-made aircraft of the 1930s and after. It is no coincidence that many of the pioneering models issued from US factories while the Europeans persevered with 'conversions' of bomber types. The cross-fertilisation of airlines and aircraft manufacturers is one of the longstanding themes in the US aeronautical scene. It was only in the USA (aided by mail contracts) that routes were sufficiently plentiful and lengthy to warrant revenue-paying services and the incentive was therefore given to manufacturers to design suitable equipment. The innovating DC-3 has already been mentioned, but in the years following World War II US long-haul transports like the Constellation and DC-7 came to dominate the world's airlines. In spite of technical innovations on the part of the British (e.g. the Comet turbojet airliner and the Britannia turboprop transport), US aircraft maintained their dominance of world airline fleets (e.g. the classic Boeing 707) largely due to their catholic design characteristics geared to fulfil American market needs which, at one and the same time, constituted the lion's share of the world's commercial aviation market. As hinted in Chapter 1, it is only now that European manufacturers are in a position to challenge US firms in the wide-bodied airliner field.

The Wave-Cycle Model

It is abundantly clear that aircraft production is inordinately dependent on military demand - to the extent of something in the order of 60 per cent in the USA and UK - and consequently, is extremely sensitive to changes in such demand. That military demand is inconstant is equally apparent by virtue of the aforementioned crises in production following the two world wars. A cyclical schema has been promulgated by Higham to account for the responsiveness of aircraft output to the variability in military markets.[14] Formulated with the UK historical record in mind, the model seems germane for other countries as well. Fig. 2.1 attempts to summarise, in crude manner, the cyclical swings common to both national industries. Appended to the oscillations or 'waves' is the terminology coined by Higham and it is this, representing phases in military demand, which has general applicability for the aircraft industry. Hinging on the perceptions by policymakers and defence chiefs of the threats to national security, the wave-cycle posits a sequence of policy responses

Emergence and Evolution

Table 2.4 :   Progression in Airliner Development

Year	Type	Passenger capacity	Cruising speed (Km/h)	Normal range (Km)
1922	DH34(UK)	8	168	400
1925	DH50(UK)	4	160	600
1928	Ford Tri-motor 4(US)	12	176	900
1933	Boeing 247(US)	10	303	803
1934	Lockheed Electra(US)	10	305	803
1935	Douglas DC-3(US)	21	305	1365
1938	Short Empire(UK)	17	257	964
1946	Lockheed Constellation(US)	51	498	3693
1949	Boeing 377(US)	70	482	4818
1952	DH Comet 1(UK)	40	803	2409
1953	Douglas DC-7A(US)	76	594	5781
1957	Bristol Britannia 300(UK)	120	562	7227
1958	Boeing 707-120(US)	132	947	4818
1964	Vickers VC-10(UK)	151	878	8078
1964	Boeing 727-100(US)	110	957	2570
1970	Boeing 747-100(US)	500	978	10650

Source: K. R. Sealy, The Geography of Air Transport, (Hutchinson, London, 1966), p.50 and A. Phillips, Technology and Market Structure,(D.C. Heath, Lexington, 1971), pp.140-4.

(reflected through military preparations) whereby the initial strategic balance is disrupted and replaced by various phases of disequilibria until a satisfactory balance is once more regained. Contracts and, allowing for a time lag, aircraft output are one manifestation of the received wisdom concerning international tension. Strategic balance translates into peacetime equilibrium in terms of aircraft procurement. In practice, that means limited budgets for new aircraft and steady-state air forces with orders issuing only to established manufacturers for replacement machines. Frequently, military business is confined to state enterprises (e.g. the Royal Aircraft Factory in Britain prior to 1914) or private contractors which compose the 'military-industrial complex' (as in the USA at the present time). The appearance of a perceived threat arouses enlarged military budgets and propels the aircraft industry into a phase of rearmamental instability. Not only are orders dramatically increased, but the industry is placed on a mass-production basis. In the initial

stages, the established manufacturers are given the
burden of meeting augmented production, but if expansion targets remain unfulfilled, other manufacturers
are brought into the programme. The UK, for example,
resorted to the motor vehicles industry in the late
1930s so as to overcome capacity bottlenecks prevalent in the mainstream aircraft industry. The phase
of maximum output – wartime equilibrium – is only
attained when the entire economy is put on a war
footing. Priority is given to aeroplane manufacture
and as many enterprises as possible are pressed into
the production effort. A leading British example of
an organisation cobbled together for such a purpose
was London Aircraft Productions Ltd. In World War II
it constructed 710 four-motor Halifax bombers; a rep-
utable record for such an unlikely undertaking.

> London Transport acts as a co-ordinator for the
> group, each member of which was responsible for
> a particular section of production. Thus,
> Chrysler Motors was responsible for the rear
> fuselage, Park Royal Coachworks for the outer
> wings, Express Motor & Body Works for the inter-
> mediate wings and tail plane, and Duples' Bodies
> & Motors for the shell and components for the
> rear fuselage. London Transport itself under-
> took the manufacture of the centre section, the
> installation of the fittings and equipment for
> the front fuselage, the installation of the
> engine and the final erection and testing of the
> finished aircraft.[15]

Naturally, on account of the excessive cost, the production commensurate with wartime equilibrium was
scaled down at the first opportunity; usually even
before the official end of war.[16] The resultant demobilisational instability was characterised by widescale cancellation of contracts as the threat to
national security had been eliminated. Enterprises
unable to divert into civil lines are faced with the
risk of bankruptcy as their military contracts dwin-
dle away. A few – generally the long-standing contractors – are allowed to survive on the strength of
a trickle of orders owing to the state's need to
ensure a 'reserve defence capability'.
    The form and intensity of those phases vary, of
course, according to country and the meshing of military requirements with technical developments. With
respect to the former, it is clear from Fig. 2.1 that
US and UK phases are not entirely synchronised:
rather, the British tended to enter rearmamental
instability and wartime equilibrium sooner than the

Figure 2.1 : The Wave Cycle and Aircraft Production

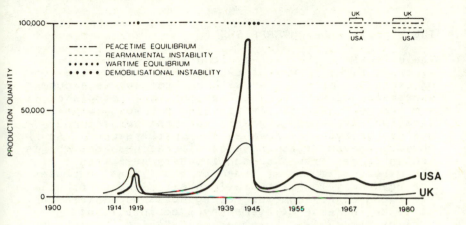

Americans. Moreover, US command of mass-production
resources was far more telling than that of the British giving rise to much higher production peaks for
the USA in the phase of maximum output in World War
II. Further, different valuations given to minimum
and necessary levels of peacetime forces result in
different ideas of steady-state aircraft production:
the UK post-1955 figure is considerably less than
that of the USA with its notions of international
responsibility while, US levels, in turn, have
trailed behind those of the USSR in the 1970s.
Arguably, the end of the 1970s witnessed a return to
rearmamental instability on the part of both super-
powers. Technical innovations also influence the
phases. A comparison of the demobilisational insta-
bilities following the two world wars evinces
detailed differences. After the earlier episode,
production was cut back to the bone because the technical development of aviation was sufficiently uncon-
vincing as to throw its whole future into question as
a genuine military arm. By way of contrast, the
inception of jet-engine technology at the end of the
second conflict meant that production of jet fighters
was effected by the USA, UK and USSR despite cutbacks
elsewhere in defence production. None the less, the
phases are discernible in the patterns of aircraft
production and act as useful indicators for relating
activity levels in the industry to changes in the
composition of military markets. What remains to be

33

debated, however, is the impact of such cyclical
swings on the individual enterprises constituting the
industry.

THE EVOLUTION OF ENTERPRISES

The effects of the wave-cycle are perceptible for
aircraft firms by way of two considerations: the form
of expansion alternating with contraction as a common
experience of such enterprises in the first place,
and the means adopted by firms - in a word, diversification - in order to ameliorate the worst consequences of cyclical down-swings in the second. An
obvious precursor to those considerations, though, is
the entry of firms into the industry as a result of
the direct stimulus afforded by the expansion phases.
One need only look to UK evidence to find proof of
the flood of new entries during World War I (Fearon
cites an increase of firms involved in aircraft production from 771 in November 1917 to 1,529 in October
1918) and the example of the co-opted motor vehicles
industry in World War II has already been mentioned.[17] The USA followed suit in that war, encour-
aging the giant automotive industry to engage in aircraft manufacture. General Motors entered the
aircraft business through conversion of five of its
existing vehicles plants to warplane output, whereas
Ford's enthusiastic entry was manifested through the
erection of a purpose-built bomber plant at Willow
Run, Michigan, for the mass-production of B-24 Liber-
ators.[18] New entries continue, for, Japanese military
build-up in the 1980s has persuaded the Yamaha motor-
cycle firm to establish an aeroengine division in
order to provide the prime movers for aerial target-
drones.[19]
    In reverting to the expansion-contraction theme,
however, that issue can be addressed through the use
of a disparate range of examples. Rising aircraft
orders impel firms to initially expand their own production facilities and, subsequently, consider acquisition of other firms if the former policy is insufficient in meeting the enlarged demand. Facility
expansion, in turn, can take two forms: the extension
of existing premises and the erection of extra facilities on new sites. Since the late 1970s boosted US
defence spending (partly in response to the Soviet
invasion of Afghanistan) has triggered a phase
approximating rearmamental instability and encouraged
aerospace firms to undertake expansion.[20] Sikorsky
Aircraft (a division of UTC), for instance, intended
to invest $100 million in its Stratford and

34

Bridgeport, Connecticut, plants mainly as a result of
the US Army choosing its UH-60A helicopter and the US
Navy opting for the SH-60B.[21] Employment was planned
to increase from 7,200 to 10,000 in the early 1980s;
a figure approaching the peak 11,307 reached in 1957
as a consequence of Korean War-related orders. At
the same time, Boeing wanted to expand its facilities
in the Puget Sound area and take on a further
6,000-7,000 workers; although in this case soaring
demand was attributed to the commercial aviation market. The launching of the models 757 and 767 airliners in the late 1970s had added 24,500 to the payroll
in 1978-79.[22] In fact, Boeing was a beneficiary of
enlarged defence spending too; and attempted to
accommodate contracts for cruise missiles by establishing new plant sites. It announced, only 24 days
after receiving the USAF contract, that it would
build a $25 million factory at Kent, Washington.
This facility would be replete with several NC
machine centres, a chemical processing plant, and an
autoclave required for bonding the missiles' wings.[23]
MD was also a recipient of the cruise missile largesse; although in its instance new plant selection
was spurned in favour of rehabilitating an existing
components factory (Titusville, Florida) to the tune
of $50 million and with the prospect of creating 600
new jobs.[24]
     If rising demand continues to outstrip existing
capacity and new facilities brought (or about to be
brought) on stream, the enterprise may circumvent
supply bottlenecks through a policy of acquisition.
In this manner, it absorbs other firms with the
requisite tools and plant that can easily be turned to
fulfilling its own contract obligations. Again, a US
example can be proffered to illustrate this situation: that is to say, the former Bell plant at Mar-
ietta, Georgia, which was reactivated by Lockheed
during the Korean War in order to produce bombers and
later, urgently-needed C-130 transports.[25] Most
acquisitions in periods of rising demand, however,
have occurred by virtue of the desire of firms to
absorb those enterprises known to have bountiful
defence contracts. It was in this light that Boeing
acquired the Vertol Aircraft Corporation of Morton,
Pennsylvania, in 1960 and thereby, entered the profitable military helicopter field.[26] In recent times,
MD purchased Hughes helicopters of Culver City, California and Mesa, Arizona in order to profit from the
US Army requirement for 515 Hughes Apache helicopters
worth more than $7 billion.[27] From a slightly differ-
ent viewpoint - that of a non-aerospace firm - aircraft manufacturers can appear as useful springboards

to lucrative defence contracts. Accordingly, Rockwell-Standard (now RI) a major automotive components manufacturer, absorbed North American Aviation in 1967. This latter, a California aircraft firm, had sales in 1966 of over $2 billion and 95 per cent of its contracts stemmed from the US Government.[28] In fact, many entries into the aircraft industry were the actions of engineering companies (usually with considerable experience of defence production) wishing to diversify their armaments portfolios. Historically, the UK warship constructors Vickers and Armstrong Whitworth provide classic examples, and the details of their aircraft interests will be recounted below. However, this pattern was emulated by the Japanese with, for example, the shipbuilder Kawasaki Heavy Industries forming an aircraft division in 1918.

As to be expected, contraction during phases of demand downswings is translated into employee layoffs, plant closure and diversification into more promising lines of business. During the era of 'détente' in the mid 1970s, the American DoD estimated that excess capacity in the aircraft firms was equivalent to 20,000 underemployed workers maintained on 'make-work' defence contracts.[29] Withdrawal of such contracts led to significant layoffs: indeed, by 1976 aerospace employment stood at 903,000, barely 60 per cent of its 1968 figure of 1.5 million.[30] The rot had started with the rundown in Vietnam-related contracts. As Table 2.5 shows, most US aircraft producers reached peak employment during the 1967-69 period, and all had suffered sizeable cuts by the early 1970s. Particularly hard pressed was Boeing which had reduced its workforce to scarcely one third of the 1968 high. The company blamed the cutbacks on a depressed commercial aircraft market as well as its failure to obtain a USAF bomber contract and a US Navy missile project, not to mention the completion of the Saturn booster rocket programme. At all events, its layoffs were held culpable for a ten per cent unemployment rate in Washington State's King and Snohomish counties (the locations of the affected Seattle, Renton, Kent, Auburn and Everett plants), a drop in hotel business there of 25 per cent, a fall off in car sales of 35 per cent and real estate sales of 40 per cent, and, to cap it all, an overall loss in state income of $1.25 billion for 1970 alone.[31] Boeing attempted to stem further job losses by dispensing with sub-contractors as far as was practicable and 'internalising' production at its own plants. Thus, it curtailed subcontracts for Boeing 747 wing boxes and landing gear doors held by Goodyear's

Litchfield Park, Arizona, plant and had them made in its own premises.[32] Turnaround in the company's fortunes arose only when commercial aircraft markets revived later in the 1970s. Ironically, though, dampening of demand for airliners in the 1980s forced the firm to shed 5,000 workers in each of 1981 and 1982; and the only promising areas for job stability were associated with defence programmes.[33]

The recent experience of Boeing illustrates an important caveat; namely, that contraction can be effected by declines in civil aviation markets as well as those following from attenuated defence contracts. In France, Aérospatiale was especially hard hit in the mid 1970s when failure to garner orders for Concorde and A300B jetliners led to the possibility of 6,000 layoffs at Toulouse. The workforce had to be hastily shifted into military helicopter production or occupied in subcontract work for Dassault fighters acquired in desperation just to provide needed employment.[34] While patently technical breakthroughs, the two civil projects were not marketable in light of the prevailing depressed airliner markets. This enterprise continued in the doldrums for several years, closing its Chateauroux works, losing FFr 487 million in 1975 alone, and finding respite only in military programmes: the Transall transport and a 35 per cent share in the Mirage 2000.[35] Britain, likewise, did not escape the painful consequences of contraction, although most of its problems arose out of difficulties attributable to shrinking defence programmes. The cutback in warplane projects following the hiatus that arose after the Korean War and Suez episodes led to the closure of aircraft factories at Blackpool, Portsmouth, Christchurch and Gloucester. Twenty years later BAe was still confronted with problems deriving from defence cutbacks: in this instance it responded by closing its Bitteswell facility with the loss of 1,000 jobs.[36]

Frequently, the plight brought on by the erosion of demand compels the firms to contemplate merger or diversification either out of the aircraft business or into another part of it deemed less risky. A prominent example of merger was the United Aircraft and Transport Corporation. Formed originally in 1929 round the nucleus of the Boeing group (manufacturer and airline), it soon merged the interests of four other aircraft firms (Stearman, Sikorsky, Avion and Chance Vought), an aeroengine firm (P & W), two propeller manufacturers (consolidated as Hamilton Standard), and three air transport ventures. While conceived in an era of buoyancy, the combine weathered the impending depression better than most other US

Table 2.5 :   Employment Cuts in the Aftermath of
              the Vietnam War

Company	Peak employment	Date	Employment in mid 1971
Beech	11,650	12/65	5,000
Bell	10,900	1969	8,000
Boeing	148,000	6/68	54,000
Cessna(Wichita)	9,500	8/68	4,600
Fairchild	13,000	6/68	7,500
GE Aircraft Group	29,000	12/69	25,000
General Dynamics(aircraft)	55,600	10/68	32,800
Grumman	36,025	12/67	25,500
Hughes Aircraft	32,107	7/67	27,437
Kaman	3,644	12/68	2,600
LTV(aerospace)	24,600	7/69	13,000
Lockheed Aircraft	99,700	9/69	71,500
MD	134,000	1967	92,854
North American Rockwell	104,000	1/65	37,500
Northrop	25,462	7/69	13,900
United Aircraft	81,600	1967	61,000

Source: Aviation Week and Space Technology, 12 July 1971, p.15.

aeronautical organisations and thus seemingly confirmed the effectiveness of merger during straitened
times.[37] The option of using merger for diversifying
into similar product lines that have more promising
markets has been pursued in more recent years.
McDonnell Aircraft of St. Louis absorbed Douglas Aircraft of Long Beach in 1967 (i.e. creating MD) owing
to its desire to add a commercial-aircraft base to
its defence interests which were jeopardised by the
rundown of Vietnam involvement.[38] Similarly, the Raytheon Company and the Beech Aircraft Corporation
agreed to merge in 1979 so that the former - preoccu-
pied with missile production - could acquire the
expertise of the latter in civil aircraft markets.[39]
Outright purchases of smaller civil aircraft manufacturers by larger aerospace firms is represented by
the cases of Fairchild Industries and Gulfstream
American. The first bought Swearingen Aircraft of
San Antonio in order to make good the evaporation of
its defence business (for the A-10A strike aircraft)
by substituting a product for the commuter and corporate aircraft market.[40] Gulfstream American, however,

bought the general aviation division of RI, located
at Bethany, Oklahoma, because it wished to consolidate its position in the commuter aircraft niche.[41]
Diversification outside of aerospace has proved
popular when all aircraft markets seem particularly
depressed. As previously hinted, such a state of
affairs was perceived as being in effect in the early
1970s. Several firms reacted, at that point, through
venturing into rail and rapid transit projects (e.g.
LTV and the Dallas-Fort Worth Airport system along
with Boeing-Vertol's manufacture of railcars for San
Fransisco and the Massachussetts Bay authority).
Indeed, Boeing entered the fields of computer services, housing, and hydrofoil boats. Perhaps its most
unusual undertaking was the plan to convert 40,469 ha
of Oregon desert into an agricultural community by
means of irrigation.[42] Not to be outdone, LTV
invested $10 million in a Colorado water-sports
resort and considered investment in Hawaii tourism.[43]
The scope for diversification, and the dependency of
it upon the wave-cycle of demand, is immediately
apparent from even a cursory examination of the Vickers experience.

Vickers as a Case Study

The firm of Vickers originated at Sheffield as a
steel and heavy engineering company in the mid-nine-
teenth century. Its first flirtation with defence
requirements occurred in the 1880s when it was
encouraged by the UK Government to lay down gun-forg-
ing capacity.[44] By the turn of the century, it had
become committed to defence production in a very
serious way having acquired machine-gun plant and a
shipyard specialising in warships. At the time of
the Boer War the company functioned as an integrated
armaments organisation producing armour plate (at
Sheffield) for warships built at Barrow, which were
armed from the firm's own gun foundries (at Sheffield
and Barrow), ammunitioned from its own shops (Erith
and Dartford) and equipped with its own brand of
light artillery to boot (from Erith). To this
impressive list of defence products (including light
and heavy ordnance, battleships, submarines) was
added an aircraft department at Erith in 1911. Massive orders for Vickers Gunbus aircraft in World War
I were instrumental in founding aeroplane production
lines at the existing Crayford works and a new site
at Weybridge.[45] Moreover, the firm bolstered its aviation interests by acquiring the Tier II firms James
Booth in 1915 (a manufacturer of duralumin used in
airships made by Vickers) and S.E.Saunders in 1918

(producer of fuselage parts). Unlike its competitor
(and, after 1927 partner through merger) Armstrong
Whitworth, this defence contractor decided to persevere with aircraft on the vanishing of wartime contracts. Aircraft manufacture, after all, was characterised by high engineering standards and "its
reliance upon scientific development, and its association with defence, was for Vickers a natural development which the production of consumer goods was
not".[46] As suggested, diversification into civil
products was less than successful.

In spite of severely curtailed orders from the
RAF, Vickers secured its aviation position in the
1920s. In the first place, it bought the Ioco company of Glasgow - a producer of oilproofed silk for
airships, and in the second, it acquired the Supermarine firm in order to diversify into seaplane manufacture. Rearmament in the second half of the 1930s
had special meaning for Vickers when its Wellington
and Spitfire designs were ordered into wholesale production. By 1939 the firm's aircraft business (valued at £8.3 million) outstripped its other defence
interests (i.e. naval armament worth £7.1 million,
land armament worth £5.1 million, and warship building worth £2.9 million).[47] During World War II it ran
aircraft factories at Chester, Blackpool, Castle
Bromwich and Swindon(South Marston) in addition to
its main complex at Weybridge and the Supermarine
Works at Eastleigh. In the postwar era the firm
maintained its defence interests on a smaller scale
(abandoning the Chester, Blackpool and Castle Bromwich sites), and tried to diversify into commercial
aircraft production. Accordingly, from the defence
viewpoint, it became a major player in the V-bomber
programme of the 1950s, evolving the Valiant type.
By the same token, the Supermarine division was
tasked with producing carrier-borne combat aircraft
culminating with the Scimitar fighter. Termination
of these programmes left the firm bereft of combat
aircraft production by 1960 (incidentally, leading to
the closure of South Marston as an aircraft factory)
and reliant, for the most part, on civil aircraft
markets. The effects of peacetime equilibrium had
strongly influenced the Vickers group, especially in
so far as government policy appeared bound to reduce
aircraft contracts even further. "In defence, the
apparent implications of the Sandys White Paper in
1957 caused Vickers to conclude that, except possibly
in naval shipbuilding, its role as a supplier of
defence equipment must rapidly diminish".[48]

The evaporation of combat aircraft orders after
the Korean War episode seemed to confirm Vickers'

belief that diversification into civil aviation was
the only long-term hope for its aerospace involvement. After all, it had produced the turboprop Viscount airliner which was a best-seller through the
1950s. However, the apparent success of civil
projects was dispelled by the end of that decade.
First of all, airliner development costs matched military aircraft programmes and were a constant drain
on company resources given the long gestation period
required before any sales revenues could be forthcoming. Secondly, markets for airliners turned out to
be just as insubstantial as those for warplanes and,
in practice, failed to provide the counter-cyclical
property needed with the wide swings in defence procurement. After realising sizeable losses on the
VC-10 jetliner project, Vickers chose to divest
itself of direct involvement in the aircraft industry
and merged its interests with those of English Electric into the British Aircraft Corporation(BAC) in
1960. Ironically, BAC made most of its profits from
the much-maligned military and not from the civil
programmes it inherited from Vickers (notably the
BAC-111 or Viscount successor).[49] Equally paradoxi-
cal, Vickers reacquired an aviation interest in 1969
when the shipbuilding group purchased Slingsby Sail-
planes; admittedly not for its place in the glider
market but rather for its mastery of glass fibre
technology which could be reapplied to submersi-
bles.[50]

CONCLUSION

This chapter has stressed the simple proposition that
technical development and market evolution of aircraft are woven together. It has been averred that
while technical change - innovation - was instrumental in determining the marketability of aircraft as a
product, it was also the case that markets served to
mould the direction of development followed by the
aircraft industry. Nowhere was market influence more
paramount than in the instance of defence contracts.
Indeed, the aircraft industry has become, to all
intents and purposes, a hostage to the vicissitudes
of military requirements. These requirements abide
by cycles which bear little resemblance to orthodox
business cycles: rather, they respond to the perceptions held by policymakers of the state of international tension. The resultant wave-cycle, quite
bluntly, apportions its largesse to the aircraft
industry precisely during the times of national inse-
curity - real or imagined. Alternate phases of

stability or peacetime equilibrium are lean times for
many enterprises in the industry and can only be
overcome provided they garner a modicum of military
business (either domestic or destined for exports) or
are able to resort to the counter-cyclical expedient
of diversifying into civil aircraft production or
even out of aircraft altogether. Commenting on the
efficacy of the wave-cycle model, Higham concedes
that it varies for individual air forces and airlines
but still allows for the making of general conclusions. Those conclusions point to the overriding
importance of the state, both as regulator of military and commercial aviation markets, and ultimately,
as a main force in the evolution of technical change.
The first of these considerations, the scope of the
market, is elaborated upon in the next chapter with
reference to civil aircraft while Chapter 4 deals
with it from the vantage point of military aircraft.

NOTES AND REFERENCES

1. See, for instance, E. Mansfield, The Economics of Technical Change (Longman, London, 1968) and
J. Schmookler, Invention and Economic Growth, (Harvard University Press, Cambridge, Mass.).
2. Books on this topic are legion; a couple of
examples will suffice here: H. Penrose, British Aviation: The Pioneer Years (Putnam, London, 1967) and C.
H. Gibbs-Smith, The Aeroplane: An Historical Survey
of its Origins and Development (London: HMSO 1960).
3. Information obtained from Bill Gunston, The
Encyclopedia of the World's Combat Aircraft (Salamander Books, London, 1976).
4. P. Lewis, The British Fighter since 1912
(Putnam, London, 4th edition, 1979), pp.161-2.
5. FI, 3 July 1976, p.23.
6. R. Higham, Air Power: A Concise History (St.
Martin's Press, New York, 1972), p.32.
7. W. G. Cunningham, The Aircraft Industry: A
study in Industrial Location (Morrison, Los Angeles,
1951), p.202.
8. D. R. Jones, 'The Beginnings of Russian Air
Power, 1907-1922' in R. Higham and J.W. Kipp (eds.),
Soviet Aviation and Air Power: A Historical View,
(Westview Press, Boulder, Colo., 1977), pp.15-33.
9. Cancellation of the entire FE 2b batch for
1918 was owing more to tardy deliveries of a state-
factory product already obsolete than to the introduction of a new design.
10. R. Freeman, Thunderbolt: A Documentary History of the Republic P-47, (MacDonald and Jane's,

London, 1978), p.141.

11. J. B. Rae, Climb to Greatness: The American
Aircraft Industry, 1920-1960, (MIT Press, Cambridge,
Mass., 1968), p.197.

12. Editorial in Air Pictorial, April 1984,
p.121. In fact, aircraft delivered in 1983 from
British factories embraced 44 Tornadoes for the RAF
from BAe Warton, three Sea Harriers (for the RN) and
twelve Hawks (RAF) from BAe Kingston, and 64 helicopters to all three services from Westland at Yeovil:
giving a total of 123 combat and training aircraft.

13. P. Fearon, 'The Formative Years of the British Aircraft Industry, 1913-1924', Business History
Review, vol.43 (1969), pp.476-495.

14. R. Higham, 'Quantity vs. Quality: The Impact
of Changing Demand on the British Aircraft Industry,
1900-1960', Business History Review, vol.42 (1968),
pp.443-466.

15. The Economist, 9 December 1944, p.782.

16. The virtually unsustainable load imposed by
maximum production is evident from a comparison of
1944 and 1945 production levels. The first year was
peak output that was cut back even before the war
ended. Figures for 1944 and 1945 are respectively:
USA (96,318 and 47,714), Germany (39,800 and 8,000),
USSR (30,000 and 25,000) and Japan (28,180 and
11,066). See E. Angelucci, The Rand McNally Encyclopedia of Military Aircraft 1914-1980, (Rand
McNally, Chicago, 1980), p.361.

17. Fearon, 'The Formative Years', p.488.

18. Rae, Climb to Greatness, p.161.

19. AW & ST, 25 January 1982, p.15. Note, tar-
get-drones are small pilotless aircraft.

20. The shock of the Afghanistan invasion was
immediately reflected in a stock prices spurt for US
aerospace firms; Northrop jumping from a quotation of
40 to 49.5 virtually overnight, and most of the other
companies faring almost as well. See AW & ST, 14
January 1980, p.21.

21. AW & ST, 3 April 1978, p.41.

22. AW & ST, 7 January 1980, p.25.

23. AW & ST, 12 May 1980, p.43.

24. AW & ST, 31 October 1983, p.26.

25. Rae, Climb to Greatness, p.199. The plant
was actually owned by the US Government.

26. Ibid, p.203.

27. Air Pictorial, February 1984, p.44.

28. J. L. Atwood, North American Rockwell:
Storehouse of High Technology, (Newcomen Society, New
York, 1970), p.18.

29. AW & ST, 24 January 1977, p.11.

30. AW & ST, 3 November 1975, p.16.

31. AW & ST, 29 June 1970, pp.14-15.
32. AW & ST, 24 May 1971, p.20.
33. FI, 27 February 1982, p.475.
34. AW & ST, 7 October 1974, p.16.
35. FI, 3 July 1976, p.3.
36. FI, 27 March 1982, p.714.
37. J. B. Rae, Climb to Greatness, p.51. Note, anti-combine legislation was instrumental in breaking up this, and other comparable ventures, in the USA.
38. G. Adams, The Politics of Defense Contracting: The Iron Triangle, (Transaction Books, New Brunswick, 1982), p.342.
39. Air Pictorial, December 1979, p.460.
40. AW & ST, 8 November 1971, p.44.
41. FI, 26 February 1981, p.553. Note, the company is now styled Gulfstream Aerospace and is contemplating the sale of its Bethany plant and concentrating its activities on the Savannah, Georgia operation.
42. AW & ST, 29 November 1971, p.44.
43. AW & ST, 10 May 1971, p.66. It also had substantial steel interests.
44. C. Trebilcock, The Vickers Brothers: Armaments and Enterprise, 1854-1914, (Europa Publications, London, 1977), p.54.
45. J. D. Scott, Vickers: A History, (Weidenfeld & Nicolson, London, 1962), pp.117-18.
46. Ibid, p.151.
47. Ibid, p.264.
48. H. Evans, Vickers: Against the Odds 1956-1977, (Hodder and Stoughton, London, 1978), p.35.
49. Ibid, p.185.
50. Ibid, pp.157-8.

Chapter Three

MARKETS FOR CIVIL AIRCRAFT

Civil aviation is, to most aircraft manufacturers and
states alike, an indivisible part of the larger concept of aerospace which is unavoidably influenced by
defence considerations.[1] However, it does establish a
distinct presence in so far as markets are concerned.
Unlike the bulk of the industry whose production
activity is tied to wave-cycles of military procurement, those aircraft enterprises pandering to civil
aviation respond to conventional business cycles.
While fluctuating in response to short-term rises and
falls in economic well-being, markets for civil aircraft have followed a generally upward trend since
World War II. Revenue-passenger miles for 'Free
World' airlines increased, for example, from 75 billion in 1960 to 162 billion in 1965, 341 billion in
1970, and 501 billion in 1975. Correspondingly,
cargo traffic witnessed a surge from 2,590 billion
revenue-ton miles in 1960, through 5,874 and 11,105
billions in 1965 and 1970, to arrive at 16,553 billion in 1975. From the mid-1970s, however, the
growth in demand for civil aircraft underwent a sharp
downturn, partly in response to recession in AICs and
debt-problems in NICs.[2] It was only in 1983-4 that
orders for commercial aircraft began to significantly
rise once more. Yet, the remainder of the 1980s
offers lucrative possibilities for aircraft manufacturers capable of meeting the demands of the market,
for, not only is the crucial North American airline
sector picking up again, but many of the world's airlines are considering replacing second-generation jet
transports with new-model airliners.
     The purpose of this chapter is to review how
this recent market environment has affected the
activities of aircraft manufacturers. In particular,
it traces the ways in which aircraft firms have
responded to what was initially for a time in the
1970s a depressing market and what is now a more

promising situation. Attempts at collaboration
between firms in order to overcome problems of risk
will be stressed, as indeed will be the participation
of states who formulate strategies aimed at overcoming the general uncertainty of the civil aviation
market. For obvious functional reasons, civil aviation is approached from two standpoints; namely, that
of commercial aviation - in a word, the airline business - and that of general aviation. The latter
embraces the markets for light aircraft and execu-
tive/business aircraft. In US parlance, general aviation covers aircraft used for "transporting company
executives, salesmen, and other personnel for business purposes, air taxi services, crop dusting, sur-
veying, advertising, photography, and recreational
and instructional flying."[3] As shall be seen, the two
branches of civil aviation affect aircraft companies
differently but are united in underscoring the vital
part played by the USA in regulating demand for non-
military aircraft.

COMMERCIAL AVIATION

Commercial aviation is the province of the air carriers, or those organisations licensed to transport
passengers or cargo on well-defined routes. The
equipment that they use, airliners, varies widely in
function and size. Some machines are capable of
ready conversion from passenger to cargo configuration depending upon the immediate requirements of the
carrier (e.g. Boeing 707 and DC-8). Others are limited to a specialised role: the Concorde as a vehicle
for rapid delivery of businessmen across the Atlantic
comes readily to mind. Much more mundane, but
equally specialised in their own way, are the civil
versions of the Lockheed Hercules and Short Belfast
used for hauling heavy freight loads. What is more,
most passenger airliners are geared to a specific
market - long-haul or short-haul, high or low-density. Thus, the Boeing 707 is optimised for long-
hauls and relatively low-density routes whereas the
Boeing 727 is designed for intermediate-distance
routes which are not unduly patronised. Conversely,
in the high-density field, the Boeing 747 caters best
for long hauls of up to 10,600km while the A300 Airbus is designed more with hauls of up to 1,600km in
mind. It should be stressed, however, that manufacturers attempt to build a degree of flexibility into
their aircraft, offering, for instance, sub-models
optimised for varying combinations of route distance
and load. The Boeing 707-120, for example, was

designed to provide accommodation for as many as 181
passengers for a range of up to 6,800km, while the
707-320 has seating for up to 219 passengers and a
range of 10,040km. Even airliners confined to a particular range category have optional load configura-
tions. To give but two examples, the short-range
Boeing 737 possesses seating for 115 passengers in
its -100 form or seating for 130 passengers in its
-200 form, while another short-range airliner, the
BAe 111 comes with accommodation for 89 in the series
475 and 119 in the series 500. Notwithstanding such
flexibility, it is possible to classify airliners by
function and size, and Table 3.1 attempts to identify
examples from among the set of aircraft in production
in the early 1980s.

The light transports are really quite distinct
from other airliners in that they are targeted at
feederliner services or regional airlines, which is
to say, the small carriers linking minor airports to
the major centres of the trunkline carriers (in this
respect they are analogous to railway branch lines).
As a result, they need to be able to utilise short
runways (hence the STOL capability of many of them)
and be eminently economical (which accounts for turboprop or piston engines). Because large size is
unnecessary, airliners of this ilk can be built by
most aircraft manufacturers and, consequently, market
success rests very much on price competitiveness. In
the 20-passenger airliner category, the best price on
offer in 1984 amounted to $1.6 million for both the
Brazilian Embraer Bandeirante and the Canadian DHC-6.
More expensive competitors were provided by West Germany's Dornier 228 ($1.9 million), Spain's CASA C-212
($2.4 million), the Short 330 and 360 ($3.1 and $4.1
million) emanating from Belfast, and the joint Span-
ish-Indonesian CN-235 ($5 million).[4]

With larger airliners operating over trunkline
routes, the advantages of propeller engines are lost.
Table 3.2 displays the airliner direct operating
costs prevailing in the 1960s for US domestic trunkline services (the last decade in which piston aircraft played a significant contribution). The
superiority of large machines such as the DC-8 and
Boeing 707 over smaller jetliners (e.g. Caravelle,
Boeing 727, BAe 111 and DC-9), turboprops (e.g. Viscount, Electra and F-27), and piston-airliners (e.g.
DC-6, DC-7, L-1049G) is readily apparent. Indeed,
the classic piston-airliner - the DC-3 - had total
operating costs more than double those applying to
most jetliners: a state of affairs attributable to
the age of the design imposing excessive maintenance
costs on the one hand and labour-intensive crewing on

Table 3.1 : Commercial Aircraft Types

Category	Example	Normal Range (km)	Normal load (passengers)
Light utility transport	PBN Islander	1,400	10
Light STOL transport	DHC-6 Twin Otter	1,775	20
Short-range airliner	Boeing 737-200	3,815	130
Short-range large-capacity airliner	A300B Airbus	1,610	331
Short-range transport helicopter	Aérospatiale Puma	620	20
Short/medium-range airliner	MD DC-9/40	2,710	125
Medium-range airliner	Boeing 727-200	4,635	189
Medium-range freighter	Lockheed L-100 Hercules	3,425	- freight
Medium/long-range freighter	Il-76	5,000	- freight
Medium-long-range airliner	Tu-154	5,280	164
Medium/long-range large-capacity airliner	Lockheed L-1011 Tristar	7,189	400
Long-range freighter	An-22	5,000	- freight
Long-range airliner	Il-62	8,000	198
Long-range large-capacity airliner	Boeing 747-200	10,650	500

Source: Jane's Pocket Book of Commercial Transport Aircraft, (Collier Books, New York, 1980).

the other. The efficacy of large jetliners on trunk-lines both within and without the USA accounted for their widescale adoption by the world's major air-lines in the period of cheap energy prior to 1973. The so-called energy crisis of that year precipitated an instant reappraisal of the effectiveness of jet-liner operations. One US study remarks on the trans-formed situation.

An increase of fuel price from ten cents a gal-lon to over a dollar caused the percentage of fuel cost to direct operating cost to rise to 50 per cent, driving the early pure jet DC-8s and

Table 3.2 : Airliner Direct Operating Costs for
             Trunkline Services (1966)

Aircraft	Flight personnel costs[1]	Fuel and oil	Direct Maintenance	Total including depreciation
Douglas DC-3	1.173	0.515	1.502	3.772
Douglas DC-6	0.658	0.542	0.500	2.125
Douglas DC-7	0.452	0.439	0.687	2.232
Douglas DC-8	0.190	0.377	0.242	1.151
MD DC-9	0.444	0.462	0.260	2.062
Lockheed L-1049G	0.585	0.540	0.389	1.883
Lockheed Electra	0.376	0.339	0.514	1.763
Vickers Viscount	0.577	0.437	0.587	2.194
Fokker F-27[2]	0.531	0.418	0.649	2.263
Sud Caravelle	0.500	0.588	0.462	2.559
BAe 111[3]	0.320	0.387	0.406	1.622
Boeing 707	0.214	0.401	0.264	1.318
Boeing 727	0.263	0.383	0.326	1.512

Notes: 1. costs throughout in cents per available seat mile
       2. costs based on local service data only
       3. then designated BAC-111

Source: Abstracted from R. Miller and D. Sawers, The Technical
        Development of Modern Aviation, (Routledge and
        Kegan Paul, London, 1968), pp.287-96.

even fan jet B-707 from regular service. The
same increase in fuel price is rendering all but
the most recent model DC-9s and high-density
configured B-727s uneconomic at present fare
levels.[5]

Figure 3.1 summarises the world fleet for the
first-generation of four-engined jetliners as of
1977. That year is particularly appropriate because
it represents a hiatus between the newly-demised era
of cheap fuel and that of expensive fuel which compelled the airlines to adopt wide-bodied airliners
offering a combination of fuel-efficient engines and
scale economies in passenger capacity.[6] The aircraft
in question conform to the long-range airliner category of Table 3.1. It is no coincidence that all
four types displayed are US built - the products of
Boeing (707 and 720), MD (DC-8) and GD (Convair
880/990) - by virtue of the pre-eminence of North

Figure 3.1 : The World Fleet of First Generation
Jetliners in 1977

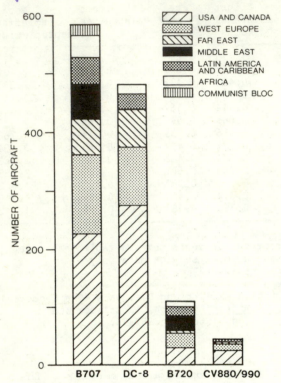

American markets. Fully 54 per cent of the four
types considered were operating for North American
airlines. In fact, as the majority of the world's
large airlines (as measured in terms of aircraft
fleets) originate in the USA, it is not surprising
that they influence airliner manufacturing to the
extent of stimulating a domestic industry to pander
to their needs (Table 3.3).

The dominance of the North American market in
the short and medium-range airliner markets is even
more telling. The density of routes serving major
cities of 500km to 1,000km apart accounts for the
huge demand for Boeing 727 and DC-9 aircraft evinced
by US carriers (Figure 3.2). Conversely, the failure
of European-made aircraft such as the Caravelle and

Markets For Civil Aircraft

Table 3.3 : Principal Airlines by Fleet Numbers, 1977

Rank[1]	Airline	Airliner total
1	United (US)	397
2	Trans World (US)	274
3	British Airways	183
4	Delta (US)	152
5	Eastern (US)	144
6	American (US)	139
7	Air France	136
8	Air Canada	119
9	Allegheny[2] (US)	107
10	Pan American (US)	104
11	Lufthansa	98
12	Braniff (US)	97
13	Iberia	86
14	All-Nippon	85
15	Western (US)	84
16	Japan Air Lines	77
17	Tarom/Romania	77
18	SAS	75
19	Alitalia	73
20	Northwest Orient (US)	68

Notes: 1. Excludes Aeroflot and Civil Aviation
          Administration of China
       2. now US Air

Source: computed from G. G. Endres, World Airline Fleets 1977,
        (Airline Publications & Sales, London, 1977).

BAe 111 to make serious inroads into the North American market acted as a major constraint on their success since other regional markets (including Europe)
were insufficiently developed to serve as substitutes. By the mid-1970s, the symbiotic relationship
between US airlines and aircraft firms had given the
latter such a commanding lead in world airliner markets that they appeared all set to monopolise the
new-generation of wide-bodied transports as well. To
that end, Boeing had sold 270 model 747s by 1977, MD
had produced 244 DC-10s and Lockheed had built 151
Tristars. In sharp contrast, the European A300 Airbus had only recorded 34 sales and the Soviet Il-86
was scarcely out of the test hangar at Voronezh. So
long as air travel remained determined by closeness

Figure 3.2 : Short and Medium-Range Jetliner
              Distribution in 1977

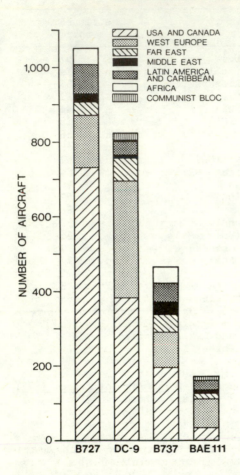

of cities containing a large proportion of affluent
citizens, US airlines would have a market advantage
over other national airlines and, to boot, would
respond by providing competitive air services which
would drum up yet further traffic growth.[7] In turn,
competition among trunkline carriers required tailor-
made equipment which effected the economies that the
carriers wanted. The resultant aircraft, the products of Boeing, MD and Lockheed alluded to, were also
suited to the requirements of non-US airlines. They
were able to out-compete the products of other

aircraft industries as a direct result of the favourable prices that occur as a concomitant of sizeable
production runs. Table 3.4 makes abundantly clear
the overriding fact that production runs of European
airliners are far shorter than American ones. Table
3.5, for its part, brings out the price advantage
usually enjoyed by US airliner producers. While the
BAe 111 was very competitively priced in comparison
to US short-range jetliners (Boeing 737 and DC-9) and
the A300 Airbus undercut the prices of some US wide-
bodied transports, the BAe 146, Fokker F-28 and A310
Airbus appeared unfavourably priced when compared to
such American competitors as, respectively, the Boeing 737, DC-9 and Boeing 757. The prospect of more
competitive prices for those European products hinges
on longer production runs and the economies of scale
that follow.

Impact on Commercial Aircraft Manufacturers

One immediate and obvious corollary of the recession
in airliner markets in the 1970s was the parlous
financial status of some aircraft enterprises. Lockheed, for instance, reputedly phased out its Tristar
wide-body airliner owing to losses of almost $2.5
billion and the prospect of sales of only 24 aircraft
a year from 1985-90 which would not make the venture
profitable.[8] Indeed, an over dependence on airliner
markets may spell doom for an aircraft firm as is
evidenced from the collapse of Handley Page Ltd in
1970. This UK firm, based at Radlett north of London, was forced into receivership with debts of $18.4
million because of its emphasis on one product, the
twin-turboprop Jetstream light airliner. The company
had forsaken defence work (whose value dropped from
$28 million in 1963 to only $7 million in 1968) to
concentrate on development of the Jetstream. However, the scale of launch costs required was underes-
timated and, devoid of military programmes as stopgap
measures, the firm foundered with the loss of 2,400
jobs.[9] Ironically, the Jetstream was resuscitated by
BAe a decade later when market prospects appeared
brighter.

It is precisely this burden of development or
launch costs which appears problematical for aircraft
firms. The gap between design and full-scale production must be covered by corporate reserves (or government launch aid) before revenues on airliner sales
are forthcoming. An enterprise undertaking diverse
projects may be better placed to cross-subsidise programmes occupying this vulnerable pre-revenue stage.
Even these diversified enterprises, however, may find

Markets For Civil Aircraft

Table 3.4 : Comparative Production Runs of Airliners:
            cumulative totals to 1976

Europe		USA	
Out of production		Out of production	
Sud Caravelle	278	MD DC-8	556
DH Comet	51	GD Convair 880/990	83
Vickers VC10	47		
Dassault Mercure	10		
In production		In production	
BAe 111	219	Boeing 727	1,195
HS Trident	117	Boeing 707/720	897
Fokker F-28	95	MD DC-9	802
Airbus A300B	23	Boeing 737	407
VFW 614	10	Boeing 747	283
Concorde	9	MD DC-10	240
		Lockheed Tristar	150
Total	859	Total	4,613

Source: AW & ST, 16 February 1976, p.22.

Table 3.5 : Airliner Price Comparisons
            ($'000 per seat), 1980

US Models		Other Models	
(twin jets)			
Boeing 737-200	92.3	BAe 111-500	84.1
Boeing 757	127.4	Airbus A300	114.8
Boeing 767	160.0	Airbus A310	160.0
MD DC-9 40/50	88.0	Fokker F-28 4000	126.5
MD Super 80	87.2		
(tri-jets)			
Boeing 727-200	89.9		
Lockheed L-1011/500	90.0		
MD DC-10 30/40	118.4		
(four-jets)			
Boeing 747-200	100.0	BAe 146-100	107.5

Source: various

summoning of the necessary resources a daunting task.
BAe, for example, is obliged in 1984-5 to find development money amounting to £30.5 million for the BAe
146, £27.5 million for the ATP, £18 million for the
BAe 125-800, and £15 million for the Airbus.[10] Boeing
went so far as to put development costs of its 757
and 767 airliners at a staggering $4 billion.[11] Both
of these firms have, accordingly, compensatory
defence programmes (amounting to sales of $2.168 bil-
lion for Boeing in 1981). Yet, Aérospatiale was
plagued throughout the 1970s by its commercial aviation projects in spite of vibrant warplane programmes. These did not prevent the enterprise from
making overall losses in several years. The loss of
$90 million in 1973, for instance, was ascribed to
the Concorde, A300B Airbus ($36 million in cost over-
runs) and Corvette light jetliner ($20 million in
losses).[12] All told, the Corvette was an unmitigated
disaster, losing FFr 900 million by the time of its
termination in 1977 and contributing "no less than 66
per cent of the total Aérospatiale deficit between
1972 and 1975."[13] Neither was the jetliner project of
sister firm Dassault an admirable venture. Its twin-
jet Mercure was cancelled after only ten had been
produced in order to contain losses on a type which
had failed to win orders. Dassault held culpable
declining airline growth rates, dropping short-haul
traffic, and price escalation as a result of dollar
devaluation and problems with suppliers in Italy
(Aeritalia), Canada (Canadair), Spain (CASA), Belgium
(SABCA) and the USA (P & W).[14] Fokker-VFW's
40-passenger contemporary, the model 614 jetliner was
also cancelled at this time: again, sales had not
materialised and the enterprise could not support
ongoing development costs. Production of the airliner terminated after only 16 had been built with
the inevitable outcome of job losses at Spire (500)
and Bremen (300).[15] Fortunately, defence contracts
mitigated the worst effects of the ill-fated venture.

> The figures could have been higher were it not
> for a redistribution by the government to VFW of
> work on other West German defence programs, such
> as F-104 Starfighter overhaul and rework, and
> minesweeper production, and the start of produc-
> tion of 25 more C-160 Transall military trans-
> port aircraft for the French Air Force.[16]

In light of the heavy costs of development, not
to mention the huge expense of failure, firms undertaking airliner projects attempt to alleviate the
inherent risks by soliciting state aid with launch

costs or through collaborative ventures with other firms. In some cases they do both, most notably the Concorde SST. Government assistance with airliner projects appears to be more readily granted when the firm in question is a state enterprise and this is nowhere more evident than in France. The French Ministry of Transport allocated $405 million for civil aviation in 1983, of which $139 million was destined for A300/310 Airbus development, $72.4 million for the new A320 and $31.8 million for the new ATR 42 turboprop airliner, while $116.5 million was destined for civil aeroengine development.[17] The whole line of Falcon bizjets and regional airliners was heavily incumbent on state launch aid. In return for Dassault agreeing to switch 55 per cent of airframe manufacture of the Falcon 50 to state-owned Aérospatiale, the government absorbed half of the costs of developing and producing the aircraft.[18] The updated version, the Falcon 900, which was due to go into production in 1986 was assisted to the extent of 30 per cent of its development costs by the French Government.[19] Such activity is not confined to France. In the UK, state-owned R-R received about $540 million in government aid during 1976-80, largely to support civil aeroengine R & D.[20]

Apart from the Concorde and Airbus projects (as much state programmes as collaborative ventures between firms), examples of firms combining their resources to build airliners have become commonplace in recent years.[21] The aforementioned ATR 42, to take but one example, is a joint Aérospatiale:Aeritalia venture with the French partner responsible for the aeroplane's wings, cockpit and final assembly (at Toulouse) and the Italian partner undertaking fuselage manufacture.[22] In a similar vein is the SF 340 commuter airliner currently being built by Saab at Linkoping and Fairchild at Farmingdale, New York. The Swedish partner is authorised to produce the aircraft's fuselage and fin, and in return for final assembly has found about two-thirds of the development costs. The US firm, meanwhile, provides the wings, engine nacelles and empennage, and the balance of the development costs.[23] In the more costly pure jet field, MD is seeking a partner to share the risks of developing a successor to the DC-9/super 80 series (i.e. the MD-80). After toying with a co-operative venture with Fokker (the MDF100), MD wants to establish a consortium comparable to the £2 billion joint venture put together by four West European governments in sponsorship of the A320 Airbus. Aiming at the market for short-range airliners (estimated at 862 aircraft by 1998), MD wishes to consolidate its

success with the 150-seat MD-80; 167 of which were
booked by American Airlines in a giant $3 billion
transaction. Despite being hailed as the deal which
put MD's commercial aviation division into a
profitable position in 1984 for the first time in 15
years, still the company cannot afford to initiate
major new airliner developments without contributions
from other firms.[24]
    The other major player in commercial aviation,
Boeing, has attempted collaborative efforts, both
officially and unofficially, since the beginning of
the 1970s. Its earlier overtures were unofficial in
the sense that the firm spread its risk load through
the incorporation of many firms into its airliner
projects as contractors and subcontractors. Thus, no
less than 53 per cent of the model 757 is built outside of Boeing, whereas three Japanese companies are
together responsible for 17 per cent of the model
767. In fact, a consortium of MHI, Kawasaki, Fuji,
Shin Meiwa and Nippi has recently joined forces with
Boeing to develop a 150-seat airliner for the 1990s.
The YXX, as it is known, will continue the precedent
set by the 767 but with the proviso that Boeing
will allow the Japanese partner much greater scope in
development of the machine (25 per cent share).
Underpinning the Japanese participation is the direct
encouragement (manifested through organisational and
financial input) of the Japanese Government and this
kind of indirect state involvement is prevalent in
other aspects of the commercial aviation business.

Commercial Aviation Markets and State Influence
In one sense, governments can directly stimulate
demand for airliners by compelling state airlines to
buy the products of the national aircraft industry.
It was in such a manner that BEA introduced the Vickers Viscount, BOAC shepherded into service the DH
Comet, Air France the Sud Caravelle, and both of
those latter, the Concorde SST. If the technical
performance of the aircraft fall short of the state
airlines requirements, governments may feel compelled
to go a step further and subsidise the operations of
the aircraft. The service records of Concorde with
British Airways and Air France, and the Mercure with
Air Inter (the French state-owned domestic airline)
attest to this course of action. Nowadays, some NICs
are following suit in obliging their own carriers to
operate domestically-made transports and, furthermore, forbidding the import of comparable machines
from the AICs. Indonesia, for one, announced in 1980
that it would prohibit the import of US aircraft

which could perform similar functions to the locally-
built C-212 turboprop airliner.[25] Brazil, for
another, attempted to guarantee a domestic market for
the Bandeirante light transport by excluding equivalent US aircraft.[26]

Even the world's single largest commercial aviation market is not free of import restrictions.
American protectionism is manifested through the
rubric of the 'Buy America Act'. Implemented originally in 1933, this act imposed penalties on US government agencies who preferred foreign equipment over
domestic equivalents. In the 1970s, the US Coast
Guard wished to adopt airliner-type aircraft for
patrol purposes and VFW-Fokker, one of the contenders
for the contract (proposing the ill-fated type 614),
reckoned that the cost penalty imposed upon it for
proffering a non-US built product would amount to six
per cent of the total contract value or "as high as
12 per cent if a losing prime US competitor in the
procurement was located in an area of heavy unemployment."[27] Eventually, much to the irritation of US
firms, the contract was awarded to Dassault for its
Falcon 20 but only after the French firm had established a US affiliate (Falcon Jet Corp) and the com-
plaints of American aircraft manufacturers had been
allayed. When the knocked-down aircraft was reassem-
bled at Little Rock, Arkansas, and then furnished
with US aeroengines and avionics, it was successfully
claimed as being more than 50 per cent US built and,
therefore, outside of the jurisdiction of the Buy
America Act.[28] While on the subject of the US Coast
Guard, it is interesting to record another instance
of a foreign purchase being challenged by US competitors invoking that protectionist measure. In this
case, Aérospatiale was able to demonstrate that even
with a six per cent cost penalty, its successful
SA-366 Dolphin helicopter was superior to the best
American entrant in the competition and, what is
more, in being assembled at Grand Prairie, Texas,
fell within the 'domestic end product' definition.[29]

American firms have also used the argument of
unfair competition as a result of state subsidies in
attempting to block the import of foreign commercial
aircraft into the US market. In 1978 Congress was
asked to consider the proposition that both Eastern
Airlines' $778 million order for Airbus aircraft and
Pan American's $480 million order for R-R powered
L-1011 Tristars was accredited to European subsidies
to aerospace enterprises and the attendant 'unfair'
financial concessions that they could, in turn, use
to tempt orders out of US airlines. Congress, in due
course, could arrive at no firm conclusions about the

validity of the complaint.[30] A more recent instance, notable in that it represents the penetration of the US market by the product of an NIC aircraft industry, is that relating to the Embraer Bandeirante. This Brazilian turboprop light airliner, mentioned earlier, was so accused by the Fairchild aircraft enterprise. Claiming that the sales of its subsidiary Swearingen's comparable aeroplane, the Metro, was adversely affected by the entry of the Bandeirante, Fairchild filed a petition with the International Trade Commission (ITC). In particular, Fairchild (supported by Beech) felt that the subsidised financial package offered by the Brazilians sufficed to push the US market share held by the Bandeirante from seven per cent in 1978 to 35 per cent in 1981. A direct consequence of this penetration, it was averred, was the running of Swearingen's San Antonio plant at only 20 per cent capacity and with only 75 per cent of its workforce.[31] The rebuttal put forward by Embraer rested on two grounds: first, that its product was unpressurised, unlike the Metro, and therefore cheaper to produce (20 to 40 per cent less) and, moreover, catering for an essentially different clientele; secondly, that the eight per cent finance rates of Embraer, while half the commercial rates required for the Metro, were still within acceptable bounds when the "after-corporate-tax cash flow costs of the two aircraft were compared." These arguments were sufficiently compelling to induce the ITC to drop its investigation on the understanding that Fairchild was not "materially injured" by Embraer.[32]

The above case serves to highlight a major form of state support for commercial aviation; namely, by way of airliner financing. Special export credits arms of governments have intervened to underwrite airliner contracts at favourable rates. Indeed, the competition among countries to facilitate such contracts may become so intense that an element of rivalry develops between the various agencies. Nowhere is this more apparent than in the wide-body airliner field. The national export credit guarantee agencies of West Germany, the UK and France supported private banks in giving a $306 million ten-year loan at fixed rates to Singapore Airlines in order that the carrier could obtain an extra six A300 Airbuses: the loan covering 85 per cent of the contract cost.[33] Prior to 1981, the Europeans and Americans had bitterly vied with each other to offer preferable financial packages. It was alleged, for example, that the Europeans managed to sell nine A300s to Toa airlines of Japan in 1980 because the US Export-Import Bank could not match the financial package, forced as it

was by the intransigence of Congress to operate with
limited funds. Before an accord was reached in 1981
among the contending states to offer standard 12 per
cent rates over ten years, the Export-Import Bank was
forced to offer 9.25 per cent rates on export credits
in comparison with the 7.5-9.0 per cent available
from the Europeans. Airliners falling under the
terms of the agreement include the US-built MD-80,
DC-10, L-1011, Boeing 757 and 767 as well as the
European-built Airbus.[34] However, the Americans do
manage to reap benefits from European finance. The
UK Export Credit Guarantee Department has been especially forthcoming in providing credits for US-made
airliners fitted with R-R engines. The Lockheed
L-1011 Tristar set the precedent: for example, a 100
per cent financial package to cover the $500 million
cost for twelve aircraft persuaded Pan American World
Airways to buy the Tristar rather than the DC-10 or
Boeing 747.[35] Other loans arranged by British banks,
but supported by the UK Government, facilitated Tristar sales to a host of airlines including TWA, Delta,
Air Canada and Air Jamaica.[36] Since the demise of the
Tristar, onus has shifted to the Boeing 757 as is
testified by a recent sale of six of those aircraft
to Air Florida.[37] It is worth recording too, that the
UK Government indirectly subsidises airliner sales
through its ownership of Shorts of Belfast. This
enterprise recently established a line of credit with
US banks (with the backing of the Export Credit Guarantee Department) in order to enable it to offer favourable financial terms in the competitive US commuter airline market.[38] The fact remains that
government support of airliner contracts is indispensable: the 85 per cent financing of Alitalia's $1
billion order for 30 MD-80s by the Export-Import Bank
in 1983 was, for example, instrumental in pulling off
the largest civil export transaction in MD's history.[39]

GENERAL AVIATION

The general aviation market is, like that of commercial aviation, dominated by the USA. Demand for general aviation is rendered feasible by a combination
of low airport costs, significant local population
with substantial average incomes, a fair degree of
industrialisation in the region and its corollary of
airports replete with technically-proficient facilities: all factors abounding in the USA.[40] All told,
the USA has more civil aircraft than the rest of the
world combined, and all except a minuscule two per

cent fall into the general aviation category.[41] Of
the 124,237 light aircraft in use in the USA in 1969,
no less than 49 per cent were single-engined machines
seating four or more, 34 per cent were smaller single-engined aeroplanes, thirteen per cent were multi-
engined aircraft and the remainder were, by and
large, helicopters. The fastest growing category (by
a factor of four since 1956) was the multi-engined
which embodies business aircraft and those fulfilling
air taxi duties. Two US light aircraft manufacturers
loom over the market - Cessna and Piper - which
together accounted for 73 per cent of all fixed-wing
general aviation aircraft manufactured in the country.[42] They are supplemented by Beech, which tends to
produce higher-value multi-engined types. A number
of other enterprises have entered the lucrative business aircraft market, several of them being subsidiaries of non-US manufacturers.

As with commercial aviation, the general aviation market experienced a tumultuous decade in the
1970s. In 1971, US manufacturers produced 7,464
light aircraft; a drop on the average figures for the
late 1960s, but still better than the production rate
applying in the 1950s (Figure 3.3). Notably, however, it took the US market twenty years to return to
the production level of 1947: a level reflecting the
boom in flying stimulated by the flight students
funded by the GI Bill.[43] The early 1970s was a period
of recession for the industry with production levels
reverting to 1960 standards. However, after 1973
demand skyrocketed, exceeding the late-1960s figures
by 1977 and peaking in 1978 with almost 18,000 aircraft built. Yet the inherent precariousness of the
market was demonstrated by the sharp reduction in
output between 1979 and 1980; a reflection of declining economic well-being. Paradoxically, by 1983 the
market situation had recovered with, for example,
both Cessna and Beech recording record sales and net
earnings ($370.6 million and $21.5 million respectively for the former firm with the equivalent figures for the latter being $204.6 million and $10 million: note, that in both cases defence sales were
down).[44] Subsequently, however, sales have slackened.

Firms were forced to take measures to counter
the effects of demand downturns in the early 1970s
and again at the end of that decade. Cessna's
response in 1971 was to close its Strother Field
facility where the assembly, painting and delivering
of its small Model 150 had been undertaken.[45] Another
light plane manufacturer, Bellanca, was forced to
suspend operations, and production of its Viking and
Champion types could only be renewed after the US

Figure 3.3 : Production of US General Aviation
Aircraft

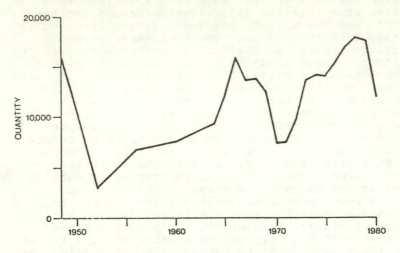

Government had agreed to underwrite the requisite
loans.[46] Despite optimistic forecasts of a market for
3,600 business aircraft in the five years succeeding
1976, many firms were caught short in the recession
at the onset of the 1980s after expanding capacity to
meet this expected surge in demand. An extemporary
solution was to extend vacation shutdowns of plants
(practised by Cessna, Piper, and Gulfstream American's Bethany, Oklahoma plants). Alternatively,
firms could redirect their business aircraft to military markets where they could be advertised as fulfilling the function of staff transports. To this
end, Gulfstream sold three of its bizjets to the USAF
as VIP transports, Cessna sold 15 Citation bizjets to
the US Navy as navigation trainers, Gates Learjet
leased 80 Lear 35As to the USAF as staff transports,
as did Beech with the loan of 40 Super King Air
machines. In the final analysis, firms could opt to
slow the development of new projects: the poor show-
ing in 1983-4 of general aviation turboprop aircraft
had the effect of persuading Beech to delay production of its Lightning while prompting Gulfstream to
delay delivery of its Commander 1200.[47]
     In emulation of airliner producers, several man-
ufacturers of bizjets have attempted to mitigate the
risk factor by pooling their resources. These collaborative efforts have typically taken on an international flavour. One of the first occurred in 1973
when the US Atlantic Aviation Corporation redesigned

the Jet Commander for IAI of Israel who then proceeded to make and market it as the Westwind (the
latest model of which is called the Astra). Other
projects have entailed manufacture in two countries.
In 1975, for example, RI and Fuji jointly produced
the Model 700 twin piston-engined business aircraft.
Basically of Japanese design, Fuji was responsible
for the manufacture of the primary structure and the
subsequent shipping of fuselage, wings and tail to
America where RI installed the US-made engines,
undercarriage, avionics and interior fittings. Eight
years later, a joint bizjet, the GP-180, was initiated by Gates Learjet and Piaggio. The US company
would produce the forward airframe at Tucson, leaving
the Italian firm to make the aft airframe, wings and
tail at Finale Ligure.[48] A prime merit of such collaborative efforts on the part of non-US firms is the
access to the US general aviation market gained by
entering into partnership with American companies.
Some non-US manufacturers attain the same end by setting up US subsidiaries. The French and Japanese
have been particularly prominent in this respect.
What is more, the state of Texas has been a principal
beneficiary of their efforts.

French subsidiaries are centred on Grande Prairie, a suburb of Dallas. About 800 workers are
employed, in the main, by the Aérospatiale Helicopter
Corporation, but with a nucleus contributed by the
Sfena Corporation and the Turboméca Engine Corporation. The first company was capitalised for $40 mil-
lion by its parent and located at this site in 1980.
Not only was it to support the sale of Dolphin helicopters to the Coast Guard (referred to earlier), but
it was to reassemble and complete to customer specifications all Astar and Twin-star helicopters manufactured in knock-down condition by the parent company at Marignane. Sfena seemingly relocated to
Grande Prairie 'by chance' because most of its business was concerned with supplying avionics to Bell-
Helicopter-Textron and not Aérospatiale, but Turboméca intentionally placed its engine support and
repair facility alongside its client Aérospatiale.[49]
While Dassault also has an American associate to support its Falcon bizjet, it is MHI which has been the
other major foreign aerospace presence in Texas.
Adopting the mantle of Mitsubishi Aircraft International after 1970, MHI shipped its MU-2 aircraft to
San Angelo beginning in 1966. The machine's fuselage
and wings were shipped from Nagoya to Texas for
installation of the engines, avionics and interiors.
Final assembly at San Angelo allowed the Japanese
parent to claim that 65 per cent of the firm's

costs were spent in the USA.[50] MHI has switched its
attention in recent years to the Diamond bizjet. As
a point of fact, the boot is sometimes on the other
foot with American firms establishing general aviation subsidiaries in foreign markets. Of special
note is Reims Aviation in France, 49 per cent owned
by Cessna, whose location enables the US company to
circumvent French import taxes. The major assemblies
of most Cessna models of light aircraft are manufactured in Wichita and delivered to Reims for final
assembly.[51] Similarly, RI gained a privileged access
to the Mexican market through its 30 per cent-owned
Aeronautica Agricola Mexicana and to which it transferred production of its crop-dusting A-9 aircraft.[52]

CONCLUSION

While, in the aggregate, playing second fiddle to
military aviation, the demand for civil aircraft is
vitally important to many of the world's leading
aerospace companies. Furthermore, as the main source
of civil aviation demand resides in the USA, it is
imperative that aircraft firms monitor cyclical
trends in US economic well-being and draw up their
aircraft projects on the understanding that only
through making inroads into the US market are they
likely to be forthcoming with a financially-success-
ful product. In so far as the US commercial aviation
market was concerned (and US carriers haul 38 per
cent of the world's total passenger traffic), the
recession of the late 1970s multiplied the attention
given to obtaining competitively-priced airliners
capable of efficient operation. In terms of the former consideration, airliner manufacturers and their
government backers responded by formulating attrac-
tive financing arrangements and attempted to out-bid
one another in wooing the airlines. Concerning the
latter consideration, much was made of the various
merits of company products. MD estimated, for example, that the maintenance costs in dollars per rev-
enue flight hour were lower for its DC-9 (183) than
those applying to the Boeing 727 (215) or 737 (225),
while in the wide-body airliner market, its DC-10
recorded $532 as opposed to the $682 of the Boeing
747 and the $689 of the Lockheed Tristar. Boeing,
for its part, makes much of the fuel efficiency of
the 767 as reflected in lower direct operating costs
than any of its competitors.[53]
    The overriding fact emerging from the general
aviation case is the sheer volume of production of
light aircraft emanating from the USA. Certain

firms, by dint of catering to this market, have emerged as specialist general aviation manufacturers. Firms such as Cessna, Piper and Beech have become, as a consequence of their commanding position in the US market, the dominant light aircraft manufacturers in the world by far. To all intents and purposes, the only possibilities for successful entry into the general aviation field by other firms is through product specialisation. In the last decade the most popular forms of product specialisation have occurred in the executive and commuter aircraft markets. Indeed, the pr fusion of bizjets on the market in the 1980s has been such as to lead to intense competition among manufacturers and, in several instances, to corporate failure. The issue of organisational survival in the face of market uncertainty is one which shall be addressed again in this book and not least in the next chapter where the whole question of corporate response to military aviation markets is reviewed.

NOTES AND REFERENCES

1. For example, the Rayner Report states "The evidence that we have had shows clearly the indivisibility of aerospace technology between civil and military applications". See <u>Government Organisation for Defence Procurement and Civil Aerospace</u>, (Cmnd. 4641, HMSO, London, 1971), p.48.

2. 'Dimensions of Airline Growth' (Boeing Commercial Airplane Company, Seattle, January 1977), pp.62-4. Note, that 1980 was for US scheduled airlines, the worst year for growth in annual traffic (-5 per cent) and only the third year since 1938 that the industry posted an operating loss. See N. K. Taneja, <u>Airlines in Transition</u>, (D. C. Heath, Lexington, Mass., 1981), p.6.

3. J. J. Warford, <u>Public Policy toward General Aviation</u>, (The Brookings Institution, Washington, DC, 1971), p.1.

4. FI, 21 April 1984, p.1081.

5. F. A. Spencer, 'A Reappraisal of Transport Aircraft Needs 1985-2000: Perceptions of Airline Management in a Changing Economic, Regulatory, and Technological Environment', NASA Langley Research Center, Hampton, Virginia, January 1982, p.111.

6. Interestingly, the usefulness of wide-bodied transports was fading by the end of the 1970s, in part owing to continued rises in fuel costs notwithstanding the fuel-efficient engines of these aircraft, partly owing to increased competition among carriers who had absorbed 370 wide-bodied aircraft in

the US alone, and also because of the declining traffic consequent upon the recession. Civil aircraft
sales dropped in the early 1980s; in 1983, for example, they declined 4.7 per cent from the previous
year. See AW & ST, 26 May 1980, p.26 and 26 December
1983, p.18.

7. For a review of airline traffic demand models, see N. K. Taneja, Airline Traffic Forecasting: A
Regression Analysis Approach, (D. C. Heath, Lexington, Mass., 1978).

8. FI, 19 December 1981, p.1812.

9. AW & ST, 19 January 1970, p.79 and 9 March
1970, p.228.

10. FI, 28 April 1984, p.1171.

11. FI, 27 February 1982, p.475.

12. AW & ST, 8 July 1974, p.20.

13. FI, 9 July 1977, p.120.

14. AW & ST, 22 July 1974, p.34.

15. AW & ST, 2 January 1978, pp.29-30.

16. Ibid, p.30.

17. AW & ST, 4 October 1982, p.32. Interestingly, $4.73 million was set aside to subsidise the
operations of the unsuccessful Mercure in airline
operations.

18. FI, 18 September 1975, p.395 and 24 July
1976, p.213.

19. AW & ST, 4 June 1984, p.67.

20. AW & ST, 13 September 1982, p.96.

21. Concorde and Airbus programmes are reserved
for Chapter 7.

22. AW & ST, 9 November 1981, p.36.

23. FI, 30 October 1982, pp.1274-5.

24. 'Firm seeks partners to develop airplane',
Winnipeg Free Press, 27 August 1984. For the pro-
fitability of Douglas, see AW & ST, 18 March 1985,
p.197.

25. AW & ST, 24 March 1980, p.11.

26. FI, 10 September 1977, p.733.

27. AW & ST, 19 January 1976, p.38.

28. AW & ST, 8 November 1976, p.19 and 10 January 1977, p.13.

29. AW & ST, 16 June 1980, p.29.

30. F. A. Spencer, 'A Reappraisal of Transport
Aircraft Needs', pp.137-8.

31. AW & ST, 20 September 1982, p.115.

32. AW & ST, 27 September 1982, p.24.

33. AW & ST, 26 July 1982, p.34.

34. AW & ST, 15 September 1980, p.17 and 10
August 1981, p.25.

35. AW & ST, 10 April 1978, p.21.

36. AW & ST, 18 January 1971, p.20.

37. AW & ST, 16 November 1981, p.34.

38. AW & ST, 6 December 1982, p.43.
39. Air Pictorial, 45 (March 1983), p.82.
Sometimes government support for airliner deals can
appear quite bizarre: for instance, the agreement by
R-R and Boeing to accept $1 billion-worth of oil in
return for selling Saudi Arabia ten Boeing 747s. See
AW & ST, 20 August 1984, p.28.
40. N. D. Baxter and E. P. Howrey, "The Determinants of General Aviation Activity: A Cross-Sectional
Analysis" in G. P. Howard (ed.), Airport Economic
Planning, (MIT Press, Cambridge, Mass., 1974),
pp.177-90.
41. J. J. Warford, Public Policy, p.2.
42. Ibid, p.10.
43. Ibid, p.23.
44. AW & ST, 17 December 1983, p.52.
45. AW & ST, 25 January 1971, p.55. During the
period from September 1969 to January 1971 Cessna's
workforce dropped from 9,200 to 4,800.
46. FI, 24 April 1975, p.671.
47. See, AW & ST, 5 July 1982, p.25; 3 October
1983, p.43; and 21 May 1984, p.15.
48. Details are available in AW & ST, 1 March
1976, pp.62-3; 22 March 1976, pp.48-9; and 2 April
1984, pp.48-9.
49. AW & ST, 18 October 1982, pp.53-61
50. AW & ST, 5 March 1973, p.9; and 12 March
1973, p.53.
51. AW & ST, 28 May 1973, p.231.
52. AW & ST, 3 May 1971, p.25.
53. N. K. Taneja, Airlines in Transition,
pp.191-8.

Chapter Four

MARKETS FOR MILITARY AIRCRAFT

As made evident in the preceding chapters, the aerospace industry and the state have historically maintained a mutually beneficial relationship.[1] In varying degrees, the state's sustained interest in the
aircraft industry revolves around the strategic
importance of the industry's output to national
defence. The militarisation of aircraft evolved from
humble beginnings and increased rapidly during World
War I. Aerial warfare was not a novel idea, as bal-
loons were utilised as observation platforms from the
eighteenth century onwards, and the Austrians actually undertook a balloon bombing raid against Venice
in 1849.[2] On 30 June 1910 Glenn Curtiss demonstrated
that it was possible to drop weapons from an aircraft
in flight, and on 20 August 1910 the first rifle was
fired from an aeroplane.[3] Naval adaptations of aviation also emerged, with a Curtiss biplane flown off
an American cruiser in November 1910, and in January
1911, another Curtiss biplane landed on a US armoured
cruiser.[4] In general however, military aviation
received a rather sceptical reception from the upper
echelons of the military establishment. In 1910, for
instance, Colonel J.E.B. Seely told a number of aviation pioneers that the UK Government, "does not consider that aeroplanes are of any possible use for war
purposes".[5] Yet with the onset of war, the military
uses of aircraft rapidly came to the forefront, and
subsequent industry output paralleled the emerging
demands of aerial combat.
    Initially, aircraft were primarily utilised as
observational platforms from which to conduct visual
and, later, photographic reconnaissance missions, as
typified by Geoffrey de Havilland's two seat BE2c
biplane (produced at the Royal Aircraft Factory,
Farnborough). Improved anti-aircraft fire stimulated
improved aircraft performance. The need to clear the
skies of intruding aircraft led to the development of

armed aircraft. From modest beginnings with pilots taking potshots at each other with hand-held pistols to the 'Fokker scourge', the fighter aircraft evolved whereby forward fuselage mounted machine guns were synchronised to propeller rotations by the Fokker developed interrupter gear. At the same time, aircraft manoeuvrability increased, as did speed as 50-100 hp power plants were progressively replaced by 200-300 hp engines. As the war continued, aircraft were pressed into new roles and their capabilities were developed accordingly. Bombing missions, originally undertaken by adapted reconnaissance aircraft and the vulnerable Zeppelin airships, were subsequently carried out by specialised light bombers (e.g. the DH-4 of 1917 and DH-9A of 1918) and heavy bombers (e.g. the Handley Page 0/400, the German Gotha and Staaken R.VI). By the war's end, the Handley Page V/1500 bomber was capable of carrying 7,500 lbs of bombs at 79-90 mph over an action radius of 1,300 miles, a notable improvement over the 0/400 which flew at 60-80 mph with a bomb load of only 1,800 lbs.[6]

Notwithstanding the laudable technological achievements made during World War I (which, in any event, would soon be eclipsed), the most significant changes concerning aircraft production occurred in its institutional environment. First of all, aircraft had become indispensable to twentieth century warfare. Indeed the sanguine visions of creating a world of "next door neighbours" gave way to the lucid realities of airpower. As Orville Wright would exclaim, "when my brother and I built and flew the first man-carrying flying machine, we thought that we were introducing into the world an invention which would make further wars practically impossible"[7], only to concede, "What a dream it was; what a nightmare it has become."[8] By virtue of its historically vindicated contributions to national defence and given that the latter falls within the purview of state activity, the aircraft industry and the state laid down the foundations of what was to become the defence market. Such a relationship, however, was predicated on the existence of a fully-fledged aircraft industry. A second major institutional change, therefore, was the creation of an industry - the aircraft industry. In the USA, for example, whereas in 1914 there were sixteen firms listed by the Census Bureau as aircraft manufacturers with a combined output of 49 planes, by 1918 production reached a wartime peak of approximately 14,000 aircraft and employment totalled some 175,000 people.[9] In Britain, likewise, the exigencies of war had transformed

aircraft production from relatively small-scale operations to true manufacturing enterprises capable of
mass production. Finally, the war experience illustrated that successful military machines required a
productive and co-ordinated industrial base. "Industrial production was as important, or more important,
to military success as tactics or strategy. Relating
its supply and procurement apparatus to a mobilised
economy had to be part of the military mission in
modern times."[10] In capitalist economies, the mobilisation effort presented particular problems in so far
as production remained outside of state authority.
The institutional integration of suppliers (e.g. aircraft producers) and the state became imperative.
The cessation of hostilities in 1918 eliminated the
immediate need for a stable integration between
industry and the military - with severe consequences
for the aircraft industry. However, the relationship
forged between defence suppliers and the state during
the war would evolve, albeit in a restricted form,
throughout the interwar years.[11]

A scant 21 years later hostilities would again
erupt and the aircraft industry would again mobilise
to meet the demands of war. As was the case in World
War I, aircraft were an important element of conflict; if anything, more vital than in the earlier
conflict. Aircraft capabilities progressed rapidly.
At the outset of war, the twin-engine medium bomber
(e.g. Bristol Beaufort) was capable of carrying a
bomb load of 1,000-1,500 lbs over a range of up to
1,000 miles at speeds averaging 200 mph; by the end
of the war, the B-25 Mitchell could carry 2,000 lbs
of bombs over a 500 mile radius, but at speeds in
excess of 300 mph. Four-engine heavy bombers
replaced the medium bombers, and the four 1,280 hp
R-R Merlin-engined Avro Lancaster night bomber could
carry a bomb load of 12,750 lbs for a 1,200 mile
radius at 160 mph.[12]

Coupled with a changing technical environment,
the institutional relationship between the aircraft
industry and the military shifted from a depression-
subsidy perspective to one of war-time mobilisation.
This was manifested in the USA through a number of
legislative actions including the approval of negotiated (as opposed to competitive) contracts with a
single contractor (in 1939) and the right to exclude
firms deemed unqualified (by the government) to
produce aircraft in quantity from the bidding process
(in 1942).[13] Despite the strengthened structural
relationships forged between industry and the state,
the termination of the war again proved extremely
disruptive. However, in contrast to the post World

War I period, the US aircraft industry would assume
an unprecedented position in the nation's defence.
In the words of the Finletter Commission,

> Our military security must be based on air power
> ... A strong aircraft industry is an essential
> element in the nation's air power. Our air
> establishment would be useless unless backed by
> a manufacturing industry skillful in techno-
> logical application, efficient in production,
> capable of rapid expansion, and strong in basic
> financial structure.[14]

Moreover, the ascendency of air power in the nation's
defence entailed significant implications for indus-
try-state relations, or more correctly, extended into
peacetime that which had evolved and matured during
wartime,

> Whether we like it or not, the health of the
> aircraft industry, for the next few years, at
> least, is dependent largely upon financial sup-
> port from Government in the form of orders for
> military aircraft.[15]

MILITARY AIRCRAFT TYPES

In general, the Tier I output of the aerospace industry targeted for the defence market may be divided
into two broad categories: piloted aircraft and non-
piloted aircraft and/or products. The latter category encompasses aeroengines, rockets, launch vehicles, spacecraft, remotely piloted vehicles (RPV),
surveilance and target acquisition drones, and a
variety of missiles. While the above constitute an
important part of the industry's defence output, the
emphasis of this chapter is on the second category,
piloted aircraft. There are two basic airframe con-
figurations - fixed wing and rotary wing - manufactured for the defence market but, among these configu-
rations, there are a myriad of aircraft types. In
1978, for example, there were 125 types of helicopters in production and more than 341 types of fixed-
wing aircraft in production.[16] The various types of
aircraft are classified on the basis of the nature of
the mission they are expected to perform.
 Two general types of fixed-wing aircraft may be
identified; namely, combat aircraft and non-combat
aircraft. The former are designed to use their own
armament for the destruction of enemy forces. In so
doing, they are expected to perform a number of

specific missions, and corresponding to these primary
missions are a variety of aircraft types of varying
capabilities. Attack aircraft are designed for
attacking surface targets of a tactical nature, as in
the case of interdiction and close air support missions. Fighter aircraft are designed to intercept
and destroy other aircraft. Bomber aircraft are
designed with the primary purpose of carrying and
releasing bombs over designated strategic targets.
In practice, individual aircraft may fulfil a number
of mission requirements. Thus, fighter-bombers are
able to intercept and destroy other aircraft, and at
the same time are able to carry air-to-surface weapons for ground attack and interdiction requirements
(e.g. the GD F-111). Similarily, the Panavia Tornado
was designed to meet the multiple mission requirements of the UK, Italy, and West Germany. In addition, combat aircraft are differentiated on the basis
of the service roles they play; hence, fighter aircraft are designed to meet the particular needs of
the air force (e.g. the MD F-15) and the navy (e.g.
the Grumman F-14). With respect to non-combat fixed
wing aircraft, a number of different types are also
available. Transports are designed to carry ten or
more passengers or equivalent cargo and are distin-
guished from utility aircraft on the basis of maximum
take-off weights in excess of 12,500 lbs (5,670
kg.).[17] There is a great variety of transport aircraft, extending from the DHC UV-18A (the military
version of the Twin Otter) with a gross weight of
12,500 lbs, to the giant Lockheed C-5A Galaxy with a
gross weight of 837,000 lbs. Utility aircraft are
generally used to carry small payloads. In addition
to transport roles, they perform "odd-jobs" and are
occasionally equipped with mission interfaces, for
example, photographic reconnaissance equipment.
Other military non-combat aircraft include reconnaissance, observation, early-warning, electronic warfare
aircraft, and trainers. In some instances, these
military aircraft simply utilise commercial airframes
suitably re-equipped for military roles, as is the
case with the Boeing E-4A/B early warning aircraft
which use a Boeing 747 airframe.

Rotary-wing aircraft - helicopters - are similarily differentiated on the basis of mission
requirements, having functions such as combat, observation, utility and transport. Specific combat versions include attack (e.g. Hughes AH-64A Apache),
anti-tank (e.g. Agusta A129 Mangusta) and anti-submarine warfare (e.g. Sikorsky SH-60B Seahawk). In a
similar fashion to fixed-wing aircraft, helicopters
frequently combine multiple mission capabilities, and

tend to be marketed to meet the needs of the individual services. In sum, the composition of defence output of the aircraft industry is generally determined by the mission requirements laid out by the military. The myriad of aircraft types destined for the defence market, therefore, may be differentiated on the basis of these requirements. What is more, there tends to be a number of potential aircraft with varying capabilities designed for specific missions. Outside of transport and utility roles, aircraft serve as platforms in a weapons system which also consists of weapons (e.g. guns, missiles and bombs) and a means of command and communication.[18]

THE DEMAND FOR MILITARY AIRCRAFT

As a part of conventional military hardware, the demand for military aircraft is dependent on the size of the defence budget. The factors determining the size of the defence budget, and thus the demand for military aircraft, are manifold and complex. Concerning the budget process, former US Secretary of Defense Robert McNamara noted, "(P)olicy decisions must sooner or later be expressed in the form of budget decisions on where to spend and how much".[19] Fundamentally, the size of the defence budget is contingent upon 'national security' considerations, which are inextricably bound up with questions concerning national sovereignty and real or perceived threats to the nation-state. Real and/or perceived threats to national security emanate potentially from both external and internal sources. It follows that the relative size of defence expenditure will generally show a positive relationship with the 'size' of the perceived threats confronting the stability and sovereignty of the state. Moreover, the perception and definition of national security will vary with the political economy and the geopolitical position of various countries. In addition to 'security' and 'nationalistic' factors, the size of the defence budget will also be affected by internal political and organisation pressures (e.g. between the military establishment and civilian groups), the potential development role attributed to defence expenditure, and the fiscal capacity of the state.[20]
Broadly speaking, therefore, the potential market for military aircraft is determined by the size of national defence budgets of the world's countries. In aggregate, this is indicated by world military expenditure and is presented in Table 4.1. In 1983, it amounted to nearly $637 billion at 1980 prices (or

Table 4.1: World Military Expenditure
(in millions of $ at 1980 prices and exchange rates)

Region	Year 1973[1]	1974	1975	1976	1977	1978	1979	1980	1981	1982	1983
USA	145237	143656	139277	137126	137938	138796	143981	153334	167673		186544
NATO Total	239988	241262	238859	233236	240340	244975	248151	256278	267118	233826	307171[3]
USSR[2]	118800	120700	122600	124200	126100	123000	129600	131500	133700	135500	137600
WTO Total[2]	128156	130866	133542	135618	137835	140073	141828	143900	146250	148635	151130
Other Europe	12025	12903	13423	14047	14029	14232	14979	15470	15348	15291	15338[3]
Middle East	19672	23431	35076	33670	37256	37017	33893	40695	45990	52350	50000[2]
South Asia	4745	4569	5006	5681	5497	5739	6220	6460	6395	7620	7865
Far East (excl. China)[2]	16730	17970	19930	21750	23220	25630	26610	27600	23790	31100	32950
China[2]	30700	35000	36300	37600	36200	40500	52700	42600	36300	37700	35800
Oceania	4802	3976	3845	3331	3848	3913	4029	4270	4488	4623	4868
Africa (excl. Egypt)	7763	9439	11416	12618	12971	13198	13526[3]	13555[3]	13390[2]	13800[2]	14100[2]
Central America	1242	1351	1502	1700	2173	2312	2468	2484	2625	2815	2825[3]
South America	7959	7998	8911	9444	10170	9980	9941	10230	10584	15745[2]	14745[3]
World Total	473732	493865	508310	514195	523539	537569	559345	563542	577978	613500	636790

Notes: 1. SIPRI Yearbook 1983
2. Estimates with a high degree of uncertainty
3. Uncertain Data.

Source: SIPRI, Yearbook 1984.

between $750-800 billion at current prices), an increase of $23 billion over the 1982 level. Over the period 1972-82, the average real growth rate of world military expenditure was 2.9 per cent.[21] Within this period, the volume increase has accelerated from an average of 2.4 per cent per year between 1975-79, to 3.3 per cent for the 1979-83 period. Geographically, military expenditure is highly variable. In terms of magnitude, the two major power blocs, NATO and the Warsaw Pact, account for about 70 per cent of total world military expenditure. The Soviet Union is overwhelmingly the major source of military expenditure within the Warsaw Pact, accounting for approximately 91 per cent of total outlays. Similarly, NATO expenditure is dominated by the USA which, in 1982, accounted for about 60 per cent of total NATO defence outlays. Overall, NATO military expenditures have experienced a dramatic increase in recent years, rising from a 3.3 per cent real growth rate in 1979-80 to an 8.2 per cent growth rate in 1982-83. In the main, this increase is spurred by the massive rearmament drive in the USA, as indicated by the US growth rate of military expenditure increasing from 3.7 per cent in 1979 to 11.3 per cent in 1982-83.[22] Table 4.2 provides a breakdown of NATO country defence expenditures (and includes France) over the period 1974-83. As can be seen, the USA is obviously the major defence market among these nations, followed by the UK, West Germany, France and Italy.

Military expenditure has also been increasing in areas outside of the two power blocs. During the 1972-83 period, for instance, the average real growth rate of Less Developed Country(LDC) military expenditure exceeded the global average and amounted to five per cent annually. As a result, LDCs increased their share of global military spending by 4.9 per cent from 18.4 per cent to 23.3 per cent.[23] To meet this increasing demand for military hardware, the share of world arms imports attributable to LDCs has increased from 71.5 per cent to 81.9 per cent over the 1972-82 period, or at an average annual real growth rate of 7.1 per cent.[24] The Middle East constitutes the largest arms market among Third World countries, with nearly $46 billion (at 1980 prices) spent on defence in 1981, and an average annual real growth rate of 11.4 per cent between 1972-82.[25] Over this period, imports grew at an average annual (real) rate of 11.5 per cent and accounted for 41.9 per cent of total world arms imports. Among the Middle Eastern countries, the largest military markets are Saudi Arabia, Iran, Israel, Iraq, Syria and Egypt. In addition to the Middle East, other LDC areas

Table 4.2: NATO Military Expenditure
(in millions of $ at 1980 prices and exchange rates)

Country	1974	1975	1976	1977	1978	1979	1980	1981	1982	1983	1
North America											
Canada	4128	4070	4341	4622	4792	4550	4703	4735	5254	5426	3
USA	143656	139277	131712	137126	137938	138796	143981	153884	167673	186544	100
Europe											
Belgium	3028	3299	3473	3562	3798	3882	3958	3995	3862	3723	2
Denmark	1417	1539	1518	1525	1584	1593	1618	1636	1683	...	1
France	20788	21709	22635	23916	25384	25962	26425	27066	27623	28042	15
West Germany	25335	25219	25044	24952	26007	26355	26692	27114	26759	27355	15
Greece	1781	2288	2508	2658	2715	2630	2276	2693	2746	2748	1
Italy	8304	7728	7687	8257	8608	9154	9578	9781	10463	10892	6
Luxembourg	36.1	38.4	41.1	40.3	43.8	45.1	52.5	54.3	54.8	55.9	neg.
Netherlands	4572	4306	4746	5237	5106	5413	5269	5325	5306	5330	3
Norway	1331	1444	1479	1507	1612	1651	1669	1686	1752	1780	1
Portugal	1572	1083	846	779	788	800	868	864	865	873	.5
Turkey	1793	2870	3295	3173	2906	2578	2442	3015	3296	3214	2
UK	23522	23490	23910	22916	23694	24744	26749	25221	26439	29443	16

Note : 1. Indicator of the relative size of military spending 1983 figures U.S.A. = 100

Source: SIPRI, Yearbook 1984.

experiencing military expenditure growth rates equal
to, or in excess of, the average for all LDCs are
Africa as a whole (eight per cent) and Latin America
(five per cent). Finally, the fastest growth in military expenditures since 1972 has occurred in OPEC
member countries, with the average real growth rate
per year (1972-82) reaching 13.3 per cent, and the
organisation's share of world arms expenditure tri-
pling from 2.4 per cent to 7.5 per cent.

An obvious limitation associated with using
aggregate military expenditure as an estimate for
demand for warplanes is that military expenditure
(the defence budget) consists of a number of spending
categories. In particular, military expenditure generally includes, among other things, outlays on military personnel (e.g. pay and various allowances),
civilian pay, infrastructure(e.g. construction),
operations and maintenance, general equipment and
supplies. The relevant component of the defence
budget in terms of aircraft demand is that portion
allocated for procurement of major equipment and
armaments, and more specifically that portion
directed towards procuring complete aircraft. In the
case of LDCs and in the absence of detailed data, a
general estimate may be formulated based on the prem-
iss that most warplanes are produced outside of the
Third World. Thus, LDCs must import most major military aircraft. Growth of arms imports by LDC area
roughly indicates the potential growth in demand for
military aircraft and is presented in Table 4.3.
Table 4.4, meanwhile, provides an indication of the
numbers of military aircraft (by type) delivered to
LDC areas over the successive periods covered in
Table 4.3. For AICs, the share of total military
expenditure devoted to procurement of major military
equipment in 1983 (or 1983-84) ranges from 14.9 per
cent in the case of Belgium to 46.9 per cent in the
case of France. However, the largest market for military aircraft is the USA. Although its procurement
component of the defence budget was significantly
less than that of France, the size of the defence
budget is far greater than that of France. As elicited from Table 4.5, there has been a general tendency for the procurement aspect of military expenditures to increase since the mid-1970s. In all ten of
the countries listed, the procurement portion of the
defence budget has increased in 1983 relative to
1974. Of particular significance has been the general increase in US procurement allocations, which
have risen to 26.1 per cent in 1983 (1983/84) from a
low of 17.4 per cent in 1976 (1976/77). In 1984,
procurement outlays amounted to nearly $62 billion,

or roughly 27 per cent of total national defence
budget outlays, while procurement budget authority
came to $86 billion or 32 per cent of total defence
budget authority.[26] In fiscal year 1971, 50.8 per
cent of total US military procurement was allocated
towards the purchase of aircraft and missiles and the
corresponding figure for fiscal year 1975 was 52.4
per cent.[27] For fiscal year 1985, aircraft procurement is scheduled to reach $41 billion (in current
dollars) or 42.3 per cent of total procurement, added
to which is a further $10.1 billion for missile pro-
curement.[28] In general, then, the demand for military
aircraft basically parallels the size of the defence
budget, and more particularly that part of military
expenditure directed towards procurement of aircraft.
Current increases in military expenditures and a
greater emphasis on procurement of military hardware
have had a positive impact on the demand for military
aircraft. As evident from the figures, the single
largest market for military aircraft is the USA.

The importance of the defence market to the aircraft industry is readily demonstrated from consideration of the dependence of its major producers on
defence production. For example, the European aerospace companies Aérospatiale , Dassault-Breguet and
MBB depend on defence demand to the extent that 50,
94, and 60 per cent respectively, of their turnover
is attributable to defence sales.[29] The major US and
UK aerospace firms are similarly dependent on the
defence market. Given such dependence, the historical pattern of military demand has significant implications for the aircraft industry. As outlined at
the beginning of this section, the demand for military aircraft is a function of military expenditure
(the defence budget). Size of the defence budget is,
in turn, a function of the real or, what effectively
amounts to the same thing, perceived threat confronting the nation-state - as determined by national
leaders and the military establishment. The size of
the defence budget, therefore, is subject to drastic
changes depending on the state of international tension. Consequently, military-industrial production
is similarily subject to volatile oscillations, which
are reflected in shifts to or from relative tranquil-
ity and war. Based on the British experience, though
applicable generally, Higham has conceptualised the
volatility of defence production (and in particular
the aircraft industry) by way of a 'wave-cycle model'.[30] As outlined in Chapter 2, that model indicates
that the magnitude and composition of output in the
aircraft industry is dependent on the state of international relations, and the perceptions of these by

Markets for Military Aircraft

Table 4.3 : Arms Imports

	Level (millions of 1981 $) and Share (in %)		Average Real Growth Rate
	1972	1982	(1972-1982)
World	20189 (100)	34424 (100)	6.1
LDCs	14431 (7.15)	28190 (100)	7.1
Africa	952 (4.7)	5144 (14.9)	8.9
East Asia	7605 (37.7)	3366 (9.8)	-5.4
Latin America	758 (3.8)	2631 (7.6)	13.9
Middle East	3880 (19.2)	14421 (41.9)	11.5
Oceania	213 (1.1)	179 (0.5)	6.3
South Asia	719 (3.6)	1730 (5.0)	9.0

Source: Derived from United States, ACDA, World Military Expenditures and Arms Transfers, 1972-82, April 1984.

Table 4.4 : Number of Aircraft Delivered between 1973-77 and 1978-82 to LDCs from Major Suppliers[1]

Aircraft Type	Cumulative 1973-77	Cumulative 1978-82
Combat Aircraft		
Supersonic	3181	3505
Subsonic	1248	565
Helicopters	2562	2435
Other Aircraft[2]	1640	1665

Notes: 1. Major suppliers included are: The Soviet Union (and other Warsaw Pact countries), United States and other NATO countries, France, and China.
2. Other aircraft include reconnaissance aircraft, trainers, transports and utility aircraft.

Source: compiled from United States, ACDA, World Military Expenditures and Arms Transfers; selected years.

Table 4.5: Expenditure for major purchases of military equipment as a share of total military expenditure, fiscal years 1974-83

Country	1974 or 1974/75	1975 or 1975/76	1976 or 1976/77	1977 or 1977/78	1978 or 1978/79	1979 or 1979/80	1980 or 1980/81	1981 or 1981/82	1982 or 1982/83	1983 or 1984/84
Belgium	8.8[1]	9.0	11.0	11.9	13.9	13.1	14.4	14.0	13.6	14.9
Canada	5.9	6.3	8.0	8.5	10.0	13.8	15.4	15.9	17.4	18.8
Denmark	19.3	19.0	19.4	21.8	16.4	16.3	18.1	17.5	16.8	17.3
France	44.7	42.6	41.1	39.2	40.2	43.0	44.5	46.0	47.8	46.9
West Germany	11.9	11.8	13.2	12.5	13.0	13.7	14.8	17.3	17.3	17.6
Italy	15.2	13.9	13.1	15.3	16.2	15.1	17.5	17.3	13.2	18.5
Netherlands	13.2	15.7	15.5	21.0	18.3	20.2	18.0	18.8	20.4	22.0
Norway	11.6	11.6	11.4	14.2	18.3	19.5	19.3	19.0	19.5	18.3
UK	17.2	19.3	20.6	22.0	23.0	23.2	25.2	26.5	25.4	28.2
USA	18.1	17.5	17.4	17.5	20.0	19.5	20.3	21.3	23.9	26.1

Note: 1. Figures are percentages.

Source: SIPRI, Yearbook, 1984.

the national elite.

The wave-cycle model identifies four general phases relating political tension and aircraft production. Peacetime equilibrium is characterised by relative calm and stability in the political sphere, while aircraft manufacturers must grapple with limited military demand for aircraft because of economic and political constraints on defence budgets. At the same time, new-generation aircraft development is limited, reflecting not only smaller defence budgets, but also the absence of an identifiable threat for which a new aircraft may be designed to counter. Upon perception of an identifiable and impending threat, the state and the aircraft industry enter a period of rearmamental instability. For its part, the state initiates the mobilisation of the economy, as manifest through rapidly expanding defence outlays and the creation of mobilisation agencies. In the USA, for example, military outlays increased from $1.2 billion in 1939 (and 13.2 per cent of federal budget outlays) to $23.6 billion (or 68.3 per cent of total federal budget outlays) in 1942.[31] Concomitantly, aircraft production capacity expanded, with factory floor space rising to a wartime peak of 16.26 million m^2 up from a scant 1.21 million m^2 in 1939 and employment increased from 76,000 to 1.7 million. Aircraft sales followed suit, increasing from $244 million in 1939 to $8.2 billion in 1944. The mobilisation period may also bring about a qualitative change in production techniques.

> In Britain, the industry started off early in the twentieth century as a foundling which was taken in by amateur gentlemen as an avocation ... as war loomed on the horizon about 1911 or 1912 the industry began to find itself moving from haphazard hobby full of hope to honest (mass production) manufacturing.[32]

Of course, such rapid expansion of industrial capacity confronts a myriad of supply constraints. To overcome these, the state may establish its own production facilities and/or convert potential factory space of other industrial sectors to wartime production, as was the case in Britain and the USA with the conversion of automobile plants to aircraft production. In terms of the composition of output, aircraft production becomes almost entirely defence oriented. Moreover, the variety of aircraft types is rationalised in order to facilitate mass production. Whereas between 1934 and 1942 the RAF had a total inventory of 75 designs (including those on order in

the USA), only eight of these were produced in quan-
tities in excess of five thousand.[33] When the entire
economy is fully mobilised, a period of wartime equilibrium exists. During this period, capacity utili-
sation is maximised, and the composition of aircraft
output is governed by strategic priorities and operational requirements as well as by supply constraints.
When the perceived threat has diminished, the state
and the aircraft industry are faced with a period of
demobilisational instability. From the latter's perspective, military demand for aircraft production
falls off rapidly and the industry is confronted with
serious questions of resource adjustment in preparing
for a return to peacetime equilibrium. Again, with
respect to the US aircraft industry, sales, production (in terms of millions of airframe pounds per
year), and employment dropped from $8.2 billion, 1.1
billion, and 1.7 million during the peak war period
in 1944 to $711 million, 24 million, and 221,000
respectively in 1946.[34] Fully half of the sixteen
leading aircraft companies identified by the President's Air Policy Commission (i.e. the Finletter Commission) did not show a profit in 1947.[35] Over this
period of demobilisational instability, defence outlay:
declined from a figure of $79.9 billion in 1944 to
$13.8 billion in 1947.[36] In terms of the
composition of output, the cessation of hostilities shifts the onus of production increasingly
towards civil products, although at least a minimum
defence capability (surge capability) is maintained
as a part of the nation's defence. Yet, as an integral component of national defence, the cyclical
nature of the demand presents particular problems to
defence planners. The need to maintain a surge capability for periods of emergency must therefore be
institutionalised in the defence budget. It is this
consideration which tempers the contemporary defence
market, and it will be addressed shortly.

THE SUPPLIERS

     The design, development and production of major
aircraft and aeroengines (and missiles) is undertaken
by a number of large corporations commonly denoted as
prime contractors. Table 4.6 presents a general
overview of the composition of output and size of the
major aircraft producers in the USA and Western
Europe. As can be seen, most major aerospace firms
are engaged in production of a number of aircraft
types, with the larger corporations generally producing more types than the smaller firms. Equally evi-

dent, is the fact that the major US aerospace companies are substantially larger than their European
counterparts. The ownership characteristics also
vary between the American and European suppliers. As
regards the former, all the major aerospace defence
contractors are privately-owned corporations. In the
European case, however, there is a marked propensity
towards state ownership, with virtually all the major
aerospace contractors having substantial state
involvement. Recently, though, the UK Government has
announced its intention to divest itself of BAe.
Political inclinations notwithstanding, the UK Government has pledged to maintain a 'special share' of
BAe to ensure at least a watchful eye on the company's future.

Another feature of the American aerospace corporation is its tendency to specialise in particular
weapons types for the particular services. Thus, for
example, Boeing, GD and RI are bomber enterprises for
the USAF. Grumman, LTV and, more recently, MD make
fighters for the Navy, while GD and MD have displayed
an affinity for manufacturing USAF fighters. In
fact, the 'dividing up' of airframe manufacturers
dates back to at least 1940. At that time, the military services allocated 'qualified bidder' firms
amongst themselves and began augmenting the production capacities of the specific firms within their
respective supplier stables. Thus, the Navy maintained jurisdiction over Brewster, Chance Vought,
Consolidated, Grumman, Spartan and part of Douglas,
while the Army scooped up Beech, Bell, Boeing,
Cessna, Curtiss, Fairchild, Lockheed, Martin, North
American, Ryan, Stearman, Stinson, Vultee and also
part of Douglas.[37]

The foregoing sections have briefly outlined the
demand for military aircraft and presented the major
aerospace corporations catering to the defence market. The following section will describe the work-
ings of the defence market. Based on the predominance of US aerospace corporations in the defence
market, and given that the single largest market for
military aircraft is the United States, the focus of
the following section will be on the USA.

THE DEFENCE MARKET: THE MILITARY-INDUSTRIAL COMPLEX

In a narrow sense, the MIC and the defence market are
synonymous. From a strategic perspective, the volatile nature of the demand for aircraft has significant implications, given the importance of aircraft
to national defence. In contrast to the period fol-

Markets for Military Aircraft

Table 4.6 : The Military Aircraft Enterprises

	Attack	Fighter	Bombers	Transports	Utility	Training	Reconnaissance	Observation	Early waiving	Electronic warfare	Patrol and Anti-Submarine	Helicopters	Missiles	Turnover
USA														
Boeing			x	x		x				x			x	$11.1[1]
GD		x	x	x						x			x	$ 7.1[1]
MD	x[a]	x	x					x					x	$ 8.1[1]
RI			x			x			x				x	$ 8.1[1]
Lockheed				x		x					x		x	$ 6.5[1]
Grumman	x	x						x	x	x				$ 2.2[4]
Northrop	x	x				x	x							$ 2.5[4]
UTC												x		$14.7[1]
Hughes												x	x	
Bell												x		
Fairchild	x					x								$ 1.1[4]
France														
Aérospatiale	x[b]			x		x						x	x	3331[2]
Dassault-Breguet	x[c]	x	x			x					x			1967[2]
Germany														
Dornier	[b]			x										662[2]
MBB						x					x			2391[2]
UK														
BAe	x[a][c]	x	x	x		x	x		x				x	3663[2]
Westland												x		506[2]
Sweden														
SAAB-Scania	x	x				x	x						x	13426[3]
Other Europe														
Fokker				x							x			516[2]
Aeritalia							x							612[2]
Macchi	x					x								
Agusta												x		503[2]

Notes: 1. Source _Fortune_ 30 April 1984 p. 44 (in 1983 $ billions).
2. AW & ST, 12 March 1984 p. 74. Figures are 1982 million European Currency Units. In 1982 1 ECU was equivalent to $0.98.
3. In Ball and Leitenberg (eds.), _The Structure of the Defense Industry_, 1983, p. 152. Figure is for 1979 and in million Skr.
4. _Fortune_ 2 May 1983, p. 238 in 1982 sales in billions of $.

lowing World War I, the USA emerged from World War II with a distinct geopolitical vision, that is to say, Pax Americana. As a part of its military role in world affairs, the United States required a strong aircraft industry. Yet, disarmamental instability left the industry in a shambles. In recognition of the industry's dependence on military demand, and consistent with the nation's global objectives, the Finletter Commission outlined the principles of what would be coined the MIC.[38] Specifically, the Commission argued,

In a freely competitive economy the number of companies manufacturing a particular product levels off at a point determined by the ordinary laws of economics. In the case of the aircraft industry, however, it would be dangerous to rely only on the operation of these laws. The demand factor fluctuates so violently from peace to war. If a reasonable degree of expansibility is to be maintained for periods of emergency, it is necessary to exercise some industry wide control in the interests of national security. It may even be desirable to keep a few marginal manu- facturers in business who might be forced out if the normal laws of supply and demand were allowed to operate...[39]

Moreover, in order to facilitate design, development and production continuity, "each company should, at any given time, have at least one type in production, one in development, and one in the design-study stage".[40]

Structure
Defence production is characterised by a highly con- centrated market structure. On the demand side, the government is the sole purchaser of defence output (although export sales are also a source of demand) and thus is a monopsonist. While the Department of Defense (DoD) is formally the single buyer, in real- ity, it consists of a number of different factions. To be specific, the various services - the Army, Navy, Marines, and the Air Force - each have particu- lar requirements and compete with each other for defence dollars and, in so doing, influence defence demand. Similarily, within the individual services themselves, there are a variety of different factions with competing objectives and visions, which also influence the nature of demand.[41] On the supply side, there are a handful of large corporations, the prime contractors, which form a monopolistic/oligopolistic structure. The structural framework of the defence market, therefore, is typified by a monopsonistic - monopolistic/oligopolistic setting.
  Defence demand is realised through the alloca- tion of prime contracts for major weapons systems. Not surprisingly, given the market structure, the allocation of these awards tends to be concentrated in the hands of the major defence contractors. His- torically, the top 100 defence contractors have gen- erally received about 60 per cent of the US military prime contract awards since World War II. In fact,

between June 1940 and fiscal year 1965, the top 50
prime contractors received from 56.3 per cent to 66.9
per cent of the total major awards.[42] The historical
legacy has remained intact to this day. In fiscal
year 1983, the top 100 defence contractors received
$89.6 billion (or 69.9 per cent) out of total mili-
tary prime contracts valued at $128.2 billion.[43] In
the same year, the top ten defence contractors, nine
of which were major aerospace corporations, received
prime contracts worth roughly $44 billion or 34.4 per
cent of the total major awards.[44] Further, the tendency for particular defence contractors to specialise in the production of specific weapons systems
obviously results in high concentration ratios in
those product areas. The evolution of the industrial
structure for selected aircraft types is depicted in
Table 4.7 and illustrates the extent of market concentration. Thus, in fiscal year 1967, for example,
the top four firms received 97 per cent of the major
contract awards for fighter and attack aircraft.
Meanwhile, the top eight firms received virtually all
the main contract awards for most military aircraft.[45] Judging from Table 4.7, it is reasonable to
suppose that the concentration ratios have increased
since 1967. It should be mentioned, moreover, that
not only are defence contracts concentrated among the
top defence contractors, but these firms are also
among the largest corporations in the United States.
Fully 75 per cent of the top 100 defence contractors
were among the top Fortune 500 list of firms, and 29
out of the Fortune top 50 were major defence firms in
1968.[46] In 1983, nine out of the top ten defence contractors were all among the Fortune top 60.[47] In general, then, the major military prime contracts are
concentrated in the hands of few large corporations,
many of which are major aircraft (and aeroengine) producers.

The obverse of concentrated defence contract
allocations is a marked dependence on defence sales
by the recipient firms, especially aerospace companies. This acute dependence on defence production is
vividly illustrated in Table 4.8 for selected US
aerospace firms. In the cases of GD, MD, Lockheed,
Grumman and Northrop, dependence is especially pronounced over the period covered, with defence sales
accounting for well over half of the firms' turnover.
Boeing, though somewhat less dependent than the other
firms, none the less, relies on defence contracts for
its survival. RI is also heavily dependent on
defence sales in the first and last period. The
smaller portion of its turnover directed towards the
DoD during the 1970s is offset by the fact that RI

Table 4.7: Competing Firms in the American Aircraft Industry, 1960-76

	1960	1968	1976
Fighter and attack planes	Lockheed, Convair, Douglas, McDonnell, Vought, Republic, Northrop, Grumman, Rockwell (L.A.), Rockwell	Douglas, McDonnell, Vought, Republic, GD (Forth Worth), Northrop, Grumman, RI (L.A.), RI (Columbus)	MD, Vought, Fairchild, GD (Fort Worth), Northrop, Grumman
Bombers	Boeing, GD (Fort Worth), Rockwell	Boeing, GD (Fort Worth), Rockwell	Boeing, RI
Military transports	Boeing, Lockheed, Douglas, Fairchild, Grumman, Convair	Boeing, Lockheed, Douglas	Boeing, Lockheed, MD
Commercial transports	Boeing, Douglas, Lockheed, Fairchild, Convair	Boeing, Douglas, Lockheed	Boeing, MD, Lockheed
Helicopters	Boeing, Lockheed, Bell, Sikorsky, Hughes, Kaman, Hiller, Gyrodyne, Cessna	Boeing, Lockheed, Bell, Sikorsky, Hughes, Kaman, Hiller	Boeing, Bell, Hughes[1], Sikorsky

Note: 1. Hughes Helicopters has been acquired by MD.
See AW & ST, 2 January 1984, p. 22.

Source: Gansler, 1980.

received NASA contracts in excess of $500 million in
six out of the ten years covered.[48] Consequently, the
structure of the defence market in the USA is best
described as a highly 'imperfect' entity characterised by a monopsonist - monopolist/oligopolist framework. The historical evolution of this structure has
given rise to a unique set of market conditions, and
it is to these that we now turn.

Defence Contracting
The crux of the defence market is the relationship
between the defence contractors and the state.
Ostensibly, in the United States, this relationship
is expected to be at arm's length, given that the
defence contractors are private corporations and outside of direct state authority. However, in their
role as 'guardians' of national security, and as 'national' assets (albeit privately owned), the defence
contractors do not expect to be compelled to do business at a loss and, furthermore, rely upon government
support to maintain capacity and ensure at least minimal profit levels. To facilitate these ends, the
institutional milieu in which defence contracting
occurs resembles an 'Iron Triangle',

> A political relationship that brings together
> three key participants in a clearly delineated
> area of policy-making; the Federal bureaucracy,
> the key committees and members of Congress, and
> the private interest.[49]

In the context of defence contracting, the relevant
participants are the DoD, the House and Senate Armed
Services Committees and Defense Appropriations Sub-
committee, and the members of Congress whose dis-
tricts contain defence firms; and the firms and various participants in the defence industry. The
outcome of these affinities is a "community of shared
assumptions" which blurs the distinctions between
public and private interest.[50] As a result, industry
may appropriate aspects of state authority, and in
the case of defence, the defence contractors play a
role in defining national security and its requirements.
    The institutionalised interdependence between
the state and the defence firms stands in sharp contrast to the usual customer-producer relationship
extant in the civilian economy. As such, and in con-
tradistinction to that posited in conventional
theory, the defence market exhibits a variety of special features. In the first place, only a select few

Table 4.8 :   Dependence on Defence Production of
              Selected US Aerospace Firms
              (DoD Contracts: Amount and % Total Sales)

Firm	1961-1967[1] $m	%	1970-1979[2] $m	%	Fiscal 1983[3] $m	%
GD	8824	67	17901	74	6818	95
MD	7681	75	18461	56	6143	76
Boeing	7183	54	12039	29	4423	40
Lockheed	10619	88	17473	56	4006	62
RI	6265	57	8322[5]	20	4545	56
UTC	5311	57	13734	33	3867	26
GE	7066	19			4518	17
Grumman	2492	67	10773	90	2298[4]	
Northrop	1434	61	6175	58	847[4]	
Raytheon	2324	55			2728	46
LTV	1744	70			1343[4]	

Notes: 1. Source: Carroll W. Purcell, ed., The Military-Industrial-Complex,
          1972, Appendix 5.
       2. Derived from Gordon Adams, The Politics of Defense Contracting
          (Transaction Books, New Brunswick, 1981). The figures
          do not include NASA contracts.
       3. Fortune, 30 April 1984.
       4. AW & ST, 23 April 1984.
       5. RI receives significant NASA contracts although these are not
          included here.

firms are actually eligible to bid on defence contracts. The DoD has a highly complex set of procurement regulations with literally thousands of pages of
text outlining the manner in which defence contracting is to be undertaken. Conforming to these regulations requires special accounting procedures as well
as specific quality-control and production procedures. In this fashion, the DoD (the purchaser) is
able to impinge upon the internal decision-making of
the firm. As a consequence, traditional supplier
decisions such as whether a particular component is
to be produced in-house or subcontracted may in fact
be made by the defence department. In view of this
highly regulated environment (a somewhat unique environment in that the regulator and the buyer are the
same), firms simply submitting a lowest bid on a particular project need not be awarded the contract. In
addition to cost considerations, defence contractors
must be 'responsible', that is, the contractor must

demonstrate its capability to perform successfully in
the defence environment - a task which presupposes
defence experience and a reasonably large resource
base.[51] That a large resource basis is required is
due to the high cost, in terms of technical expertise
and time, of preparing contract proposals. The proposal of LTV submitted to the Navy for a new aeroplane consisted of 194 bound volumes totalling some
82,000 pages (and yet the company failed to win the
contract).[52] The above example points to another
aspect of the defence market which has grave implications for defence firms and generally differentiates
this market from civilian ones. Specifically, competition among defence contractors for a particular
proposal usually involves an 'all or nothing' situation. While civilian firms compete and advertise to
capture relative market shares, there is no comparable situation for military prime contract awards:
rather, the DoD mostly selects a single supplier to
produce the entire requirement.[53] Firms, therefore,
are required to allocate substantial resources for
developing new products (i.e. major aircraft and
weapons systems) embodying extensive technological
sophistication (and thus significant R & D efforts)
and present these proposals in a highly structured
way, yet without any assurance of a possible market.
The complexity of the process presents a unique environment of uncertainty in the defence market. Thus,
in contrast to the civilian economy,

> (T)he weapons acquisition process is character-
> ised by a unique set of uncertainties which dif-
> ferentiates it from other economic activity. To
> be sure, uncertainty is a pervasive feature of
> all economic activity, and most of all the
> uncertainties in weapons acquisition have their
> commercial counterparts. But there is unique-
> ness in both the magnitude and the diverse
> sources of uncertainty in weapons acquisition.[54]

Indeed, not only is there an inherent technological
uncertainty, but a myriad of political and bureau-
cratic pressures ultimately colour the acquisition
process.[55]
Figure 4.1 indicates that the lion's share of
defence contracts is awarded on a non-competitive
basis. Approximately 90 per cent of total dollars
allocated to defence contractors is done on the basis
of negotiation, and the remaining 10 per cent is
allocated on an open format. Ostensibly, the DoD is
pledged to make use of competitive bidding in the
awarding of defence contracts. Notwithstanding this

Figure 4.1 : Trends in the Awarding of Department of Defense Contracts

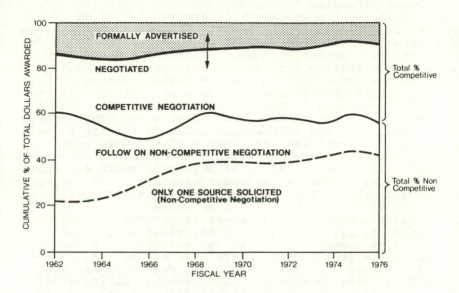

commitment, most defence contracts are awarded under 'exceptions' to competitive bidding requirements. Among these exceptions are: public exigency, experimental, developmental, or research work, specialised capital investment, critical schedules, prior investments, and national security and/or industrial mobilisation considerations.[56] The last consideration is generally held as sacrosanct. Yet even detractors of the existing procurement patterns recognise the need for some flexibility on this account as the recent US Senate proposals to increase competitive bidding on defence contracts duly attests. But two exceptions to the proposed Bill, which is designed to increase competition in the award of defence contracts, are made explicit. In the first place, it may be necessary to award the contract to a single source in order "to maintain an essential industrial capacity, achieve industrial mobilisation or establish or maintain an essential research capability". Secondly, exception is justified when, "disclosure of the agency's needs to more than one source will compromise the national security."[57] However, the institutionalised interdependence of the defence contractors and the state (the Iron Triangle) acts to make the determination of "essential" and "national security"

extremely problematic - in so far as the individuals
making these decisions belong to a "community of
shared assumptions".

In fact, most contracts are awarded on an exclusively non-competitive basis, owing to either a sin-
gle-source solicitation, or as a negotiated follow-on
contract. Moreover, the extent of non-competitive contracting displays a positive relationship
with the size of the defence contract in question. A
DoD report revealed, for example, that in fiscal year
1972, contracts in the $100,000 realm had 57.9-59.6
per cent of the dollars awarded on a non-competitive
basis, while the corresponding figure for the $1 mil-
lion to $10 million range was 60.8-68.9 per cent.
Significantly, those contracts in excess of $10 milli
(39.2 per cent of the total dollars), which encompass
virtually all major aerospace contracts, had 76.8 per
cent of the contracts allocated on a non-competitive
basis.[58] Obviously, defence contracting is a special
kind of business. The extent of non-competitive
awards is also a product of the stage of the contracting process. Frequently, a number of major
aerospace corporations compete in the initial phases
of a future aircraft programme. Thus, for example,
LTV (V-1100), Northrop (P-530, P-610), GD (GD-401),
Boeing (Boeing-618) and Lockheed (X-27) all responded
to the USAF Systems Command Aeronautical Systems
Division (ASD) request for proposals for a lightweight fighter. Of these, the ASD recommended the
selection of the GD and one of the Northrop designs
as the competing prototype developments, and awarded
$37.9 million and $39 million respectively for this
purpose. Subsequently, the two firms went all out to
win the contract with the eventual winner being the
GD-401 (restyled the YF-16 and later, the F-16).

At the point when a particular prototype (contractor) is selected for full-scale engineering and
production, the market structure is significantly
altered. Although only two competitors may be vying
for a single contract, competition may be extremely
intense, so much so that, "competition in the limiting case of only two rivals may be just as effective
from a behavioural standpoint as competition among a
few firms."[59] However, once a contractor is selected,
the government is 'locked in' to a single source of
supply for the duration of the project. The market
structure is, therefore, radically transformed into a
monopsony-monopoly situation. Much of the government's previous bargaining leverage is lost owing to
the highly specialised nature of capital investment
associated with major aircraft production. In preparing for the renewed B-1B programme, for instance,

RI invested $150 million for production machinery and an additional $150 million for facility construction, including an $83 million final assembly plant at Palmdale, California.[60]

In the circumstances, the firms are able to pass the burden of cost-overruns and technical problems on to the purchaser, the DoD. The all or nothing nature of defence contracting coupled with the transformation of the market structure upon the award of a major contract induces firms to 'buy-in'. This entails a firm submitting a low initial bid for a particular project, then, assuming its proposal is technically acceptable, renegotiating the terms of the contract once selected as a prime contractor. A successful buy-in can guarantee the firm a stable production rate for many years. Notably, however, the genesis of most production contracts rests in antecedent R & D contracts. It is in this light that Boeing, Lockheed and MD reportedly employed some 6,000 specialists to formulate their proposals for the C-5A programme.[61] Successful competition for these contracts is essential, since "a contractor that gets a project to the prototype stage often has a procurement package that is almost unstoppable."[62] Attesting to the strength of the momentum is the case of the B-1 bomber. In 1977, after $6.1 billion had been spent and four prototypes nearly completed, President Carter suddenly cancelled the project, denouncing it at one point as "wasteful".[63] A project of the magnitude of the B-1 is not easily quashed, however, and it was subsequently re-established by the Reagan administration with a cost estimate of over $20 billion.

A salient characteristic of the defence market for aircraft is that the contract terms rest primarily on the grounds of technical criteria at the virtual expense of cost-competitive (price) criteria. This technological imperative promotes, "rapid technical change, in which every component part of successive weapons systems is pursued up to and beyond the state of the art."[64] Underpinning this technological imperative is substantial state underwriting of aerospace R & D expenditure, as evidenced in Table 4.9. Clearly, throughout the 1970s the technological dynamic of the industry was driven by the liberal provision of R & D monies to the main aerospace defence contractors. In virtually all instances, US Government sponsored R & D exceeded that undertaken by the firms themselves. The fiscal year 1983 figures on DoD prime RDT & E contract awards (those with a net value over $25,000) further vindicates the technological predominance of major aerospace defence

contractors. Of the top ten award recipients, nine
are major aerospace corporations with contracts valued at greater than $7.3 billion.[65] As was the case
with the distribution of prime military production
awards, prime military RDT & E contracts are concentrated among the top defence contractors which tend
to be aerospace corporations. This positive relationship lends credence to the importance of antecedent R & D to future production contracts. The concentration of R & D contracts in the hands of the
major contractors, therefore, reinforces the concentration of defence production.

The dimensions of technological change in the
aircraft industry, including the defence segment of
the business, are discussed in Chapters 2 and 6, and
thus will only be considered here from the perspective of defence contracting. Technological competition in the aerospace defence market emphasises the
progressive improvement of a particular set of performance characteristics.[66] Coined "baroque" by Kaldor, this technological dynamic is characterised by
trend improvements and the multiplication of roles,
and results in aircraft which can fly at greater
speed with greater and more effective payloads. By
virtue of the historic relationship between the military and the defence contractors, the pattern of
technological change is 'conservative' in that neither the prime aerospace defence contractors nor the
generals are prepared to develop revolutionary weapons systems which would undermine their own institutional basis. (Noteworthy in this respect is the
ongoing saga of the relative merits of long-range
manned bombers in an era of ICBMs). This technological change is motivated by a number of factors.
From the perspective of the prime contractors, it is
the desire to capture major defence contracts which
are awarded, by and large, on technical grounds.
From the DoD perspective, there is the imperative to
stay ahead of the enemy. In terms of the latter, the
DoD defines a 'mission' for which a major aircraft
may be developed. The determination of this 'mission' is based in varying degrees on the perceived
threat confronting the nation's security. In the
absence of detailed information concerning the enemy's capabilities, the DoD is forced to formulate
threat scenarios, which may or may not be realistic.
The problem in ascertaining what constitutes a plau-
sible threat and what does not is that the relevant
information may be sensitive and thus not divulged.
While it is expected that the military defines the
mission requirement and awards R & D monies to potential suppliers to design and develop an appropriate

Table 4.9: Dependence of US Aerospace Firms on State Sponsored R & D

Firm	Total Sponsored by US Government, 1970-79 ($ million)[1]	Total Company-Sponsored 1970-79 ($ million)[1]	Fiscal 1983 DoD Prime RDT & E Awards[2] ($ million) and Rank
Boeing	5622.8	1884.1[3]	1703.5	1
GD	3614.4	207.8[3]	643.5	7
Grumman	2306.0	3119.0	131.8	28
Lockheed	4982.8	473.6	9,22[7]
MD	6571.4	1634.3	647.3	5
Northrop	821.7	229.3[4]	245.5	16
RI	6884.4	638.9[5]	1171.7	2
UTC	2252.8	2781.1[6]	339.4	10

Notes:
1. Derived from Gordon Adams, The Politics of Defense Contracting, 1981.
2. AW & ST, 18 June 1984 p. 85.
3. For the period 1973-79.
4. For the period 1971, 1973-79.
5. For the period 1973-79
6. For the period 1972-79
7. Lockheed Missiles and Space Co. ranked number 9, while Lockheed Corp. ranked number 22. Their respective awards were $509.2 million and $194.4 million.

weapons system, the institutional interrelationship between the military and industry has bridged the gap between the two stages. In effect, defence contractors have internalised the process, since defining a mission often presages the definition of a new weapons system. A Raytheon (a major aerospace defence contractor) representative aptly reveals this state of affairs.

> The day is past when the military requirement for a major weapons system is set up by the military and passed on to industry to build the hardware. Today, it is more likely that the military requirement is the result of joint participation of military and industrial personnel, and it is not unusual for industry's contribution to be a key factor. Indeed, there are highly placed military men who sincerely feel ` that industry currently is setting the pace in the research and development of new weapons systems.[67]

Two levels of technological evolution may be discerned. On the one hand, there is the successive improvement of a particular aircraft type as indicated by varying marks (e.g. F-16A, F-16C). On the other hand, there is a compelling force driving weapons systems to the fringe-of-the-art. Hence, the USAF's advanced tactical fighter programme, the replacement of the F-15 air superiority fighter, is expected to incorporate the most advanced technology, including the use of very-high-speed-integrated-direct technology, to integrate avionics systems and advanced composite materials.[68] Similarily, the US Army's current LHX helicopter programme advocates technological advances in rotor design, composite structures, flight control systems, drag reduction, propulsion, mission equipment and cockpit automation and integration.[69] Equally indicative of contemporary technological change in aircraft is the multiplicity of mission requirements and increasing reliance on avionics systems. In terms of the latter, whereas about ten per cent of the engineering effort on the Army/Bell AH-1 (one of the helicopters to be replaced by the LXH) was devoted to avionics, the corresponding figure for the LHX is expected to be around 50 per cent.[70] With respect to the former, the LHX is being designed to replace eight existing types of helicopters utilised in light utility, scout and attack roles. An industry spokesman captured the essence of the technological imperative of the LHX in these words: "We are working at the cutting edge of technology across the board ... there is not one area in which we're not challenging our technical capabilities."[71]

The technological imperative built into the defence market does have a number of serious side effects. Most obvious has been the rapid escalation of programme costs. The LHX, for example, will be the most expensive helicopter programme ever undertaken by the Army, with development costs pegged at $3 billion and procurement costs at more than $30 billion.[72] The projected cost of the LHX is, in fact, a logical outcome of the general trend pervading all major aircraft developments. As technical complexity has increased so too has costs. A caveat is in order, however, in that it is difficult to draw a strict comparison between say the Supermarine Spitfire of 1936 (cost of about $300,000) and the Panavia Tornado of the later 1970s (cost of around $10 million) since in many respects they are qualitatively different products. The fact remains, though, that cost escalation is universal.[73] The origins of cost increases are manifold. In part, unit costs may increase due to continued improvements in aircraft capabilities. The Navy's decision to equip its F/A-18s with forward looking infrared and laser spot trackers is estimated to add approximately $2 million to the aircraft's $24.1 million (in 1982) price tag.[74] On the other hand and perhaps more importantly, there are costs associated with working at the technological frontier and attempting to integrate multiple systems into a single aircraft as is blatantly evident in the massive cost overruns of the Lockheed C-5 and GD F-111 programmes. The B-1 programme, moreover, had a cost escalation of 18 per cent over seven years which, in view of the sheer scale of the venture, amounted to $3 billion dollars. In the case of the Panavia Tornado, the decision to increase engine thrust resulted in a ten-fold increase in development cost over the original estimates.[75] In most major aerospace programmes, in fact, there is a constant revision of technical criteria and specifications which escalate development costs, and which necessitate constant contract negotiations (and frequently result in cost-plus type contracts). Many defence development contracts have these cost-growth clauses imputed at the outset. Fairchild's recent contract for the USAF next generation trainer provides an example. The contract award to Fairchild is a 'fixed-price' contract for $104 million for the design, development, fabrication, test and delivery of prototype aircraft. Its terms allow the service to absorb 85 per cent of cost increases during the

programme up to a maximum of 125 per cent cost
growth, beyond which Fairchild is wholly responsible.
Total costs for the trainer programme are estimated
at $3 billion. In addition to the cost growth prob-
lems arising from technical complexity, programme
stretch-outs also result in cost overruns. In the
case of the A-10 attack aircraft, the primary cause
of cost growth was attributable to programme slippage, which resulted in cost increases of 17 per
cent.[76] Slippage in this case was largely ascribable
to a reduction in production rate of from 20 to 14
machines per month. To offset the problem of cost
growth, be it of technical origin or programme management, the DoD has increasingly instituted multiyear funding contracts, as opposed to the historical
use of annual allocations, to allow contractors to
order long-lead-time requirements and realise economies of scale, quantity purchase benefits and greater
production continuity. The savings may, in fact, be
quite substantial. At the micro level, Grumman estimated that multiyear contract savings on the purchase
of power unit nose landings for a combat aircraft
amounted to 41 per cent (or about $5 million). At
the macro-level, programme saving can be significant.
In the above case, the multiyear procurement award
was expected to allow the Navy to procure 39 E-2Cs
for the price of 35. In reference to smaller countries, the acceleration of production costs has compelled them to enter into international joint ventures in order to share the burden of development and
production outlays over longer production runs.
Given the importance of technology to contemporary
defence aircraft, and given the political aversion to
technological dependence in key strategic industries,
European nations have banded together to attempt to
increase production runs and spread development
costs, as is evident in the current European military
helicopter programmes: EH-101 (Italy-UK), PAH-2
(France-West Germany); and NH-90 (Italy, West Germany, the Netherlands, France and perhaps the UK).
As an indication of the relative disparity in production runs, the LHX's development cost of $3 billion
is expected to be spread over programme procurement
of some 5,000-6,000 aircraft, whereas the PAH-2 procurement has been tentatively set at 400 aircraft.

The Kurth Follow-On Imperative: The Strategic-Politi-
cal Interface
Conforming to the Finletter Commission's assessed
need to maintain a "reasonable degree of expansibility" for periods of emergency, the awarding of prime

military aircraft contracts in the recent period has conformed to a follow-on imperative.[77] Major aircraft manufacturers require relatively constant design, development, and production activity in order to keep vital design and production teams together. From a strategic perspective, it is argued that at least a minimum surge capability is required for national security. Simply, surge capability is the ability to rapidly expand production in periods when threats to national security loom large. The precarious nature of defence demand, as encapsulated in the wave-cycle model, requires some institutionalised basis by which a degree of stability may be afforded to the aircraft industry while, at the same time, vouchsafing national security. As we have stressed, the state's principal means for accomplishing this task is through the allocation of prime military contract awards. As a matter of course, all DoD requests for funding for particular programmes must be approved by Congress. Defence spending on major prime contract awards to large aerospace corporations possesses an important feature not lost on astute Congressmen. In contrast to the diffuse nature of many social welfare expenditures (e.g. unemployment benefits or health services), major defence awards are a very visible and positive form of government expenditure. For example, the $20.5 billion B-1B programme is expected to generate 4,700 jobs at a newly constructed Palm-dale, California, facility (costing $83 million) and utilise 5,300 subcontractors including a $1.5 billion award to LTV Corporation.[78] By the same token, failure to win such awards, or cancellation of them, has a negative impact on the communities hosting the firms in question (recall Table 2.5). The cancellation of the original B-1, for example, was expected to result in over 10,000 layoffs at RI alone, never mind the thousands of subcontractors dependent on the programme.[79] The pervasiveness of political influence on defence expenditures has been systematically studied by R. J. Johnston.[80] In particular, Johnston has attempted to ascertain whether states represented on the relevant committees and subcommittees will receive a greater per capita allocation of defence dollars, under its various spending categories, than the states not represented on those committees. By comparing the mean per capita expenditure per state Johnston discovered that, in terms of prime military supply and R & D contracts, there is evidence of substantial pork-barrel activity in the House and Senate Armed Services Committees. Thus he concludes, "The main contracting sectors, apparently are the major areas of pork-barrel politics within the defence budget ... (and) the main pork-barreling for these contracts appears to take place in the House Armed Services Committees and its Subcommittees".[81] Indeed, at the end of a long career as chairman of one of those committees, Mendall Rivers (Democrat-South Carolina) wryly noted that the rationale underpinning the location of a Lockheed plant in his state reduced to: "I asked them to put a li'l old plant here."[82] Given that for every billion dollars of defence purchases an estimated 35,000 jobs are created, and that ten states (including the important electoral college states of California, Texas, and New York) receive in the order of 65 per cent of the total prime military contract awards, political influence on the contracting process is inevitable.[83]

The twin concerns of maintaining a strategic surge capability and a politically acceptable level of development and production activity conflate in the follow-on system. Table 4.10 indicates the allocation of selected prime military contract awards for a number of the large aerospace firms over the period fiscal years 1981 to 1985. As is evident, all the major aerospace firms have been kept relatively active with a number of major programmes. In all years covered, with the exception of RI in 1981, each main aerospace corporation has received major contracts amounting to at least $500 million, with most receiving in excess of a billion dollars since 1982. It is fairly obvious then, that a concerted effort is being made to ensure relatively high activity levels in those firms. A problem occurs when scheduled production (and/or development) runs are nearing their completion. It is at this stage that the follow-on imperative becomes operational. The follow-on system basically parallels the broad tenets laid down by the Finletter Commission's report to the President. In order to counter the inherent instability of government policy and the business cycle, state procurement policies have evolved in such a manner that successive weapons systems 'follow' each other on the production line. Specifically, as one production line begins to phase out manufacture of a particular aircraft (or missile) type, a government contract is soon awarded to ensure that the factory remains continuously active. As argued earlier, R & D contracts are vital antecedents to production contracts, and thus are also amenable to the basic precepts of the system. The follow-on system, therefore, was responsible for the revitalising of Boeing throughout the postwar period with successive defence orders for the B-50, C-97, KC-97, B-47, B-52 and KC-135 underpinning the firm's success well into the 1960s.[84] In the

Table 4.10 :   Selected Prime Contract Awards to Major
              Aerospace Corporations

(dollar values in brackets - in millions)

	Fiscal 1985[2]	Fiscal 1984	Fiscal 1983	Fiscal 1982	Fiscal 1981
Boeing[3]	KC-135 (986) B-52G/H(229) CH-47 (498)	KC-135 (552) B-52G/H(149) CH-47 (358)	KC-135 (496) B-52G/H(389) E-3A (217) CH-47 (236)	KC-135 (271) B-52G/H(389) E-3A (310.3) CH-47 (310)	KC-135 (119) B-52G/H(459) E-3A (335)
GD	F-16 (2,655)	F-16 (2,655)	F-16 (2,334)	F-16 (2,330)	F-16 (1,995)
RI	B-1B (8,220)	B-1B (6,360)	B-1B (4,737)	B-1B (2,093)	
Lockheed	C-5B (2,238) TR-1/U-2(365) P-3C (522)	C-5B (1,367) TR-1/U-2(218) P-3C (312)	C-5B (803) TR-1/U-2(195) C-5A (196) P-3C (318)	C-5 (270) C-5 (202) TR-1 (153) P-3C (461)	C-5 (178.5) TR-1 (125.3) P-3C (348)
MD[4]	F-15 (4,228) KC-10A (718) F/A-18 (2,818) AV-8B (1,010)	F-15 (1,655) KC-10A (811) F/A-18 (2,527) AV-8B (1,015)	KC-10 (919) F-18 (2598) AV-8B (1,033)	F-15 (1207) KC-10A (360) F/A-18 (2623) AV-8B (896)	KC-10A (327) F-15 (1101) F/A-18 (2054) AV-8B (331)
Grumman	F-14 (1001) EA-6B (440) E-2C (404) A-6E (276)	F-14 (1021) EA-6B (527) E-2C (371) A-6E (244)	F-14 (1,140) EA-6B (345.1) E-2C (346) A-6E (249)	F-14 (1,206) E-2C (285) EA-6B (288) A-6E (295)	F-14 (925) E-2C (261) A-6E (252) EA-6B (228)

Notes: 1. The figures were derived from AW & ST annual reports on the DoD aerospace
          budget. The programme dollar amounts awarded for the various fiscal years
          was assumed to be the figures reported in AW & ST as the previous year's
          award. For example, the fiscal 1984 figure was taken from the fiscal 1985
          issue, which lists the administration's current request, and the previous
          year's figure.
       2. Administration's fiscal 1985 request, subject to change.
       3. The Boeing B-52G/H, and Boeing B-52H programme.
       4. The F/A-18 programme also involves Northrop, and the AV-8B programme involves
          BAe.

Source: Compiled from AW & ST various issues.

later 1960s and early 1970s, Boeing was again in a
precarious position, facing reduced demand in both
civil and defence markets. Company employment
plunged from a peak Vietnam War level of 148,000 to
54,000 by mid-1971.[85] The firm's fortunes took a turn
for the better, however, with the receipt of E-3 and
E-4 aircraft procurement awards from the DoD.[86] Similarly, Boeing's Vertol Division lost two successive
major helicopter awards and was subsequently awarded
a CH-47 upgrading contract. Kurth went so far as to
examine the allocation of prime contracts throughout

the 1960 to 1972 period. The follow-on model appears
relevant in no less than eleven out of twelve major
contracts during the period examined.[87] The selection
of the GD F-111 against military advice was occasioned by that firm's Convair division recording
losses of some $400 million. The awarding of this
contract to the firm literally saved it from impending bankruptcy.[88] Evidently, the follow-on system is
alive and well in the 1980s, for, phase out of
the A-10 attack aircraft at Fairchild's Farmingdale,
New York, plant was prompty co-ordinated with the
planned phase in of the USAF next generation trainer
(T-46A) with a scheduled production run of 650 aircraft. Choice of Fairchild for the trainer rested
partly on the grounds "that Fairchild's A-10 production is winding down in 1985, and the (trainer) production will fit in after that date."[89] To ease the
transition, the DoD awarded Fairchild $29 million for
termination costs.[90] Other comparable machinations
concern the apportioning of work between Lockheed and
MD on transports (C-5 and C-17 respectively; the latter of which is now projected to go into full-scale
production at the Long Beach plant) and MD and Northrop on tactical fighters (F-18).[91] The foregoing
evidently indicates that technological superiority
and the supposed 'all or nothing' nature of defence
contracts must at least be tempered by inevitable
political influence.

In addition to formal budget allocations by the
DoD, contractors can rely on Congress to provide minimal funding to help tide over their fortunes. Thus,
the state may prolong production contracts or provide
R & D monies through the use of 'add-ons'. Specifically, these are subsidiary allocations, not necessarily requested by the military, but added as sup-
plementary contracts following political lobbying.
LTV's A-7D aircraft procurement programme underwent
several contract extentions. For example, LTV
received a $115 million contract to supply 24 A-7D
aircraft to the National Guard (despite the DoD not
requesting funds) as a direct result of Congress
overriding President Ford's decision to withdraw
funds from the programme.[92] Similarily, Congress
authorised $53.9 million for the procurement of
eleven AH-1S helicopters despite the Reagan administration's decision not to procure the aircraft. The
Congressional action came at a time when Bell, the
AH-1S manufacturer, was undergoing extensive layoffs
at its Fort Worth facility.[93]

The interplay of strategic interest and political sensitivity is also apparent where questions of
foreign sources of supply are concerned. From a

strategic perspective, there is a general preference
to buy defence items from domestic suppliers since
the advent of hostilities may place the nation in a
precarious position if supplies are somehow trun-
cated. From a political perspective, defence dollars
are visible evidence of government activity, and thus
are a means to influence votes. Imports remove this
tangible source of political jockeying. Furthermore,
defence contracts can be disbursed in the name of job
creation. In light of the above, it is not surprising that a number of restrictions are invoked to
secure the domestic market for indigenous producers.
The most obvious of these is the 'Buy America Act'
(noted in Chapter 3) which provides domestic producers with a six per cent cushion against foreign competition. In fact, domestic producers may at times
enjoy as much as a 12 per cent cushion if they happen
to be located in areas experiencing high unemployment.[94] More importantly, the 'specialty metals
clause' of the Defense Appropriations Bill effectively closes the US defence market to foreign firms
because nearly all arms components include some specialty metals.[95] To give an example, the replacement
for the CT-39 (Rockwell Sabreliner) in the USAF had
to be assembled in the United States and use an airframe produced in the USA.[96] Similarily, in a sudden
turn of events, the UK Martin-Baker ejection seat
selected (following a competition) for the F/A-18 was
subsequently rejected by a Congressional edict, and
replaced by an American produced seat. Political
sensitivity to foreign sourcing of defence equipment
is no less pervasive elsewhere, as the current UK
trainer competition makes manifest. The UK Ministry
of Defence reinstated the Hunting Firecracker into
the RAF trainer competition (after it had been eliminated) because of political upheaval over the decision to drop the only British designed aircraft in
the competition.[97] Clearly, whether for questions of
national security or expediency, the expenditure of
large sums of public funds is a highly politicised
affair and nowhere is this more evident than in the
procurement of military aircraft.

NOTES AND REFERENCES

       1. Chapter 7 will develop more fully a number of
contemporary themes dealing with state-industry relationships.
       2. Charles H. Gibbs-Smith, Aviation: An Histori-
cal Survey From its Origins to the End of World War
II, (Science Museum, HMSO, London, 1970), p.179.

3. David Mondey (ed.), The Complete Illustrated Encyclopedia of the World's Aircraft, (A & W Publishers Inc., New York, 1973), p.19.

4. Ibid, p.19.

5. Peter Fearon, 'The Formative Years of the British Aircraft Industry, 1912-1924', Business History Review, Vol. 43 (1969), p.479.

6. Gibbs-Smith, Aviation, p.176.

7. Ibid, p.225.

8. Cited in Jane's 1984-85, p.67.

9. John B. Rae, Climb to Greatness: The American Aircraft Industry, 1920-1960, (MIT Press, Cambridge, Massachusetts, 1968).

10. Paul A. C. Koistinen, 'The "Industrial-Military Complex" in Historical Perspective: World War I', Business History Review, Vol. 4, (1967), p.389.

11. See Paul A. C. Koistinen, 'The "Industrial-Military Complex" in Historical Perspective: The Inter War Years', Journal of American History, Vol. 56, (1969-70), pp.819-839 and Randolph P. Kucera, The Aerospace Industry and the Military: Structural and Political Relationships, (Sage Publications, Beverly Hills, California, 1974).

12. Gibbs-Smith, Aviation, pp.203-216.

13. Randolph P. Kucera, The Aerospace Industry and the Military, p.24.

14. Finletter Commission, 'Survival in the Air Age' in Carroll W. Purcell (ed.), The Military-Industrial Complex, (Harper & Row, New York, 1972) cited on p.179, 182.

15. Ibid, p.183.

16. SIPRI Yearbook 1979, Table 2:3, p.66.

17. Bill Gunston, Jane's Aerospace Dictionary, (Jane's, London, 1980). The actual cut-off point is subject to variation. For example, AW & ST classifies the Beech RU-21J as a utility aircraft even though its gross weight is 15,000 lb. (AW & ST, 12 March 1984, p.136).

18. See Mary Kaldor, The Baroque Arsenal, (Hill and Wang, New York, 1981), Chapter I.

19. Cited in Arnold Kanter, Defense Politics: A Budgetary Perspective, (University of Chicago Press, Chicago, 1975), p.5.

20. For an elaboration of some of the factors affecting the size of military expenditure see David K. Whynes, The Economics of Third World Military Expenditure, (University of Texas Press, Austin, 1979), Chapter 2.

21. United States, Arms Control and Disarmament Agency (ACDA), World Military Expenditures and Arms Transfers 1972-82, April, 1984, p.3.

22. SIPRI, Yearbook 1984.

23. United States, ACDA, p.1.

24. Ibid, Table A, p.3.

25. Ibid, p.7.

26. AW & ST, 11 February, 1985, p.17.

27. Helena Tuomi and Raimo Vayrynen, _Transnational Corporations, Armaments and Development_, (St. Martin's Press, New York, 1982), p.20.

28. AW & ST, 5 November 1984. The missile procurement figure does not include Navy missiles. All figures used are those approved by the Appropriation Conference.

29. Figures are taken from Nicole Ball and Milton Leitenberg (eds.), _The Structure of the Defense Industry, An International Survey_, (St. Martin's Press, New York, 1983). Note, the figures refer to 1977.

30. Robin Higham, 'Quantity vs. Quality: The Impact of Changing Demand on the British Aircraft Industry, 1900-1960', _Business History Review_, Vol. 42, (1968), pp.443-466.

31. Carroll W. Purcell (ed.), _The Military-Industrial Complex_, Appendix 9.

32. Robin Higham, 'Quantity vs. Quality', p.445.

33. Ibid, p.453.

34. Finletter Commission, 'Survival in the Air Age', p.188.

35. John B. Rae, _Climb to Greatness_, p.190.

36. Carroll W. Purcell, ed., _The Military-Industrial Complex_, Appendix 9. Graphically, Figure 2.1 attempts to summarise the process.

37. Randolph P. Kucera, _The Aerospace Industry_, p.24. It will be recalled that the USAF, as a separate service, was not created until 1947.

38. The expression, the MIC, was first used by President Eisenhower in his farewell address.

39. Finletter Commission, 'Survival in the Air Age', in Carroll W. Purcell (ed.), _The Military-Industrial-Complex_, (1972), pp.184-185.

40. Ibid, p.195.

41. For an intriguing account of the internal divisions within the DoD and the USAF in the context of the F-16 project, see Ingemar Dorfer, _Arms Deal: The Selling of the F-16_, (Praeger, New York, 1983).

42. Carroll W. Purcell (ed.), _The Military-Industrial-Complex_, 1972, Appendix 10. During the period described in the text, the figures are not strictly comparable due to reporting changes and methodological changes. None the less, the thrust of the argument remains valid.

43. AW & ST, 23 April 1984, p.166.

44. Ibid, p.166. The extent of market concentration in the USA is by no means unique. In Italy

for example, the top 10 companies account for 42.5 per cent of total Italian defence sales. Sergio A. Rossi, 'Italy' in Nicole Ball and Milton Leitenberg (ed.), The Structure of the Defense Industry, p.221.
45. Jacques S. Gansler, The Defense Industry, (MIT Press, Cambridge Massachusetts, 1980), p.42.
46. Gavin Kennedy, Defence Economics, (Duckworth, London, 1983), p.156.
47. Fortune, 30 April 1984, p.44. The ninth ranked defence contractor, The Howard Hughes Medical Institute, did not have a Fortune ranking listed.
48. Gordon Adams, The Politics of Defense Contracting: The Iron Triangle, (Transaction Books, New Brunswick, USA, 1981), p.394.
49. Ibid, p.24.
50. Adams argues that these shared assumptions are fostered through a "revolving door" of personnel transfers between industry and government. In fact, between 1981 and 1983 some 2,000 Pentagon employees left for jobs with defence contractors. The extent of the flow has caused some alarm, prompting congressional members to move towards passing legislation to impede the flow. Fortune, 18 March 1985, p.139-140.
51. J. F. Gorgol, The Military-Industrial Firm: A Practical Theory and Model, (Praeger, New York, 1972).
52. Jacques S. Gansler, The Defense Industry, 1982, p.296.
53. Recently, the USAF has split the procurement of aeroengines for the F-15 and F-16 between P & W (F100-220) and GE (F110). In fiscal year 1985, GE received 75 per cent of the procurement award and is scheduled to capture 54 per cent in fiscal year 1986. The split contract is intended to increase competition and ensure the maintenance of a fighter engine industrial base. AW & ST, 14 January 1985, p.16.
54. Merton J. Peck and Frederic M. Scherer, The Weapons Acquisition Process: An Economic Analysis, (Harvard University Press, Cambridge, Mass., 1962), p.17.
55. See for example, Gordon Adams, The Politics of Defense Contracting, and Michael R. Gordon, 'Are Military Contractors Part of the Problem or Part of the Solution?' in Lee D. Olvey et al. (eds.), Industrial Capacity and Defense Planning, (D.C. Heath and Company, Lexington, Mass., 1982), pp.93-102.
56. Jacques S. Gansler, The Defense Industry, p.75 and Gordon Adams, Politics of Defense Contracting, p.21.
57. AW & ST, 30 January 1984, pp.22-23.
58. Jacques S. Gansler, The Defense Industry, p.297, footnote 26.

59. F. M. Scherer, The Weapons Acquisition Process: Economic Incentives, (Harvard University Press, Cambridge, Mass., 1964), p.48.
60. AW & ST, 1 August 1983, p.34.
61. Gordon Adams, The Politics of Defense Contracting, p.96.
62. Michael R. Gordon, 'Are Military Contractors Part of the Problem or Part of the Solution?', p.95.
63. AW & ST, 4 July 1977, p.14-16, and 1 August 1983, p. 34.
64. Mary Kaldor, The Baroque Arsenal, p.18.
65. AW & ST, 18 June 1984, p.85.
66. Mary Kaldor, The Baroque Arsenal, p.20.
67. Gordon Adams, The Politics of Defense Contracting, p.98.
68. AW & ST, 19 November 1984, p.46.
69. AW & ST, 14 January 1985. Special issue on advanced helicopter technology.
70. Ibid, p.43.
71. Ibid, pp.41 and 43.
72. AW & ST, 3 September 1984, p.46.
73. For the evolution of combat aircraft costs, see Mary Kaldor, 'Technical Change in the Defence Industry', in Keith Pavitt (ed.), Technical Innovation and British Economic Performance, (Macmillan, London, 1980), pp.100-121.
74. AW & ST, 6 September 1982, p.14.
75. AW & ST, 20 December 1982, p.24.
76. AW & ST, 12 July 1982, p.18.
77. James R. Kurth, 'The Political-Economy of Weapons Procurement: The Follow-on Imperative', American Economic Review Papers and Proceedings, Vol. 62, (1972), pp.304-311.
78. AW & ST, 1 August 1983, pp.34, 52, 59.
79. AW & ST, 4 July 1977, p.14.
80. R. J. Johnston, 'Congressional Committees and the Inter-State Distribution of Military Spending', Geoforum, Vol. 10, (1979), pp.151-162.
81. Ibid, p.158.
82. Cited in Robert W. DeGrasse Jr., 'Military Spending and Jobs', Challenge, Vol. 26, (1983), pp.4-15.
83. The jobs created figure is from AW & ST, 11 February 1985, p.19, while the state expenditure is from DeGrasse, p.8.
84. J. B. Rae, Climb to Greatness.
85. AW & ST, 12 July 1971, p.15.
86. Gordon Adams, The Politics of Defence Contracting, p.231.
87. James R. Kurth, 'The Political-Economy of Weapons Procurement'.
88. I. F. Stone, 'Nixon and the Arms Race', in

Carroll W. Purcell (ed.), <u>The Military Industrial Complex</u>, 1972, pp.221-235.

89. AW & ST, 12 July 1982, p.18.
90. AW & ST, 23 August 1982, p.16.
91. See, for example, issues of AW & ST for 25 January 1982, p.19; 12 March 1982, p.47; and 9 August 1982, p. 68.
92. AW & ST, 12 May 1975, p.17.
93. AW & ST, 11 October 1982, p.23.
94. AW & ST, 15 December 1980, p.19.
95. AW & ST, 17 January 1983, p.16.
96. AW & ST, 20 June 1983, p.27.
97. AW & ST, 21 January 1985, p.25. In the event, the Brazilian Tucano was selected by the RAF, albeit built under licence by Shorts of Belfast.

Chapter Five

SUPPLY FACTORS AND INDUSTRIAL LOCATION

In his seminal work on the location of the US aircraft industry, Cunningham asserts that certain
unique qualities associated with its geographic distribution; namely, "the absence of response to the
traditional factors of location" combined with "its
strategic and vulnerable nature", make for a subject
of inquiry which is, at one and the same time,
divorced from the standard precepts of economic geography while being of vital importance for the
national economy and polity.[1] In essence, Cunningham
is making the point - brought out in the last chapter
- that as a creature of the state, the aircraft
industry's location is determined for the most part
by the whim of governments. It is all very well to
aver that aircraft enterprises, as manufacturing
operations, locate at given sites because of locational considerations (unique to the industry or otherwise), but the simple fact that the enterprises are
likely to depend on government orders for their survival (and 'cost-plus' contracts to boot) means that
the marginal efficiencies involved in selecting opti-
mal plant locations are totally overwhelmed by the
need for the enterprises to convince the state of the
technical attributes of their own designs. As we
have intimated, this central truth of the techno-
logical-imperative overrides the kind of marginalist
economic thinking which pervades location theory.
    While demand considerations constitute the cru-
cial factors for aircraft enterprises, they do not
manifest themselves in ways that present a readily
identifiable spatial focus. In other words, demand
does not reside in a geographical market centre:
rather, it is to be found in the aspatial polity
which, while occupying a spatially-determinable capital, sets procurement goals that mean delivering of
the aircraft product to bases and installations
throughout the state and even beyond to garrison

forces overseas. The evidence for aircraft firms
gravitating to the national capital in order to be
more accessible to policymakers is very scanty
indeed. Cunningham's example of the Glenn L. Martin
Company's decision to move from Cleveland to Baltimore in 1929 and thereby ensuring, among other
things, "proximity to the military markets in Washington" is perhaps an exception to the rule that the
'Iron Triangle' does not need a geographic market
centre.[2]
    None of this is to say that supply factors are
unimportant to the aircraft industry: in fact, quite
the reverse applies. Because labour costs at airframe plants can equal the costs of materials, they
are of vital interest to all aircraft manufacturers.
And, more to the point, because labour is spatially
uneven in its quantity and quality, it forces firms
to contemplate a geographical dimension in the formulation of plans to establish plants. In view of the
predominance of the wage bill in production costs,
this factor tends to outweigh any other supply factor
as a locational consideration. Owing to the industry's requirement for such scarce labour, the tendency is for it to gravitate to major agglomeration
centres containing well-established trades and engineering structures or, alternatively, to evolve on
'green-field' sites, where the local environment is
conducive to the maintenance of a pool of skilled
workers. In both instances, establishment of aircraft plants has been triggered, to a large extent,
by the existence of local entrepreneurs (a supply of
human capital, as it were) well versed in expertise
which subsequently became germane to this particular
industry. The question of entrepreneurial talent
introduces the notion of the effects of locational
inertia, which is to say, the outcome whereby many
aircraft firms were located in the centres in which
their founders 'cut their teeth' in associated industries. Of special note were men who had previously
worked in automotive engineering, coach-building and
boat-building (recall the similarities between wooden
craft, be they coaches, powerboats or primitive aircraft fuselages) and frequently, they set up their
aircraft operations in the vicinity of those formative industries. This kind of 'seed-bed' development
has been recognised in the locational literature.[3] So
long as the firm is small, underfunded and technologically immature, it will have precarious prospects, and the entrepreneur will best serve his
interests through 'hedging his bets' and remaining in
close contact with his previous employer.
    Historically, the locational inertia in the

formation of the aircraft industry was especially telling when such associated industries decided to diversify into aircraft manufacture and created aeronautical divisions of their own. Almost invariably, these aircraft departments were lodged in existing premises belonging to the organisation or, very much the same thing, in plant extensions of those premises. Understandably, as an arm of the MIC, aircraft manufacture was taken up by firms already prominent in defence production. Vertically-integrated arms producers such as Vickers instituted aircraft manufacture at existing sites: the Crayford machine-gun shops for aeroplanes and the Barrow shipbuilding complex for airships.[4] Other UK defence contractors established warplane factories on sites as geographically proximate as possible to existing works. Thus, naval shipbuilders William Beardmore, Harland & Wolff and J. S. White all sought factory space as close as possible to their shipyards at Dalmuir, Belfast and Cowes respectively. The Royal Navy even went one step further, actually using the slips of Malta Dockyard to build Felixstowe F3 flying boats in 1918.

The fact remains, therefore, that with the exception of labour and the amalgam of entrepreneurship and inertia encapsulated in the term agglomeration, supply factors coming to bear on the aircraft industry are not especially pertinent to locational analysis. As Cunningham stresses, the aircraft industry is a consumer of semi-manufactured materials and has "no reason for becoming material-oriented".[5] Not only are the materials fabricated in the airframe plant of high value in relation to weight – and therefore dismissive of transport costs – but the plethora of components and parts which go into the finished aircraft derive from a vast number of enterprises spread throughout the spatial economy. The dispersed nature of the supplier firms, and their very number, deny a geographical focus or 'locational pull' to the airframe plant in its assembly operations. This is why the industry has never been overly concerned about minimising the distance of its interindustry linkages.[6]

Given this context of demand pre-eminence in the first place, and a supply concern which is not primarily spatial in the second, the object of the present chapter is to provide an overview of the factors of production applicable to the aircraft industry and, then, to extract those elements of the supply-side that are genuine locational factors. To this end, a brief discussion of the construction materials used by the industry is followed by an outline of the role played by labour in the production process. At that

juncture, the locational aspect is made explicit. A
number of factors which conspire to create an air-
craft-plant site are enunciated and the chapter con-
cludes with a review of the attempts made by governments to steer aircraft plants to particular
locations; in a word, regional policy.

INDUSTRIAL CHARACTERISTICS

The aircraft industry is, first and foremost, a high
value-added sector demonstrating high levels of productivity. One indication of this situation is the
fact that in 1970, for instance, each American aerospace worker produced an average $26,000 of sales,
while his French counterpart produced $13,750, his
West German co-worker turned out $13,200 and the
British worker was responsible for sales worth
$11,350.[7] More modern comparative output figures have
been expressed in European Currency Units, a better
standard of comparison for the non-US aircraft industries.[8] For example, 1978 figures suggest that, at
33,667 units, the turnover value per employee of
French workers was higher than the productivity of
aerospace workers in West Germany (22,787), the USA
(21,366), the UK (14,941) and Italy (14,473).[9] By the
beginning of the 1980s, French supremacy in the productivity stakes was confirmed with a sales-to-em-
ployment ratio of 75,000 units; a marked improvement
on the 52,000 figure for the USA or the 46,000 of
Japan, the 45,000 of West Germany and the 32,000 of
the UK.[10] It virtually goes without saying, of
course, that such national indices of productivity
are only composites of the performances of individual
enterprises. French labour efficiency, for example,
was underpinned by an astounding 117,000 units per
man for Dassault and a very respectable 65,000 units
for Aérospatiale. The most productive US firms were
Boeing, P & W, MD and Lockheed (with 64, 55, 53 and 52
thousand units respectively); but they failed to
equal the two leading French enterprises. In fact,
only two other firms approached the American level of
'best-performance' firms; namely, Kawasaki (62,000)
and MBB (50,000). Major organisations of the likes
of GD (40,000), BAe (31,000), R-R (36,000), GE
(42,000), and MHI (42,000) appeared to perform only
moderately well in the productivity ratings.[11]
    As with any other manufacturing industry, the
performance of the aerospace sector, whether considered on a national or corporate basis, is affected by
the scale and timing of production. By the former is
meant the economies of scale phenomenon. Sizeable

production runs averaged over relatively fixed overheads are conducive to enhanced productivity figures.
Conversely, limited production runs averaged over the
same commitment to overheads is tantamount to low
productivity and, indeed, accounts for the relatively
poorer performance of European industries and firms
(with the aforementioned exception of the French)
when compared to those of the USA. But even the
Americans are not immune to the cost escalation (and
productivity drop) which follows from production cutbacks. GD, for instance, estimated that a slowdown
in production of F-16 fighters from fifteen to ten
aircraft per month was sufficient to add $3 billion
to the contract cost notwithstanding the fact that
procurement totals remained intact.[12] Timing comes to
bear on productivity in terms of 'learning curves',
that is to say, workers acquire greater expertise
with experience as a project unwinds. MBB aptly
illustrates this point when it notes that the first
A300 Airbus manufactured by its Hamburg plant
required 340,000 man-hours of work in contrast to the
78,000 man-hours entailed in the construction of the
87th copy, and the 56,000 man-hours anticipated for
individual airliners when the production run exceeds
three hundred.[13] In part, this marked improvement in
productivity is attributable to enhanced experience,
but it is also due to technological progress, especially the greater use of computers (CAD/CAM) and the
further application of composite materials. The
first example of technical change, incidentally, was
also lauded by Boeing. That company thought the
application of CAD/CAM in wing construction was
directly responsible for the Boeing 767 production
costs materialising at 50 per cent less than
expected.[14] The application of composites, meanwhile,
is addressed in the next sub-section.

Materials
Primary materials, as such, play little part in the
manufacturing activities of airframe plants: instead
metal 'skins' and forgings have traditionally been
supplied by one or two specialist forges which cater
for the entire materials needs of a national aircraft
industry. These secondary products - steel alloys,
aluminium sheet and castings, and magnesium castings
- are high in value and low in relative transport
costs. One organisation, Interforge of France, supplies most of the European demand for large forgings.
With a 67,000 tonne hydraulic press, Interforge possesses the largest press outside the USSR which has
two 75,000 tonne presses. American needs are met, in

the main, by two USAF-owned presses operated by Wyman-Gordon and Alcoa.[15] In recent years, however, the use of materials in aircraft construction has dramatically changed. Technological developments have centred around the application of titanium on the one hand, and composites on the other.

The advantage of titanium is its strength, being twice as strong as aluminium. Offsetting that advantage, though, is the fact that it is 60 per cent heavier than aluminium. It was first used in the 1950s in military aviation where weight drawbacks were less important than in civil aviation (excessive weight in the latter tended to curtail payload and thus affected the costs:revenue ratio). Commencing with the airframe of the North American F-100, titanium was also used in the airframes of Boeing's B-52 and MD's F-4; and not least, in P & W's J57 engine. While high-performance aircraft of recent years have used more titanium (e.g. the Lockheed SR-71 'spy plane' is almost entirely made of the metal), the largest single market has been that of aeroengines. The B-1 supersonic bomber makes extensive use of the material both in its airframe (125,000 lbs of mill products) and its engines (17,600 lbs). The B-1's structure is 21 per cent titanium, while the F-14 is 24.4 per cent and the F-15 is 26 per cent.[16] As a result of programmes such as these, American titanium producers have undertaken major expansions: American Cyanamid adding 10,000 tons of capacity, Oregon Metallurgical extending sponge plant by 50 per cent and ingot capacity to 16 million lbs, TIMET investing $50 million, and RMI increasing ingot capacity by 20 per cent. Even UK producer IMI Titanium (the only UK producer and the world's third ranking) was establishing a Denver office to serve the American market.[17] Expansion plans were equally apparent in Japan. A subsidiary of MHI was aiming to produce 500 tonnes of titanium monthly to supplement the 30,000 tonnes already produced annually in Japan (in contrast to the US figure of 22,000 tonnes and the USSR level of 35,000 tonnes).[18]

In spite of this expansion, however, titanium contributes a mere four per cent of the materials used in the average aircraft in comparison to the 82 per cent contribution of aluminium and the 13 per cent of steel (the residual one per cent being made up of fibreglass). Yet by 1985, a typical subsonic 'new-generation' aeroplane may be constituted mostly from composite materials: that is, a whopping 65 per cent of the aircraft composed of composites and only 17 per cent of it made of aluminium, 15 per cent of steel and three per cent of titanium.[19] The

114

advantages of composites are generally summed up as half the weight and twice the strength of aluminium. They have been used since the 1960s in the form of bolt-on parts (e.g. control surfaces) which could easily be removed and replaced, but only in the 1980s have they emerged as primary structural components of airframes. The revolutionary Learfan 2100, the subject of detailed scrutiny in the regional policy section of this chapter, was designed around graphite-reinforced epoxy wings, empennage and fuselage. In the military arena, the Anglo-American AV-8B has an airframe which is 26 per cent composite by weight. Strides are also being made in helicopter manufacture. Already, there are viable composite rotor blades and the acceptance of transmissions, drive shafts, rotor hubs and control components of the same material is imminent. A helicopter made largely of composite materials (i.e. 85 per cent) is regarded as the next major breakthrough in rotorcraft technology.

Composites come in many varieties: carbon epoxies, graphite, fibreglass, carbon fibre reinforced plastics (CFRP), boron fibre reinforced plastics (BFRP) and glass reinforced plastics (GRP) are perhaps the more prominent. They all suffice to give weight and fuel savings; for example, they offer a weight saving of 25 per cent over the previously used materials when built into Boeing's 757 and 767 airliners. Translated into operating costs, that can mean savings of 22,000 gallons of fuel per year in the case of the Boeing 757. Initially, research focused on asbestos composites in the UK and glass fibres in the USA, but later attention switched to carbon fibres in the former and boron fibres in the latter. Carbon (i.e. CFRP) enjoys widespread availability and is cheap to produce, but boron (i.e. BFRP) is twice the strength of carbon. However, it is expensive ($180 per lb) compared to carbon ($90 per lb) and even titanium ($150 per lb), and therefore finds a market mainly in warplane production (e.g. the Grumman F-14 and MD F-15) where costs tend to play second fiddle to technical criteria.[20] MD is, accordingly, embracing composite technology with gusto, investing $100 million in composite manufacturing facilities at St. Louis and Long Beach in order to annually process 400,000 lbs of composite materials for its AV-8B and F-18 programmes.[21]

Components and Parts
The new composite materials were introduced into aircraft construction by way of bolt-on parts and only later adopted as primary structural materials. In so

doing, the process highlights the fundamental role
played by components and parts in the aircraft industry. Furthermore, these components and parts come
from a wide-ranging assortment of industries, firms
and locations. An input-output study of processing
sector inputs for Boeing of Washington, for example,
arrived at the following order of industries supplying that firm: other aerospace ($750.3 million in
1967), electrical equipment ($316.5 million), busi-
ness services and trade ($58.6 million), light fabri-
cated metals ($39.7 million), aluminium ($29.1 million), finished plastics ($28.1 million) and printing
and publishing ($27.2 million).[22] Interestingly, only
$164.3 million of this total of $1.37 billion in processing sector inputs originated in the local region:
the remainder was obtained from outside Washington
state. Of the regional purchases, the main stimulus
was given to the aluminium industry, followed by purchases from other aerospace firms. Yet, in light of
the predominance of extra-regional linkages, the
principal suppliers of Boeing were found to reside in
two concentrations: Hartford, Connecticut, and southern California. The first was important because it
housed P & W; the main source of Boeing's aeroengines. The second figured prominently presumably
because many aerospace firms are located there.[23]

In fact, most modern aircraft programmes draw on
a host of components suppliers that are located virtually randomly in relation to the site of airframe
assembly. Four examples are selected for the purposes of explication. As an example of an aircraft
using nationally-made inputs for all but a minor
aspect of construction, the PZL organisation set up
to produce the An-28 is considered. This Soviet-designed twin-turboprop airliner is a successor to the
An-24 and PZL has been assigned authority to manufacture all Warsaw Pact requirements for it. Final
assembly at Mielec is a culmination of manufacture
undertaken elsewhere in Poland (Figure 5.1). The
fuselage is built in Lublin, the licence-built Glush-
enkov TVD-10B engines derive from Rzeszow, hydraulics
are produced at Wroclaw, control surfaces and landing
gear are made at Krosno, while Warsaw is responsible
for aircraft equipment.[24] By current standards, the
An-28 programme entails few supplier linkages: a much
more extensive network of linkages is evident from
the TSR-2 programme. This aircraft, a product of
BAC, was brought to the production stage in the
mid-1960s but was then cancelled on the grounds of
cost escalation. Table 5.1 highlights the array of
suppliers as the aircraft was poised for production.
Apart from airframe assembly at Preston and

aeroengine construction at Bristol, the vast majority
of contractors hailed from the London area, especially the suburban new towns. The same general pattern emerges for subcontractors, although the linkages to the London area are leavened by those to
primary-metals suppliers in the West Midlands and in
Sheffield. On the whole, however, the TSR-2 case
illustrates the fact that the airframe plant may be
located at a site eccentric in relation to the geographic centre of gravity of the components and parts
suppliers.

Supplier linkages can extend to a continental or
indeed, international scale as is evident from our
next two examples, both the products of Boeing,
namely: the civil 757 programme and the military
NATO/AWACS venture. The first, graphically represented in Figure 5.2, requires inputs from suppliers
in 15 states as well as the home state of Washington
where the airliner is assembled. What is more, Boeing also calls upon the services of suppliers in Australia, Canada, Japan, Spain and the UK. As a point
of fact, about 53 per cent of the 757 derives from
sources outside of Boeing, including most of the
fuselage. Body sections of the airframe originate in
Maryland by courtesy of Fairchild-Republic, Oklahoma
as a product of RI (Tulsa) and Texas, through the
efforts of LTV. The engines are either obtained - as
with earlier Boeing aircraft - from P & W in Connecticut or from R-R, which commands the energies of a
number of factories in Britain. While retaining
prime responsibility for the wing, Boeing still calls
on Tennessee's Avco for wing centre sections, New
York's Schweitzer for wing tips, and Australia's HDH
for wing inspar ribs.[25] When all the avionics and
instruments suppliers are added to these airframe
structural suppliers, the spatial extent of linkages
from Puget Sound is truly pervasive.

The NATO/AWACS venture involved Boeing in the
manufacture of a batch of E-3A 'surveillance' aircraft which were jointly funded by the NATO members
(excluding Britain which opted for its own AWACS variant of the Nimrod) and stationed at Geilenkircken in
West Germany. Ultimately, a derivative of the Boeing
707, the E-3A differs in being stuffed with sophisticated electronic monitoring equipment. Consequently,
a large part of the project cost revolves around supply of avionics and other systems. To complicate the
supplier situation further, the international nature
of the project demands a production work-sharing
scheme which placates the individual members of NATO.
The outcome is the industrial collaboration programme
summarised in Table 5.2. That table pinpoints the

Figure 5.1 : Production Linkages for An-28

suppliers drawn upon because of the political complexion of the venture: in other words, contractors
outside the USA who are involved because it is a
NATO effort. The prime contractor, of course,
remains Boeing, and much of the avionics as well as
the aeroengines are American sourced.[26]
     A final point worth making with respect to the
extent of spatial linkages is that, more often than
not, factories providing parts for aircraft assembled
by a particular company are also participants in the
same business organisation. In other words, a firm
may utilise its own far-flung facilities to provide
much of the mass of inputs required in aircraft
assembly. The PZL example is a case in point, but
the practice extends beyond state-monopoly aircraft
enterprises. A dramatic example in the American context is that offered by RI, the prime contractor for
the USAF's new strategic bomber, the B-1B. Fulfil-
ment of the contract for 100 aircraft by the late
1980s will require workforces of 22,000 at the company's plants: 8,500 at El Segundo (California), 4,000
at Palmdale (California), 7,500 at Columbus (Ohio)
and 2,000 at Tulsa (Arizona).[27] Final assembly in
California notwithstanding, major components and

TABLE 5.1   Contractors and Subcontractors of TSR-2

Contractor	Location	Subcontractor	Location
BAC	Weybridge*	Elliott Bros	Borehamwood*
	Preston		Sydenham
Bristol Siddeley Engines	Bristol	S. Smith	Basingstoke*
	Leavesdon*	Decca	Heysham
Plessey	Titchfield	STC	London*
Ferranti	Edinburgh	Dowty	Cheltenham
	Manchester		Coventry
EMI	Hayes*	Martin Baker	Denham*
AEI	Coventry	Plessey	Ilford*
Mullard Electronics	Crawley*	HS Dynamics	Hatfield*
S.Smith & Sons	Barkingside*	Aviation Tool	Hounslow*
Cossor	Harlow*	J. Booth Alum.	Birmingham
Ekco	Southend*	T.J. Brooks	Leicester
Marconi	Basildon*	Ceramic aircraft components	Southall*
General Precision Systems	Aylesbury*	Darchem	Durham
Elliott Bros	Rochester	Diac	Croydon*
Kollsmans Instruments	Southampton	Electro-Hydraulics	Warrington
Vinten	Bury St Edmunds	GKN	Birmingham
Williamson Mfg.	Willesden*	Sir G. Godfrey & Partners	Feltham*
AGI	Croydon*	H.M. Hobson	Wolverhampton
Wray Optical	Bromley*	IMI	Birmingham
Fraser Nash	Kingston on Thames*	Lucas GTE	Birmingham
ML Aviation	Maidenhead		Liverpool
Microcell	Camberley*	D. Napier & Sons	Luton*
MB Metals	Portslade	High Duty Alloys	Redditch
Normalair	Yeovil	Firth Vickers	Sheffield
Stargate Engineering	Blackpool	Daniel Doncaster & Sons	Sheffield
Sperry	Bracknell*	Firth Derihon Stamping	Sheffield
Triplex	Birmingham	Mark Bridge Iron & Steel	Leeds
Palmer Aero Products	London	Hughes Johnson Stamping	Olbury
		Tubes Ltd	Birmingham
Serck Radiations	Birmingham		
Teddington Aircraft Controls	Merthyr Tydfil		
Ultra Electronics	Acton*		
Vactric	Morden*		
Ransome & Marles	Newark		

Note : * 'London-area' location

Source: G. Williams et al, Crisis in Procurement: A Case Study of the TSR-2, (RUSI, Whitehall, 1969), pp. 74-5.

Figure 5.2 : Distribution of Boeing 757 Work in the USA

Table 5.2 :   International Suppliers to NATO/AWACS

Company	Location	Product
AEG Telefunken	Saarbrucken	racks, consoles, cabinets, flight-deck parts
	Ulm	radar components
Boeing of Canada	Winnipeg	tailcone
Diehl Elektronik	Nurnberg	special test equipment
Dornier	Oberpfaffenhofen	mission system installation and check
ESG	Munich	software development
Fleet Industries	Fort Erie, Ontario	vertical fin, rudder, nacelles, power pack
Liebherr-Aero	Lindenberg	antenna hydraulic drive
Litton Systems Canada	Rexdale, Ontario	on-board test monitor subsystems
Siemens	Munich	data displays and controllers
Standard Electrik Lorenz	Stuttgart	data processing system components

assemblies derive from company facilities in the US
industrial heartland, a fact which speaks volumes in
dismissing the relevance of material transfer costs
for aircraft plants.

Labour
While locational costs incurred in obtaining material
inputs may appear trivial for airframe operations,
the same cannot be said of labour. Simply put, managers of airframe plants locate irrespective of the
sites of their components suppliers but they are, in
contrast, very conscious of labour supply in choosing
to locate an airframe facility. Labour, in combination with agglomeration, plays an important part in
determining plant locations. As long ago as 1939 the
ratio of wages and salaries to value of product converted into percentage terms stood at 37.7 for the
industry in the USA, and only 12 out of 71 main
industries in the Census of Manufactures recorded a
higher level.[28] This essential labour-intensive

characteristic of the industry remains intact as modern economic-geography texts attest.[29] Several
aspects of labour stand out as significant in the
aircraft industry: first, the sizeable quantity
required; secondly, the orientation towards higher
skills; thirdly, the tendency towards stability of
employment among the workforce and finally, the differential impact of those quantitative and qualitative considerations on firms' manpower costs and the
resultant drive to cut labour costs. Confirmation of
the sheer quantity of labour required is readily
forthcoming from the 1.2 million or more currently
engaged in US aerospace activities. However, a better intimation of the relative importance of labour
is got from measures of manpower per plant. Table
5.3 shows, for example, that in the early 1960s, the
typical UK Tier I airframe plant employed 2,692 workers when the aggregate manpower undertaking aircraft
manufacture numbered 129,250.[30] Plants employing in
excess of two thousand people are sizeable entities
by any standards and necessitate, in consequence, a
substantial labour pool to support them. As shall be
shown in reference to government plant dispersal policies, a major concern was to find labour sheds with
reserves of potential workers of this (or even
greater) magnitude.[31]

The skill mix of the industry's manpower is
equally distinctive. In World War II skilled labour
constituted 41.3 per cent of all labour required in
US airframe manufacture, whereas semi-skilled labour
made up 46.5 per cent, unskilled labour contributed
7.7 per cent, and the residual 4.5 per cent consisted
of clerical and managerial staff.[32] It was the presence of skilled and semi-skilled labour in abundance
that induced many aircraft firms to establish themselves either in New York or the Los Angeles metro-
politan area during the formative decades of the
1920s and 1930s. In recent years the bias towards
quality manpower has kept pace with the tempo of
technological change experienced by the industry. By
the mid-1970s American aerospace workers were composed of 453,000 production workers, 165,000 scientists and engineers, 63,000 technicians and 253,000
'others' including clerical staff. Clearly, the number of 'technical' workers was encroaching on the
traditionally-large factory workforce, skilled or
otherwise. This pattern continues to the present
day. It was noted, for example, that the employment
growth for technicians in 1980 was a hefty 13 per
cent, while for scientists and engineers the growth
rate recorded a respectable 10.7 per cent. In marked
contrast, however, demand for production workers had

Table 5.3 :   UK Aircraft Firms and Plant Size, 1962

Firm	No. of plants	Average plant labour force
Aviation Traders	2	800
Beagle Aircraft	2	650
BAC	12	2,917
Handley Page	3	2,000
HS Aviation	20	3,275
Scottish Aviation	1	1,850
Shorts	3	2,333
Westland Aircraft	5	2,200
National Average		2,692

been a paltry three per cent.[33]
    One consequence of the industry's need for
skilled labour is its desire to retain it despite the
fluctuations in activity levels imposed upon aerospace by the wave-cycle and business cycle. The
essential defence nature of aircraft manufacture
comes to the fore in this respect. Hartley and Corcoran have noticed that cancellation of government
defence projects rarely results in a commensurate
decline in employment. The two workers note that
cancellation of projects in 1965 employing 30,000 in
the UK aircraft industry should have resulted in the
loss of 25,000 jobs and the closure of five plants.
Yet, layoffs one year later only amounted to 7-8,000
and a single plant had been closed. The only conclusion to be drawn is that a substantial proportion of
the 'redundant' workforce are intentionally retained
and, in so being, perhaps under-employed. In line
with the behaviour of the 'Iron Triangle' mentioned
in the last chapter, they assert that firms might
even overstate the scale of redundancies in order to
"influence the decisions of vote-maximising governments".[34] At any rate, cost-based pricing whereby
product price is determined by total outlays plus an
agreed-upon profit margin is hardly conducive to production (labour) cost controls during activity slow-
downs. However, the evidence indicates, in a circum-
stantial manner, that fixed-price contracts may
induce firms to be more sensitive to production outlays, including a greater tendency to shed labour in
periods of demand downturn. Yet, the relationship

between reluctance to shed surplus labour and defence contracts should not be over-emphasised in view of the findings of Hartley and Corcoran that industries producing clocks, glassware, iron castings, ships and cars are even more reluctant than the aircraft industry to dismiss workers during lean times.[35] The common thread, shared by all those industries, is the need for at least a modicum of skilled labour which, by dint of its scarcity value, compels firms to procrastinate where layoffs are concerned.

Paradoxically in view of the just stated assertion that aircraft firms are loth to dispense with skilled (and thus, expensive) labour, they may still be amenable to tapping supplies of cheap labour if, by so doing, they materially reduce production costs (e.g. see Chapter 8 with respect to Boeing's agreement with Indonesia; also P & W has established duplicate production lines in the USA so as to overcome potential labour disruptions). Unsurprisingly, the attraction of cheap labour is especially telling for firms operating in civil aviation markets. In other words, firms of this kind may not enjoy the cost-based pricing endemic in defence markets and, therefore, are much more conscious of marginal savings in production costs. Among Tier III firms, for instance, the overhaul subsidiary of IAI - Bedek - stresses its competitive position as a result of the cheaper labour prevailing in Israel. During the 1970s this firm was bidding for airliner overhaul contracts on the basis of $6 per man-hour labour costs in contrast to the standard rate of $10 per man-hour in Europe and the $14.50 in the USA.[36] From a slightly different focus - that of chronic labour shortage at home - Pilatus Aircraft of Switzerland was obliged to have the wings for its B4 glider made in India.[37]

Entrepreneurship

Effective entrepreneurship continues to act as a main force in the aircraft industry, as is attested by the formation of new companies attempting to market appealing designs. In the UK in recent years, such entrepreneurs have set up firms to produce revolutionary observation aircraft (Edgley Optica), basic trainers (NDN Turbo Firecracker) and aerobatic light aeroplanes (Trago Mills SAH-1). In the USA, the achievements of entrepreneurs such as the late William P. Lear in both formulating new types of bizjet and forming companies to manufacture them are well-known and far-reaching. The desire of an entrepreneur to create a new aircraft company has obvious

geographical repercussions. On the one hand, the new
firm may be set up in the resident community of the
entrepreneur, but, on the other, it may settle on a
location which the founder has selected as a result
of the persuasion and support of state authorities.
This latter aspect comes to the fore in terms of
regional policy and will be dealt with then. The
former aspect, however, is best illustrated by highlighting the case of Wichita, Kansas. In the words
of Rae:

> The astonishing rise of Wichita, Kansas, as the
> nation's principal center for the manufacture of
> private planes started in the early 1920s.
> Wichitans attribute the rise to the city's loca-
> tion in the heart of a vast plain constituting
> the largest natural airport in the country, but
> this claim could be made for any number of
> places in the same approximate longitude. The
> Wichita achievement was fundamentally entrepre-
> neurial. A well-financed beginning attracted
> talent to the city and became the stem from
> which other companies proliferated.[38]

The process underway in Wichita combined pioneer
entrepreneurial efforts with a 'copy-cat' effect
which induced agglomeration of aircraft firms. The
initial enterprise, the Wichita Airplane Company,
attracted design talent of the likes of Lloyd Stearman and Walter Beech, both of whom later departed to
form their own company in partnership with Clyde
Cessna. By the 1930s all three were operating companies of their own, although Stearman's enterprise had
been absorbed into the Boeing empire. Today, in
addition to the Wichita division of Boeing which is
integrated into the Seattle company's military and
civil ventures, the two firms in Wichita, between
them, account for the lion's share of the world's
output of light aircraft. Only the Los Angeles area
can challenge Wichita as a multi-firm aerospace centre of world stature, but this agglomeration centre
grew to commanding importance largely as a result of
firms relocating there from the US Eastern Seaboard.
Of the numerous firms eventually locating in Los
Angeles, Donald Douglas pioneered the way by intentionally choosing the area for its good climate (conducive to flight testing) and plentiful supply of
skilled labour.[39] His actions in 1921, give him claim
to being the first aircraft entrepreneur to actually
engage in locational decision-making.

LOCATIONAL IMPLICATIONS

Douglas was, of course, searching for a suitable site
for aircraft manufacture, a procedure which still
occasionally distracts the attention of the industry's managers. Prior to Douglas's precedent, little
consideration was given to determining special sites
for plants and for good reason: space for landing
grounds was scarcely a problem when aircraft were
small enough to be trucked to a convenient piece of
flat ground for aerial testing. Consequently, any
industrial premises, more likely than not, the engineering shops or body-building works of the original
diversifying firm, served to house aircraft assembly.
Subsequently, of course, the drawbacks of cramped
urban locations were recognised and firms tended to
transfer to sites with plenty of room for airfields
adjoining the airframe facilities. Nevertheless,
these relocations were generally minimum distance
moves: in the UK, for example, DH moved from London
(Edgware) to one of its satellite towns (Hatfield),
Gloster transferred from Cheltenham to its outskirts
(Brockworth), while Armstrong Whitworth moved in two
stages out from Coventry (Parkside to Whitley to Bag-
inton). They fulfilled the purpose of seeking room
for operations without undue change in locale. It is
worth emphasising, though, that many firms persevered
with cramped urban sites in spite of the mounting
difficulties: Avro (at Manchester) and Handley Page
(in London) persisted in building large bombers in
subassemblies at urban factories and painstakingly
transporting them to suburban airfields for reassem-
bly (Woodford and Radlett).[40] In the UK, at least,
very few firms relocated to sites at some remove from
their original premises, but one of the few was
Shorts which moved from Rochester to Belfast and is,
incidentally, an integral component of the Northern
Ireland regional policy case addressed later in this
chapter.
    In the USA relocations were much more common,
especially those involving firms forsaking eastern
sites for California in the 1930s. Since World War
II, however, long-distance relocations have been
rare. Chance Vought (LTV) opted to quit Bridgeport,
Connecticut, for Dallas, Texas, in 1948 owing to the
obsolescence of its old facilities and the prospect
of existing newer facilities in Texas along with better flying weather.[41] Yet America has thrown up a
contemporary example of site selection-cum-reloca-
tion; namely, the case of Piper Aircraft. The incentive for relocation occurred in the mid-1950s when
the firm's existing plant at Lock Haven,

Pennsylvania, reached saturation point. Eventually a
site for a new plant was chosen at Vero Beach, Florida. Four factors were influential in the decision.
In the first place, the equable climate not only
facilitated flight testing but also minimised heating
costs in factories which are, of necessity, areally
extensive one-storey structures. Secondly, the new
plant was devoid of a design division (a function
which was continued in Pennsylvania) and required a
mainly unskilled workforce for which the nonunionised
tradition of Florida conspired to present attractive-
ly-priced labour. Thirdly, the state was something
of a tax haven, having no personal or corporate
income taxes and inheritance tax, not to speak of the
below-average property taxes. Finally, the Vero
Beach site was a former naval air station and thus
endowed with a well-equipped airport and suitable
space to accommodate a 45,000 m^2 factory building.
The enthusiasm of the local municipality in granting
clear title and long-term leases to the land added to
its attractions.[42] Indeed, the locational advantages
of Florida impressed themselves upon Piper as the
years unfolded. By 1973, it had decided to build
another Florida plant - at Lakeland - to produce an
aircraft type developed at Lock Haven.[43] Two years
later, it was publicly musing over the possibility of
abandoning Lock Haven in view of the lower labour
productivity in the original centre.[44] By 1984 it
took the plunge, so to speak, deciding to close its
two Pennsylvania factories (the metal-parts plant at
Quehanna as well as Lock Haven) and transferring to
Florida in its entirety.[45] Interestingly, another denizen
of the industrial-heartland, Bethpage (New York)-
based Grumman has also chosen to expand in Florida.
In this case, the company purchased the old Fairchild
facility at St. Augustine in order to rebuild ex-mil-
itary HU-16 amphibians as G-111 civil machines. The
availability of an existing airport plus the nearby
location of Grumman's other Florida factory at Stuart
were reasons proffered for the choice of St. Augustine.[46]

Strategic Relocations
In truth, however, plant relocations undertaken as a
consequence of private enterprise decision-making
have been overshadowed by those undertaken as a
result of government fiat. In these instances, strategic considerations far outweighed any issues of
location cost. The USSR offers the supreme example
of aircraft industry location and relocation on the
basis of national security. As early as the second

five-year plan of the mid-1930s, the government was aiming to decentralise the aircraft industry away from the Moscow area. This led to the construction of the Gorki fighter plant (GAZ No 21) and the Voronezh bomber plant (GAZ No 18) as well as three large aeroengine plants at Zaporozhe and Rybinsk.[47] The essential spur to decentralisation, however, arose out of the German invasion of the country in 1941. In spite of the exigencies of wartime, most plants west of the Leningrad-Moscow-Stalingrad line (including much of the plant in the first two cities) were evacuated to cities in the east which heretofore had not undertaken aircraft manufacture (Figure 5.3). Soviet railways are reputed to have carried 1.5 million waggonloads of plant, machinery and personnel to the new centres and transferred 1,523 factories, many of which were GAZ units.[48] Moscow, for one, was denuded of its aircraft plants: the fighter factory, GAZ No 1, and the aeroengine facility, GAZ No 24, were both transferred to Kuibyshev; Kazan received the bomber-maker GAZ No 22, Irkutsk became host to another bomber plant - GAZ No 39 - and Tashkent benefited from the re-establishment of GAZ No 84, the transport aircraft manufacturer. While aircraft production had regained its prewar level in Moscow by the end of the war, the region embracing Kuibyshev had experienced a five-fold rise in activity; the tempo of activity had increased eleven-fold in the Urals, while Eastern Siberia's production rate had increased by a phenomenal factor of thirty.[49]

Dislocations as a result of World War II were also widespread in the case of France, Britain and the USA. In these cases, however, the changes were less relocations than redistributions; which is to say, the original firms remained in situ but were responsible for operating government owned-plants as 'branch' establishments in regions outside of the 'war zones'. The French and British cases were bound up with capacity expansion during the phase of rearmamental instability prior to the war. Nationalisation of the French aircraft industry in 1936 was accompanied by initiatives to set up new capacity in the south, away from Paris. The efforts, such as they were, did not materially influence the French distribution of production until after the German occupation and postwar period of reconstruction. The present situation of Aérospatiale's orientation to Toulouse and Marignane (on the outskirts of Marseille) is an obvious legacy of those prewar efforts to integrate strategic considerations into aircraft production.

British attempts at plant dispersal also have

Figure 5.3 : Soviet Evacuations of Aircraft Plants

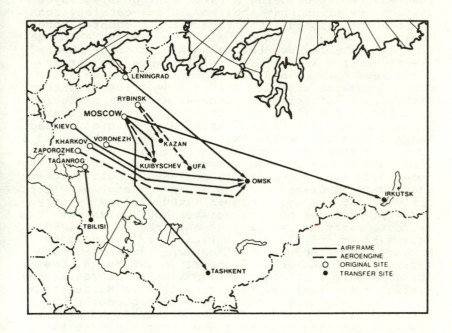

had far-reaching implications. The current focus of
BAe military aviation is Preston - a product of a
prewar-induced engineering firm's attempts to enter
aerospace (i.e. English Electric) at government instigation provided it received a government-built aircraft factory (Samlesbury) in a 'safe' (from bombing)
region. The UK Government was disturbed about the
concentration of aircraft capacity in London and the
South-east and, accordingly, drew up the so-called
'shadow' factory scheme in 1935.[50] Its aim was, quite
simply, to decentralise defence industries, including
aircraft plants. The new plants were to be devoid of
R & D facilities: rather they would mass-produce
standard designs of the established firms. The division of responsibilities meant that the private firms
would design aircraft and initiate production in
their own facilities, but should the design warrant
wholescale adoption, this would be undertaken in
state-built 'shadow' factories under the supervision
of the original firm. The 'shadow' factories were,
in fact, what the Americans came to call

'government-owned company-operated' plants. Added to
the requirement of being outside easy bombing range
was the criterion that they should be near (but not
in) centres of population from which adequate labour
could be drawn.
Figure 5.4 shows the 'shadow' factories managed
by established aircraft firms. Vickers ran three
complexes: Chester and Blackpool in the North and
Castle Bromwich in the West Midlands. The first consisted of a main assembly line at Hawarden and a secondary line at Byley; the second was centred on a
primary assembly line at Squires Gate with a supple-
mentary line at Stanley Park, whereas the third was a
massive centralised complex which built 11,939 Spit-
fires and 305 Lancasters between 1940 and 1945.[51]
Such productivity required a correspondingly large
investment in plant: Avro's Yeadon plant had a floor
space of 136,277 m^2, employed 11,000 (53 per cent
women), had three housing estates and a fleet of 160
buses to ferry the workers to and from their
houses.[52] One of the most unusual (and temporary
because it resided in a national park) was Shorts
flying-boat plant at Windermere. Selected in view of
its access to sheltered, inland waters for flight
testing and access to towns (and labour) by courtesy
of the railway, the plant produced 35 Sunderlands
between 1942 and 1944. Another set of 'shadow' factories was turned over to the automotive industry
when car-making firms were co-opted into the aircraft
production programme. They, likewise, were located
in the West Midlands and north of Britain: Rootes
Securities, for example, ran large plants at Speke
(Liverpool Airport) and Blythe Bridge near Stoke-on-
Trent, whereas Austin Motors built Lancaster bombers
at its Longbridge (Birmingham) Works and then assembled them at the Marston Green 'shadow' factory.
Although most of these plants abandoned aircraft manufacture after the war, the current aerospace centre
at Chester is really the Hawarden 'shadow' factory in
disguise and complements Preston as an inheritance by
BAe of the dispersal scheme.
The US version of strategic dispersal centred on
a 'Defence Zone' which was at least 200 miles inland.
Moreover, burgeoning growth of existing aerospace
centres on the coast led to labour shortages and the
desire to tap under-used manpower resources in the
interior. The outcome was a number of 'branch'
plants in the Great Plains and mid-West (Figure 5.5).
Costing almost $4 billion ($3.5 billion of which was
government funded), many of these plants were on a
huge scale. The War Department's need for B-24 bombers resulted in three giant factories: Tulsa (ran by

Figure 5.4 : UK Shadow Factories of Aircraft Firms

Douglas), Fort Worth (managed by Consolidated, the
precursor to GD), and Willow Run (operated, as in
Britain, by the co-opted automotive industry - in
this case by Ford). The last site employed 42,000
and necessitated the construction of an express high-
way from Detroit to Ypsilanti simply to get the workforce to the factory.[53] Two other large bomber-assem-
bly plants were built by the US Corps of Engineers at
Omaha (for Martin) and Kansas City (for North American). A number of Tier III factories were also built

131

by the government. Known as 'modification centres',
they were sites where aircraft off the production
lines were finished in accordance with operational
military requirements. Several locations new to the
aircraft industry hosted such centres, including:
Elizabeth City, North Carolina (managed by Consolidated); Daggett, California (under Douglas supervision); Phoenix, Arizona (ran by Goodyear Aircraft, a
subsidiary of the tyre company); and Birmingham, Ala-
bama (operated by the Bechtel-McCone construction
company).[54] As with all the other countries engaging
in strategic dispersal, many of the wartime US sites
became permanent fixtures in the postwar aerospace
sector.

REGIONAL POLICY

The government record of redistributing industry (and
not least the aircraft industry) during the war was
instrumental in stimulating regional industrial policy after 1945. Essentially, the policy adopted
everywhere was to provide incentives to private firms
to influence their choice of location. Italy went
one step further by compelling public enterprises to
locate a portion of their capacity in the depressed
Mezzogiorno.[55] It was hardly surprising, therefore,
that on the formation of Aeritalia as a result of
merger, its headquarters were placed at Naples and
the Italian Government promised the southern
depressed region a new R & D centre and aerospace
factory capable of employing 13,000.[56] The other
principal Italian state-owned aircraft company - Agusta - was responsible for an expansion plan which
explicitly recognised the need to shift aerospace
investment to the south. The first outcome of this
plan was the opening, in 1981, of the Industria Aeronautica Meridionale at Brindisi Airport. This subsidiary of Agusta was tasked with overhaul of aircraft and manufacture of helicopter parts as well as
the fabrication of rudders and vertical stabilisers
for the Lockheed L-1011 Tristar. Another subsidiary
was to be set up for the production of aluminium and
magnesium castings for use in airframe plants.[57]
     The usual pattern with aerospace activities,
however, is for regional incentives to emanate from
regional authorities who proffer them with the intent
of attracting private companies. The examples of
Northern Ireland, British Columbia and Belgian Flanders are cases in point and are outlined below. Yet,
even the USA has within it regions that have resorted
to incentives aimed at attracting aircraft companies.

132

Figure 5.5 :   US War-Built Branch Plants

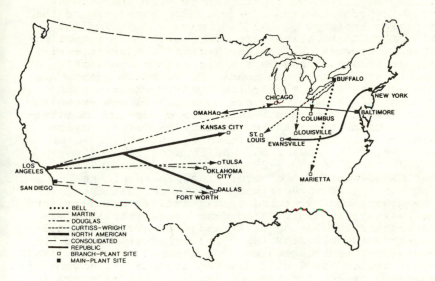

Mindful of the publicity associated with high-tech-
nology industries, the Government of Puerto Rico
offered tax concessions (and the prospect of low-cost
labour) to the Ahrens Aircraft Corporation of Oxnard,
California. A new venture, Ahrens had developed a
four-engined turboprop utility transport (the AR-404)
almost to the flight-test stage when it agreed to
transfer to Puerto Rico for certification and production of the machine. Housed at the former Ramey Air
Force Base, the island government "arranged financing
for an initial production run of 18 aircraft as part
of an effort to offset the impact of the base's closing on local employment".[58] The second prototype flew
in 1979 and the Puerto Rico Government appeared willing to provide loan guarantees to would-be customers.
By the middle of 1982 about 65 staff were employed on
the project and a factory was tooled up and poised
for production. Certification difficulties, however,
resulted in the failure of the venture and its abandonment of the island. That setback was not the end
of the AR-404, though, for plans were afoot in 1984
to have the aircraft (renamed the KM 180) built in
Sweden. Backed by the Malmo City Council and the
Swedish Investment Bank, the project was to be

implemented from a purpose-built plant in that city.[59]

Northern Ireland

Aircraft construction here effectively dated from the late 1930s when shipbuilder Harland & Wolff formed a partnership with the Shorts aircraft concern of Rochester, England and commenced to build bombers and flying-boats at a plant alongside its Belfast shipyard.[60] After many vicissitudes, Shorts was taken into public ownership in order to ensure its continuance. Completion of the military Belfast-transport programme in 1966 forced it into subcontract work: initially with Fokker and MBB in a collaborative effort to build the F-28 jetliner and then with MD for manufacturing the outer-wing panels of the F-4 fighter. Subcontracts kept Shorts in business throughout the 1970s and by the end of that decade it was making, in addition to F-28 wings, the landing gear doors for Boeing's 747 and the inboard flaps for the 757, the ailerons, spoilers, wing-tips and galley doors for the Lockheed L-1011, the forward engine nacelles for the R-R RB.211 engine, and the entire engine nacelles for the BAe 146. At the same time, its own series of light transports were coming to fruition; exemplified by the sale of 18 C-23A Sherpas to the USAF in 1984 which was worth $165 million and, best of all, guaranteed 1,000 jobs for a year. All these efforts required continual injections of government funds: the company received $43 million in 1980 from the UK Government in order to cover losses of $40 million in 1978-9 and to finance the development of its model 360. Similarly, the Northern Ireland Department of Economic Development (Shorts' controlling shareholder) committed £30 million in 1984 for the firm's role in developing the wing of the new Fokker F100 airliner.[61] Notwithstanding the difficulties of maintaining Shorts, the UK Government was keen to augment the province's aerospace sector by subsidising the ill-fated Lear Fan project. The brainchild of William Lear, this centred on the model-2100 twin-turboprop business aircraft; a revolutionary design entailing an airframe made almost entirely from graphite/epoxy and Kevlar composite materials, and an arrangement whereby the two engines independently drive a pusher propeller mounted in the tail. The UK division of the enterprise - Lear Fan Ltd - was a wholly-owned subsidiary of Lear Avia Corporation of Reno, Nevada. The intent was to pursue R & D and testing at the US location, leaving Northern Ireland responsible for manufacturing production aircraft. The initial capitalisation encompassed $80 million, of which $50 million derived from UK Government sources ($35 million for industrial grants and loans and the balance from loan guarantees).[62] By 1982, the enterprise employed 560 at Carmoney and Aldergrove in Northern Ireland and 400 at Reno. It was, however, desperate for development money, and there was talk of Beech Aircraft on the one hand, and a group consisting of American and Saudi investors on the other, coming forward to inject the necessary capital. The latter was sucessful and a reconstituted company - Fan Holdings Inc - was registered in Delaware and offered the prospect of 2,800 jobs in Northern Ireland by 1987. Minority shareholders included the Northern Ireland Department of Economic Development (with five per cent equity), Lear Avia, and the New York-based Oppenheim partnership. The UK operation was promised a further $30 million from the government on the understanding that private investment would be in the order of twice that amount. Consequently, Lear Fan Ltd purchased a 45,000 m² factory at Antrim which, owing to its previous use as a synthetic-fibre facility, was particularly well-suited with environmental controls for handling composite materials. Plans envisaged building of the first 42 aircraft in Northern Ireland as components and their subsequent dispatch to Reno for final assembly. With copy No 43, complete production and assembly would take place in the UK and the aircraft flown 'green' to the USA for outfitting: the Northern Ireland operation would represent about 70 per cent of total production man-hours. Unfortunately, structural problems with the airframe (ironically, not involving the revolutionary composites but the gearbox) in 1984 imposed delays on certification and forced the company to lay-off most of its UK workforce. A renewed attempt at certification was thwarted by cash-flow problems which led to the demise of the firm in 1985. The fact that the innovative nature of the project obliged Beech, Cessna, and Gates-Learjet also to introduce composite business aircraft projects was small consolation for the technical difficulties confronting Lear Fan as the pioneer in the field.

British Columbia.
The mixed results of Northern Ireland's attempts to build a regional aerospace industry can be compared with the even less auspicious experience of British Columbia. This Canadian province attempted to establish a regional aerospace core based on the Trident venture. The Trident Aircraft Company originated as

a private firm in Vancouver, formed in 1970 to manufacture a redesign of the US Republic Seabee amphi-
bian which was renamed the Trigull. Encountering
financial difficulties virtually from the outset, the
provincial government rapidly stood in to provide,
under the aegis of the British Columbia Development
Corporation, enough resources to keep the project
functioning. At its instigation, the federal government also became involved and later, in 1978, the
federal Enterprise Development Board pledged support
worth $6 million.[63] At the same time, British Colum-
bia agreed to contribute another $1 million and the
company claimed that it could find $950,000. How-
ever, the federal government could rescind its contribution if there was a 'material change in risk'
and it was through such a loophole that the Enterprise Development Board withdrew its pledge. The
decision of Trident to internalise components manufacture owing to difficulties with suppliers was
interpreted by the federal government as an unwar-
ranted risk burden. The direct result was the closure of Trident's new Victoria plant (paid for by
British Columbia Development Corporation) in January
1980 and the dismissal of 100 employees. The attempt
to create a regional aircraft industry from scratch
had met with ignominious failure.

Belgian Flanders.
Undeterred by such experiences as those offered by
Northern Ireland and British Columbia, the Belgian
Government has designated Flanders as the site for
future aerospace developments. The impetus for this
stance follows from the perceptions of the Flemings
that the Walloon-portion of the country has received
disproportionate aerospace investments. In particular, they point to two projects: Belairbus and the
F-16 offsets. The first embraces Belgium's participation in the Airbus and translates to a state funding of in excess of $30 million to SONACA for A310
wing-parts production. By the same token, the government (along with Fabrique Nationale) acquired
SONACA in Wallonia in order to guarantee production
of F-16 components. These initiatives were visual-
ised as part of a regional development strategy for
Wallonia which included the construction of a $12
million titanium-casting plant for aerospace products. In an attempt to arrive at regional balance,
the Belgian Government had ordered Merlin transports
from Fairchild on the understanding that the US firm
would provide offsets which would be distributed 40
per cent to Flanders, 40 per cent to Wallonia and 20

per cent to Brussels. Such a sop to Flanders was
regarded as insufficient with the result that 64 manufacturing firms combined to form FLAG - the Flemish
Aerospace Group - in order to promote regional aerospace development. In February 1983 FLAG was vindicated when the Belgian Government announced that offsets from any military programmes must be directed to
Flanders.

The main attention for regional development in
the north, though, revolves round the Foxjet project.
Emulating Lear Fan in many respects, the Foxjet
ST-600 is a twin-turbofan business aircraft designed
by an American, Tony Fox, the President of Foxjet
International of Minneapolis. Conceived in 1977, the
ST-600 was to be built in a planned 9,000 m^2 factory
in Minneapolis. Its selling point was the fact that
it was light (about one-third the weight of the competing Cessna Citation) and, therefore, cheap. It
was powered, however, by two engines of revolutionary
design which, as it transpired, led to teething trou-
bles in the certification process. Plans to build
the aircraft in the USA were abandoned and, instead,
onus was shifted to Belgium. In 1984 the Belgian
Government stated that a $80 million factory would be
built at Zutendael in north-east Belgium to manufacture the ST-600. The Foxjet project in combination
with a proposed helicopter plant employing 2,000 (a
by-product of military offsets) is anticipated to
form the core of the Flanders aerospace industry.[64]

CONCLUSION

In historical terms, the aircraft industry evolved as
a 'spin-off' of other related engineering activities
and, consequently, tended to locate in the same
industrial milieu even to the extent of adopting
inner-city premises ill-suited for extension. This
pull of inertia was strong enough to retain many aircraft enterprises within the agglomeration after due
allowance was made for the extensive space requirements of the industry and the virtual necessity of
relocation to suburban sites. Agglomeration centres
were also replete with appropriate supplies of
labour, the only locational factor of any real significance to the industry. Certainly, the desire to
minimise spatial linkages to supplier industries was
not a cause for selecting a site in an agglomeration
where this industry is concerned. None the less, the
quest for labour was sufficient stimulus to engender
interest in relocation and accounts, along with the
climatic factor, for the rise of southern California

as a main world centre of aerospace. When combined
with state strategic interests, the labour requirement was a powerful instrument for geographic redis-
tribution of the industry not only in the USA, but in
the USSR, Britain and France as well. Today, governments continue to influence the location of the
industry, although their interest is generally
couched in the language of regional development and
not that of defence planning. Interestingly, the
forthcoming regional policy has often been incumbent
on the action of entrepreneurs who have taken the
active part of designing aircraft which are then
built at public expense in return for the state having the right to locate the production facility in a
preferred region. In itself, this fact highlights
the continuing importance of entrepreneurship in the
industry and, more so, the crucial role played by
such people in technological advance. The equally
self-evident fact that entrepreneurship and technological change are not always commercially rewarding
is also extracted from the regional policy experience. Why technical change is vital to the fortunes
of the industry is the subject of the next chapter.

NOTES AND REFERENCES

    1. W. G. Cunningham, The Aircraft Industry: A
Study in Industrial Location, (Morrison, Los Angeles,
1951), p.2.
    2. Ibid, p.42.
    3. See, for instance, M. J. Taylor, 'Industrial
Linkage, "Seed-Bed" Growth and the Location of
Firms', University College London, Geography Occa-
sional Paper 3, September 1969.
    4. Recall Chapter 2 for an overview of Vickers'
aeronautical initiatives. Exceptions to this trend
have occurred. Grumman, for example, built a new
airframe plant at Savannah, Georgia in 1967: a site
markedly removed from its principal plant at Bethpage, New York. The plant was subsequently sold to
Gulfstream.
    5. W. G. Cunningham, Aircraft Industry, p.18.
    6. A fact brought out by Erickson, who points to
the wideranging geographical effects of purchases
made by Boeing. See R. A. Erickson, 'The Regional
Impact of Growth Firms: The Case of Boeing,
1963-1968', Land Economics, vol.50 (1974),
pp.127-136.
    7. AW & ST, 17 August 1970, p.11.
    8. In 1979 one European Currency Unit was valued
at $1.37; in 1980 it stood at $1.39.

9. 'The European Aerospace Industry: Trading Position and Figures', EEC Commission, Staff Working Paper, Sec. (80), 1237, Brussels, 23 September 1980, pp.50-64.

10. FI, 1 January 1983, p.11.

11. FI, 16 January 1982, p.138.

12. AW & ST, 2 June 1980, p.9.

13. AW & ST, 6 October 1980, p.15.

14. AW & ST, 13 April 1981, p.52.

15. AW & ST, 29 March 1976, p.9.

16. FI, 11 September 1975, p.373.

17. AW & ST, 26 April 1982, p.82.

18. AW & ST, 25 May 1981, p.13. Note, the UK had, in 1975, a capacity of 2,500 tons of titanium per year; 1,000 tons of which was earmarked for the aircraft industry. The USSR produces 80 per cent of the world's sponge titanium, supplying the needs of Italy and West Germany in addition to its own requirements.

19. AW & ST, 26 April 1982, p.78.

20. FI, 11 September 1975, pp.375-6.

21. AW & ST, 2 August 1982, p.84.

22. R. A. Erickson, 'The Regional Impact', p.130.

23. R. A. Erickson, 'The Spatial Pattern of Income Generation in Lead Firm, Growth Area Linkage Systems', Economic Geography, vol.51 (1975), pp.17-26.

24. FI, 11 February 1984, p.388.

25. AW & ST, 20 February 1982, p.44.

26. AW & ST, 10 November 1980, pp.74-5.

27. All told, 58,000 people in 3,000 firms are expected to be working on the $20.5 billion contract. See AW & ST, 25 January 1982, p.19.

28. W. G. Cunningham, Aircraft Industry, p.29.

29. For example: R. C. Estall and R. O. Buchanan, Industrial Activity and Economic Geography (Hutchinson, London, 4th edition, 1980), p.105 and, incidentally, for the effect of climate see p.204.

30. Calculated from information in FI, 30 August 1962, pp.309 ff.

31. Cunningham asserts that wartime plants used 10,000 or more workers; some ballooning to require 30,000. As a result "location in or near a large city was essential". See W. G. Cunningham, Aircraft Industry, p.22.

32. Ibid, p.21.

33. AW & ST, 3 November 1975, p.16 and 6 July 1981, p.55.

34. K. Hartley and W. S. Corcoran, 'Short-run Employment Functions and Defence Contracts in the UK Aircraft Industry', Applied Economics, vol.7 (1975),

pp.223-233. Quote from p.223. It should be noted, however, that labour 'hoarding' is much less prevalent in the USA than in Europe - as is attested by the figures in Table 2.5.

35. Ibid, p.230.

36. AW & ST, 4 June 1973, p.56.

37. AW & ST, 29 October 1973, p.66.

38. J. B. Rae, Climb to Greatness, (MIT Press, Cambridge, 1968), p.15.

39. Ibid, pp.10-11.

40. Certain UK firms located in non-metropolitan centres from the outset and so space limitations were rarely an issue in their expansion, e.g. Westland at Yeovil.

41. J. B. Rae, Climb to Greatness, p.188.

42. Jane Lancaster, 'Piper Aircraft's Vero Beach Plant: An Analysis of Locational Determinants in Light Aircraft Manufacturing', The Southeastern Geographer, vol.7 (1967), pp.22-33.

43. AW & ST, 26 March 1973, p.67.

44. FI, 20 March 1975, p.445.

45. FI, 19 May 1984, p.1316. Ironically, concentration also entailed dispensing with the Lakeland facility.

46. AW & ST, 30 June 1980, p.69. Incidentally, the plant at Stuart, another former naval air station, had initially been chosen by Grumman for testing its E-2 AWACS aircraft as the lack of iron in the soil did not interfere with magnetic testing. In the early 1980s Stuart was rebuilding OV-1 aircraft and making parts for the F-14, E-2C, Boeing 767 and CH-53. See AW & ST, 14 September 1981, p.135.

47. Alexander Boyd, The Soviet Air Force since 1918, (MacDonald and Janes, London, 1977), p.36.

48. Ibid, p.187.

49. Ibid, p.203.

50. W. Hornby, Factories and Plant, (HMSO, London, 1958).

51. M. J. F. Bowyer, Action Stations 6: Military Airfields of the Cotswolds and the Central Midlands, (Patrick Stephens, Cambridge, 1983), p.101.

52. B. B. Halpenny, Action Stations 4: Military Airfields of Yorkshire, (Patrick Stephens, Cambridge, 1982), p.198.

53. J. B. Rae, Climb to Greatness, p.159.

54. W. G. Cunningham, Aircraft Industry, pp.94-5. It is interesting to record that strategic relocation is not quite dead: in the 1970s the Chinese were keen on transferring aerospace facilities away from the disputed border with the USSR. See AW & ST, 19 January 1976, p.19.

55. Good reviews of Italian regional policy

include: V. Cao-Pinna, 'Regional Policy in Italy' in
N. M. Hansen (ed.) <u>Public Policy and Regional Economic Development</u>, (Ballinger, Cambridge, Mass,
1974), pp.137-179 and E. Nocifora, 'Poles of Development and the Southern Question', <u>International Journal of Urban and Regional Research</u>, vol.2 (1978),
pp.361-78.

    56. AW & ST, 31 May 1971, p.73.
    57. AW & ST, 21 April 1980, p.141.
    58. AW & ST, 15 November 1976, p.48.
    59. The Ahrens story can be assessed from FI, 15
May 1982, p.1225; 17 July 1982, p.118; and 21 April
1984, p.1081.
    60. An abortive attempt by Miles Aircraft of
Reading, England to set up a second production line
for Messenger aircraft at Newtownards was cancelled
by the ending of hostilities after only a few aeroplanes had been delivered. See John Corlett, <u>Avia-
tion in Ulster</u>, (Blackstaff Press, Belfast, 1981),
pp.78-9.
    61. See AW & ST, 14 April 1980, p.44 and 8
December 1980, p.52. Also FI, 10 March 1984, p.614;
24 March 1984, p.734; and 18 August 1984, p.96.
    62. A series of articles deal with this issue.
See AW & ST, 21 July 1980, p.22; 13 December 1982,
p.27; 31 October 1983 and 4 June 1984, p.25. Also:
FI, 11 September 1982, p.774; 25 September 1982,
p.923; 14 January 1984, p.65; 28 January 1984,
pp.277-9 and 3 March 1984, p.561. It is of interest
to note that the enticements of regional development
planners nearly resulted in another American aircraft
firm moving to the province in 1980. Cabair Sales
Ltd, the UK distributors for Gulfstream American,
announced that the US manufacturer would relocate
part of its production process to the UK - "probably
Northern Ireland". The relocation never came to
pass. See <u>Air Pictorial</u>, April 1980, p.122.
    63. <u>Financial Post</u>, 29 December 1979.
    64. Information germane to Flanders is found in:
FI, 18 September 1975, p.402 and 31 March 1984,
p.797. Also: AW & ST, 16 May 1977, pp.57-9; 31 March
1980, pp.92-3; and 2 February 1981, p.11. In addition: <u>Toronto Globe and Mail</u>, 5 July 1984.

Chapter Six

TECHNOLOGY AND INDUSTRIAL ORGANISATION

The crucial interaction between technical change and
the evolution of the aircraft industry was recounted
in Chapter 2. The object of this chapter is one of
refinement, that is to say, to specify the ways in
which typical aircraft enterprises rely on technology
for their well-being. What is more, the vital dependence on technical change necessitates certain strategies on the part of enterprises, as business organisations, in order to vouchsafe their own survival.
That subject is also the purview of this chapter. In
short, corporate ploys for gaining access to, and
making use of, aerospace technology will be highlighted. To that end, the chapter is divided into
two broad areas: the first outlines a conceptual
framework wherein the interaction between technology
and business organisation can be accommodated, the
second reviews the practical means for sharing technology which have been adopted by aircraft firms.
Accordingly, the former stresses the importance of
the interplay between endogenous R & D and exogenous
R & D in the operations of a characteristic aircraft
firm, whereas the latter considers such matters as
international and national co-production arrangements
and subsidiary ventures. Reference to the role of
the state in these considerations is unavoidable.
    Clearly, the fortunes of industrial organisa-
tions are inextricably bound up with the rate of
technical change, or, the degree of 'technological-
imperative', to put it in terms familiar to the aircraft industry. Yet, equally apparent is the 'environmental' milieu within which the industrial
organisations are found. Environmental factors
include a temporal dimension; namely, fluctuations in
demand imposed by the wave-cycle and business cycle,
as well as a political factor which embraces the
influence of the state both directly in terms of regulating demand and indirectly by way of influencing

142

industrial location. The structural contingency
model intentionally postulates that 'environment' and
technology have the effect of determining the shape
of industrial organisations as a result of their
interaction.[1] In according technology a central role,
it can reconcile both motivations for technical
change: the 'technology-push' whereby innovations
from within the aircraft industry determine subsequent
market activity and the 'demand-pull' by which the
market imposes specifications delimiting new designs
produced by the industry.[2]

A STRUCTURAL CONTINGENCY FRAMEWORK

The essence of the structural contingency model is
that technology bridges the environment and the
industrial organisation. In other words, technology
can be a component of the environment when it is con-
strued as emanating from a source external to the
enterprise in question. Alternatively, technology
can be part-and-parcel of the enterprise when it
forms a dynamic component of the focal organisation.
Advocates of the structural contingency model have
tended to adopt mutually-exclusive stances, claiming
that technology is either exogenous or endogenous to
the enterprise; but, conceptually, there is no reason
to suppose that technology cannot be envisaged as
being part-exogenous and part-endogenous. Indeed, a
comprehensive view of the importance of technology to
the aircraft industry necessitates such a compromise
view. In practical terms, it means that attention
must be directed evenly to endogenous R & D and
exogenous (to the firm) R & D.
 Of equal significance is the allowance for feedback effects between industrial organisation and
technology. Put otherwise, the simple proposition
that technology (R & D) leads to product or process
innovation which, in turn, shapes the production
activity and organisation of the firm needs to be
placed in context. On the one hand, the format of
the firm has some bearing on the generation and
acceptance of technical change: conceivably, for
example, a large firm well-endowed with resources
will be more susceptible to promoting R & D and then
adopting the resultant innovations than would a small
firm strapped for resources. On the other hand, the
economic attributes of the firm – the fact that it is
specialised or diversified, an independent operation
or subsidiary operation – also greatly influence the
attitudes to technology. Diversified firms, for
instance, may be in a position to take risks with

innovations that would not be contemplated by specialised firms: the former can divert resources from
other arms of the organisation to cover the losses
that may ensue; that is, they can pursue a strategy
of cross-subsidisation unavailable to the latter. In
sum, the type of feedback, or modification imposed on
technology (R & D) by the firm, is dependent on the
history and environmental conditions within which
individual enterprises operate. It is impossible to
predict deterministic behaviour applicable to all
firms in the aircraft industry: at best, general
strategies which firms may follow are made logical
when related to the interactions outlined by the
structural contingency framework.

The basic framework within which all aircraft
firms have to function is outlined in Figure 6.1.
The unbroken lines connect the origins and destina-
tions of primary stimuli while the broken lines indicate that the format of technological change is, at
one and the same time, incumbent on demand and a
determinant of it. The first case arises from the
specifications – military operational requirements,
for example – defined by the customer and passed on
to the R & D team for bringing to fruition. The
desire for technical supremacy expressed by air
forces has obliged aerospace R & D teams to compete
in terms of performance increments wherever warplane
contracts are concerned. The second is occasioned by
innovations formulated by aerospace engineers and
designers which have an immense impact on the perceptions of the customer: introduction of the jetliner
convinced airlines of the need to obtain such equipment virtually overnight and created a new market at
the expense of that for piston-engined machines. In
short, the opposing stimuli between technological
change and demand conform to 'demand-pull' and 'technology-push' motivations for innovation. The direct
edge linking technological change to industrial organisation allows for the possibility of the formation
of aircraft firms as speculative ventures to market
an innovative product: the example of Lear's companies in the bizjet field are cases in point. Most
aircraft enterprises, however, evolve and grow as a
result of their access to the market; hence, the link
connecting technological change to industrial organisations via the demand intermediary. The other major
'environmental' player is, of course, government. It
can come to bear either as a main force in formulating demand or alternatively, as the direct instigator
of the aircraft firm when the latter is set up as a
state undertaking. Feedback effects emerge from
these primary relationships: the firm can invest in

Figure 6.1 :   A Structural Contingency Framework

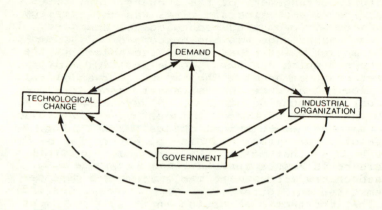

technological change by independently summoning
resources for the purposes of R & D, or, it can do so
by way of government subsidies. Whichever route is
adopted, the outcome is a fresh round of technical
advance which, in turn, triggers a new set of circumstances for the markets and the firms.

     Missing from such a framework is the distinction
between exogenous and endogenous R & D on the one
hand, and the explicit manner in which the form of
industrial organisation influences the firm's attitude towards adoption of subsequent innovations. Is
the 'technological change' box of Figure 6.1
ensconced within the firm or does it function partly
inside and partly outside of it? Does the size of
the enterprise influence the receptiveness of management to succeeding innovations? These questions have
already been aired, but the structural contingency
framework needs adjustment to expressly account for
them. The precedent set by Phillips is germane here.

The Phillips Eclectic Model
Phillips noted that aerospace belonged to a select
group of industries (electrical equipment, communications, chemicals, motor vehicles, machinery, and
instruments) which were characterised by high market
concentration and rapid technical progress. Rather
than concluding that large firms propagate technological change, he averred, after studying the US

civil aircraft industry, that changes in the technological environment were key players in altering the
structural arrangement of the industry. In other
words, the size of aircraft firms was not a significant factor in promoting technological change:
instead, such change was the outcome of adjustments
in the market which arose out of technological
advance and which, in turn, compelled firm expansion
to meet customer needs. The impetus forwarded by
technological advance was, moreover, generated for
the most part outside of the focal organisations constituting the civil aircraft industry. Only in subsequent rounds of technical change, market adjustment
and reaction of firms, did size of enterprise become
an issue. At that point, the firms of commanding
stature could ensure that barriers to entry were
imposed on new firms. The whole line of thinking is
systematised in Figure 6.2.[3]

The important distinction in this, Phillips'
Eclectic Model, is that between the two boxes representing technical change: one box, building on the
work of Schumpeter and Galbraith, allows for exogenous R & D undertaken quite independently of corporate goals for market control; the other, accommodates endogenous R & D undertaken by the firm in
order to further its market penetration. In Phillips' conception, the former encapsulates the work
undertaken by private inventors, government establishments, private research institutions and univer-
sities. It is, therefore, outside of the control of
the firm and, possibly, dissociated from any sense of
belonging to the concerned group which identifies
itself as serving the interests of the aviation community. The R & D pursued by the aircraft firm, however, is done to counter the efforts of other firms
which might eventually conspire to undermine its market position. As a risk-reducing activity, commitment by firms to endogenous R & D is always tempered
by the thought that 'short-cutting' and using exogenous R & D is an expedient ploy which can save on
development costs. At any rate, exogenous R & D
enriches the R & D efforts of existing firms and also
induces the entry of new ones: the two forms of business organisation together formulating the product
and process innovations that shape the market.

The resultant market structures proceed to
thrive on the strength of the performance advantages
gained as a consequence of the application of new
technology (provided, of course, that the innovation
does not represent a 'false-start').[4] Aircraft firms,
or at least some of them, also benefit from the adoption of the innovation and the incorporation of its

Figure 6.2 :   Phillips' Eclectic System

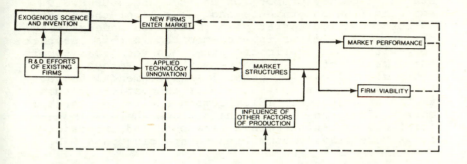

advantages into the aeroplane product. Yet, the
eclectic nature of the accomplishments of firms needs
underscoring. Harking back to the Schumpeterian cre-
ative-destruction argument, Phillips maintains that
new firms tend to displace older firms in as much as
they offer a dynamic new competitive force in the
market. Indeed, only the innovation-adopters among
the old firms will tend to survive: the others will
be driven out of business owing to their tardy commitment to technological advance. This pattern is
subject to modification, however, if the existing
firms have had ample time to corner a portion of the
market which remains loyal to their product. In this
case (and now technical change is de facto a subsequent round of innovation application) the advantages
of firm size can come to bear. The broken lines in
Figure 6.2 comprise the feedback system. In effect,
two loops close the model. The first trends back
from market performance - that is, the emergence of
demand opportunities - to new firm formation. A
dynamic, growing market which has shown itself recep-
tive to innovations can elicit entrepreneurial initiatives that take material form in the establishment
of new firms geared to incremental innovations.
Enhancement of the stock of competing firms serves to
heighten the competition for customer allegiance
among the aircraft producers and leads to further
market improvements. The second feedback loop
extends via the achievements-of-firms box to the
motivation for continual replenishment of endogenous
R & D. Quite simply, firms that have prospered from
prior innovation will be encouraged to try again.

Some of the rewards of that prior effort could be passed on to sources of exogenous R & D in order to facilitate the process of cross-fertilisation. As stated, a goodly proportion of the exogenous R & D emanates from government, and the role of the state in both moulding market performance and underwriting the success of firms is accommodated in this feedback loop within the rubric of 'other non-technical supply and demand factors'. That somewhat amorphous category also allows for general 'environmental' factors. All in all, the steady stream of innovations germane to the aeronautical field, combined with an unstable market situation, led to the outcome whereby industrial concentration became paramount and the major firms were heavily committed to spending on R & D.

The Evidence
After analysing the stream of innovations affecting US civil aircraft operations between the late-1920s and the mid-1960s, Phillips was convinced that, firstly, the numbers of airliner manufacturers had declined sharply over the years in question and, secondly, that the surviving manufacturers have experienced wide swings in market shares. Without the palliative of massive orders for warplanes, the probability of many more exits from aircraft production could not be discounted.[5] The US aircraft industry was, in effect, benefiting from the subsidies flowing from a giant defence establishment and the military R & D commensurate with that military stance. The overwhelming trend towards industrial concentration and the consonant disinclination of new entries into the market was traceable from an examination of the product innovations - the successful airliners - which garnered an element of market control for their manufacturers. Pinpointing in chronological order the Ford Trimotor, Douglas DC-2, DC-3, Lockheed L-10, Douglas DC-4, DC-6, DC-6B, Lockheed Constellation series, Boeing 707, 720, Douglas DC-8 and Boeing 727, Phillips demonstrated that, at the time of their entry into airline service, these aircraft offered definite operating-cost advantages over alternative machines. In consequence, their impact on the market was such as to induce 'copy-cat' effects. In Phillips' words, operating savings "supplemented in most instances by other performance improvements and by the demonstrated effect of new types of planes on passenger demand, were such that the new aircraft were demanded for replacement of existing models as well as for fleet expansion".[6] It is abundantly clear that 'technology-push'

innovations are seen as the prime movers in US civil aircraft development.

The firms fortunate enough to marshal the innovations reaped the accompanying benefits and acted to thwart the successful entry of newer, smaller aircraft manufacturers. Nevertheless, the maxim of 'once successful, always successful' did not seem to apply, as the failure of Ford (propagator of that early success, the Trimotor) duly attests. Also, the highly successful Lockheed and Boeing companies, formulators of a string of innovative airliners, were not immune from backing market failures. Boeing, for example, produced the models 307 and 377 piston-airliners which were commercial disasters, losing out to the Douglas DC-6 family, and would have bankrupted the company if alternative defence contracts had not saved the day. Lockheed, for its part, virtually failed with the burden of the L-1011 Tristar and relied upon government for salvation. The roles were reversed later. Boeing more than recouped its share of civil markets when it introduced the 707: Douglas which had dominated the piston-engined field had to resort to defence production to stave off collapse. The fact remains, though, that firms were deterred from entering the airliner market: GD refrained after approaching financial disaster with its ventures into the jetliner arena (the Convair 880 and 990), settling instead for more lucrative warplane programmes.

Exogenous R & D. In terms of civil aircraft, Phillips points to the crucial part played by US government agencies in providing the basic R & D for innovation development. All of the formative work on aeroengines, for example, came from government-funded research. Much of the incentive for state support came, in fact, from the desire to underpin military technology but it sufficed, none the less, to cross-fertilise civil aircraft developments. The affinities of Boeing's C-97 military transport and its model 377 airliner for one, and the KC-135 aerial tanker and the model 707 for another, are cases in point. However, perhaps the best example of the reliance of existing US aircraft manufacturers on exogenous R & D was the inception of the turbojet. This technological breakthrough was pioneered in the UK and Germany and was taken up in the USA (and USSR) as a derivative innovation.[7] Development of jet engine technology emphasised a persistent feature of aeronautical innovation; namely, that so much of it derived from the efforts of individual inventors. Indeed, Miller and Sawers are altogether dismissive of the record of endogenous R & D in the formulation of effective product innovations in aeronautics. They proffer the stark comment that of the principal innovations "only those of two types of flap can wholly be credited to the employees of aircraft manufacturers".[8]

Highlighting three major phases of innovation in aircraft design, Miller and Sawers ascribe the frantic years 1908-12 and, again, 1930-33 to the stimulus emanating from the civil aircraft market, leaving the fruitful 1942-47 period as the sole representative of military-led development. The earliest period was congruent with the flowering of pioneer inventors and aviators: men who responded in particular to the potential for private aircraft in France. The second phase was largely triggered by the competition among American airlines, while the third was, naturally enough, a product of the exigencies of war. Among the major innovations coming to the fore at the end of the 1920s were the variable-pitch propeller and the stressed-skin metal airframe. The former was largely the outcome of inventors working privately - Hele-Shaw, Beacham, Turnbull and Caldwell - while the latter was the outcome of combined private research and company R & D (Junkers and Northrop both formed their own companies to exploit the advance after pioneering it; while Dornier and Rohrbach pioneered the process innovation while working for the Zeppelin company). The major product of the 1940s phase was, as intimated, the jet engine and its associated wing redesign (swept-back wings). As with the others, individual initiative was crucial. Whittle, working on his own, was a major pioneer in jet technology as was von Ohain, whereas wing innovation rested mainly on the work of Busemann and Betz at the University of Göttingen.[9] Even where product innovations result from R & D endogenous to the industry, they do not necessarily arise out of the efforts of firms ensconced in the market. According to Miller and Sawers, many innovators in airliner design were warplane producers who wished to diversify into civil aviation. Prior to its DC-2 success in 1932, Douglas had only built military aircraft while Vickers, the designer of the world's first turboprop airliner (the Viscount), had (as recounted in Chapter 2) based its aviation interests on defence products.[10] Those examples might, figuratively speaking, coincide with the entry of new firms as posited in the Eclectic Model but, in reality, they were established aircraft firms whose evolution and R & D impetus had stemmed from the military branch of the market.

Entry of New Firms. The aforementioned examples of Douglas and Vickers emphasise the relative ease whereby firms can enter the civil aircraft market should they be blessed with resources acquired from other markets (defence, in this instance) and a general familiarity with aircraft R & D (the indivisibility of civil and military R & D noted in Chapter 3). The situation can apply in reverse of course, with airliner manufacturers breaking into the military market. In this respect, the sale of bizjets to air forces has been mentioned and, by the same token, manufacturers of light aircraft for general aviation purposes have also prospered from defence contracts. The Canadian DHC concern, for instance, received modest prosperity from the development of STOL 'bush' planes after World War II. It leapt to prosperity, however, when those light aircraft were adopted by the US forces during the Korean War as utility transports. A total of 980 Beaver planes, nearly 58 per cent of total output, were bought by the USAF and US Army and this precedent led to purchases of DHC-3 Otter, DHC-4 Caribou, DHC-5 Buffalo and DHC-6 Twin Otters in large numbers by the US forces.[11]

As a result of protection accorded by governments, some enterprises are given the opportunity to develop designs which will challenge the supremacy of existing market leaders. Nowhere is that situation more apparent than in the current market for light airliners, the so-called 'commuterliners'. In the market for small commuterliners (10-20 passengers), the market leaders of the 1970s (Beech, DHC, Government Aircraft Factories, PBN, Piper, and Shorts) have been faced by the competition of 'new' entries in the 1980s (BAe, Cessna, Dornier, Fairchild) compelling some of them to retaliate by innovating 'follow-on' products. As Table 6.1 shows, the original innovators Beech, PBN and Piper responded by introducing new aircraft designs to coincide with the introduction of 'new' entry products. Other original firms, however, have stuck to their 'tried-and-tested' designs and hoped to retain their market share by a combination of marginal improvements applied to the aircraft and financial inducements offered as a result of scale economies realised over sizeable production runs. The table indicates that, on the whole, the older designs are lower-priced than the newer products of the same firms or 'new'-entry firms. Where this is not the case, the higher price tends to indicate a successful product enjoying price 'inelasticity' within a well-established market

Table 6.1 : Small-Commuterliner Market

Type	Company/Source	First Flight	Basic Price ($m,1984)
Super King Air	Beech (US)	1972	1.87
Twin Otter 300	DHC (Canada)	1965	2.10
Nomad N24A	Government Aircraft Factories (Australia)	1975	1.20
Islander	PBN (UK)	1965	0.38
Chieftain	Piper (US)	1973	0.46
Skyvan	Shorts (UK)	1963	1.20
Jetstream 31	BAe (UK)	1980	1.70
Caravan 1	Cessna (US)	1982	0.65
228-200	Dornier (W. Germany)	1981	1.70
Metro III	Fairchild (US)	1981	2.20
C99	Beech (US)	1980	1.45
1900	"	1982	2.85
B300	"	1983	2.34
Turbine Islander	PBN (UK)	1980	0.73
T-1040	Piper (US)	1981	0.87

Source: Flight International; 1 September 1984, p.412.

Table 6.2 : Medium-Commuterliner Market

Type	Company/Source	First Flight	Basic Price ($m,1984)
212 Aviocar	CASA (Spain)	1971	2.40
Bandeirante	Embraer (Brazil)	1968	2.10
330	Shorts (UK)	1974	3.30
Dash 8	DHC (Canada)	1983	5.20
340	Saab-Fairchild (Sweden/US)	1983	5.30
Brasilia	Embraer (Brazil)	1983	4.70
360	Shorts	1981	4.10

Source: Flight International, 1 September 1984, p.412.

niche. None the less, some of the original market leaders have opted to divert their efforts to a different market because either the competition in the first market is becoming too intense or the firm feels that better prospects will be forthcoming from 'new'-entry status in a fresh market. This trend is discernible in the medium-commuterliner market. As evinced from Table 6.2, both DHC and Shorts redirected their subsequent design efforts to the 'up-market' commuter sphere once their initial commuter-liner ventures (the Twin Otter and Skyvan) had been brought to maturity. The far fewer competing products in this market is a pointer to the less-intensive competitive environment (and also to the greater R & D cost involved in designing a larger aircraft). Interestingly, however, the original market leaders in the medium-commuterliner field have responded in a manner comparable to some of their counterparts in the small-commuterliner market, that is, they have brought out 'follow-on' designs. Embraer and Shorts itself are cases in point.

Role of the State. The state has had far-reaching consequences in two respects: first, by facilitating the provision of exogenous R & D for the ultimate betterment of aircraft firms and, secondly, through deliberately restructuring those aircraft firms to make them more amenable to technological progress. The first aim is achieved both directly and indirectly. In the indirect sense, governments maintain state research institutions whose mandate is to pass on aeronautical findings to aircraft designers: the US NASA, the British Royal Aircraft Establishment (RAE), and the Soviet Central Institute of Aerodynamics and Hydrodynamics (TsAGI) all fulfil this function. It is not always a particularly fruitful relationship, however, as the nature of pure research is not easily grafted onto product design.[12] Consequently, governments resort to the provision of specific R & D monies as a second, less indirect way of fomenting innovation in aircraft design. As to be expected in view of the symbiosis between the state and defence contractors brought out in Chapter 4, public monies are particularly munificent in warplane development. Table 6.3 lists the top ten recipients of RDT & E awards from the US DoD in 1983 and it also gives examples of the budget requests put forward by the firms for 1984. Three companies each received in excess of one billion dollars in state-aid for military aerospace development, and a further six benefited to the tune of over half a billion dollars each. A single project, the B-1B, was the subject of a request for three-quarters of a billion dollars in RDT & E support. Multiplied over a number of years- the ten years typically required to design a modern combat aircraft - and the level of exogenously funded R & D is truly staggering. While the gigantic American MIC devours vast sums of public funds for military aviation, the more modest aircraft industries of the EEC are not sluggards where state-supported R & D is concerned. The £2 billion A320 Airbus programme has been mentioned, and will be again in Chapter 7, but the amount of public money put into the UK industry is illustrative of government backing for national aerospace R & D. Even twenty or more years ago, the UK Government was reputed to be averaging £9 million per year in support of civil aviation projects.[13] A paper presented to the House of Commons in the mid-1970s suggested that in the previous nine years, sums of £300 million and £350 million had been made available by the state to support civil airframe programmes and military aviation R & D respectively. The then Minister responsible for the aircraft industry stated to the House that in the period since 1965 some £350 million had gone to subsidise civil aircraft while £450 million had been sunk into warplane R & D.[14] For its part, the industry suggested that the lion's share of state support had been earmarked for just two projects: Concorde (absorbing £548.4 million since 1964) and the RB.211 aeroengine produced by R-R for the Lockheed L-1011 Tristar (£189.4 million). Excluding those two programmes, they implied that state largesse had been confined to an investment of £52.8 million in a decade, £36.7 million of which was repaid.[15] Arguably, most projects stood or fell on their commercial merits and the willingness of firms to take risks in backing them: a significant few, however, were brought to completion as a result of government intervention. Clearly, the risk-burden associated with product innovation was being shouldered entirely by the state in those instances.

Governments have agreed to absorb the risk burden in direct proportion to the rise in project development costs. In a telling passage, Miller and Sawers highlight the escalation in cost of engineering development (Table 6.4). The rise seems inexorable: the £2 billion price tag put on the A320 Airbus and the sum in the order of $4 billion that Boeing attributes to the development of the 757/767 new-generation of jetliners are mere continuations of past trends. Unable to summon the resources necessary to cover development costs, firms have either to go

Table 6.3 :   US Aerospace RDT & E Awards

Firm	Award ($'000)	Examples of Budget Requests
Boeing	1,703,491	
RI	1,171,720	B-1B bomber, $749.9 million
Martin-Marietta[1]	1,048,660	
TRW[1]	669,331	
MD	647,323	AV-8B tactical fighter, $118.2 million
		F-15 fighter, $117.8 million
		F-18 fighter, $27.2 million
GE[2]	645,426	
GD	643,504	F-16 fighter, $107.4 million
Hughes	627,333	AH-64 helicopter, $28.3 million
Lockheed	509,219	
UTC[3]	339,431	

Notes: 1. missiles and avionics only
        2. aeroengines only
        3. helicopters and aeroengines

Source: Aviation Week, 14 March 1983, pp.10-11 and 18 June 1984, p. 85.

cap-in-hand to the state for subsidies or, alternatively, they may be forced out of the airframe business. Prior market success is no guarantee for smoothing the progress in overcoming obstacles where development costs are concerned. The failure of Britten-Norman is salutary in indicating the consequence of a shortfall in development funds. This British firm had spent about $3 million on R & D associated with its highly-successful Islander light transport. Nevertheless, it owed $600,000 of a $1.32 million production loan from the UK Government, not to speak of $6.72 million to a commercial bank. Inability to service the bank loan resulted in receivership for the firm in 1971. Britten-Norman, the organisation established by a duo of entrepreneurs, was subsequently purchased by the Fairey engineering company and, on its bankruptcy in 1976, by Pilatus Aircraft of Switzerland. The original firm had been capitalised for only $250,000 and was unable to finance R & D without incurring a loan burden which eventually crippled it.[16] Ironically, the Islander was built in four countries (the UK, Belgium, Romania and the Philippines) largely to contain aircraft production costs. The machine was commercially successful, PBN handing over copy number 1,000 to the customer in April 1982, but 'follow-on' product innovations were clearly beyond the financial capabilities of the original innovating organisation.[17] Another firm confronted by similar cash-flow problems was R-R, but its size prevented the stoppage commensurate with commercial failure which was the lot of Britten-Norman. The aeroengine giant had over-extended itself in attempting to develop the RB.211. On its entering receivership in 1971, it was immediately nationalised by the UK Government in order to maintain its commitments (and ensure a national aeroengine capability). Prior to collapse, the state had invested $213.6 million in the RB.211 programme, but a further $72 million was needed simply to fulfil development targets. Problems with the development programme had pushed up individual engine costs from the $840,000 agreed with Lockheed as the sale price to $1,104,000: resulting in a whopping loss to R-R for each engine built.[18] The scale of the dependence of R-R on subsidies to cover development costs is apparent from the bill introduced in the UK House of Commons in 1980 which aimed at immediately raising the borrowing limit of the company from £750 million to £1.5 billion with the prospect of another £500 million over the succeeding five years.[19]

Merger. Governments have actively intervened to promote restructuring of aircraft firms in an attempt to make them more competitive all round. A significant aspect of the augmented competitiveness is the ability to command greater resources for R & D. The merger of separate business organisations into a single, larger enterprise is a tactic much favoured by governments. In Britain, government encouragement of mergers came about in the 1950s when a combination of reduced defence contracts after the 1957 Defence White Paper and increasingly expensive project development costs compelled a rationalisation of the industry. Already UK aircraft production had fallen from a figure of 2,000 completed airframes in 1953 to 510 by 1960 and the Government was no longer prepared to support a large number of airframe manufacturers either with production contracts or R & D subsidies for the next generation of aircraft. Of its own volition, the industry commenced merger steps in the phase of demobilisational instability after World War II. Two groups coalesced: General Aircraft and Blackburn forming an airframe group and Cierva and Saunders-Roe (Saro) forming a helicopter combine.[20] The Government began to force the pace when in 1957

Table 6.4 :   Escalation in Engineering Development Costs

Period	Type	Cost ($'000)
1920s	Lockheed Vega airliner	25
1930s	Douglas DC-3 airliner	300
1940	Douglas DC-4 airliner	3,300
1945	Douglas DC-6 airliner	14,000
1947	Boeing B-47 bomber	29,000
1950s	Douglas DC-8 airliner	112,000
1950s	MD F-4 fighter	468,000
1960s	RI XB-70 bomber	1,500,000

Source: Miller and Sawers, The Technical Development of
Modern Aviation, p.267.

it insisted that a contract to produce a jetliner for
BEA be split 67.5 per cent to DH, 22.5 per cent to
Hunting and 10 per cent to Fairey, with the three
companies forming a working consortium (the Trident
eventually materialised).[21] A similar consortium-ar-
rangement to produce the only major new warplane
requirement was used as an excuse by the Government
in 1959 for forcing the creation of BAC. Centred
around the TSR-2 programme, BAC was based on the
merger of English Electric Aviation and Vickers-Arm-
strong (Aviation) Ltd. Junior partners which joined
in 1960 to officially launch BAC were Hunting and
Bristol (the ownership breakdown being in the ratio
of 40:40:20 English Electric - Vickers - Bristol;
later the first two bought out Bristol). At the same
time, Hawker Siddeley Aviation Ltd was prodded into
becoming an integrated manufacturing organisation
rather than the loose holding company it had been
hitherto. Figure 6.3 summarises the merger process
which culminated in 1960 with two large UK airframe
producers and five smaller manufacturers which
remained immune from the larger mergers (Beagle,
Handley Page, Scottish Aviation and Shorts - as aeroplane producers - and Westland as a helicopter specialist).[22]
      It is not without irony that BAC, the product of
government machinations, should have virtually foundered in the succeeding decade as a result of govern-
ment-project cancellations (TSR-2, PT428 missile and
OR351 next-generation combat aircraft).[23] Cancellation of missile R & D led to the closure of the Luton
factory inherited from English Electric in 1962 while

Figure 6.3 : The UK Pre-Nationalisation Mergers

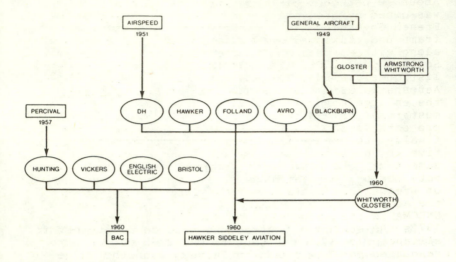

the scrapping of TSR-2 resulted in the abandonment of
military work at Weybridge and Bristol and its concentration on Preston. Fortunately, the firm persevered with a civil project, the BAC-111, and by a
judicious allocation of parts manufacture to Bristol,
Luton (Hunting's plant), Hurn and Weybridge was
enabled to keep these facilities operating. A problem that arose as a by-product of merger became evident in connection with the TSR-2 cancellation.
Observers felt that the programme was delayed by up
to two years owing to the distraction of management
with issues of organisational restructuring.[24] The
delay might have contributed to the cost escalation
which was used by the Government as the basis for
cancellation. In the final analysis, though, BAC and
HS survived because they were large enough – as a
consequence of merger – to absorb losses on the scale
of TSR-2 (which employed 20,000 men).[25] Other firms,
devoid of either the extra resources consonant with
merger or state predilection to support them, were
unable to survive. The examples of Britten-Norman
and Handley Page have been touched on elsewhere, but
Beagle had also collapsed by 1970 and Shorts was only
kept in being because of its sensitive Northern Ireland location. Therefore, in a European context,
merger appeared to be the only option capable of
overcoming the problem of acquiring the resources

necessary for innovating major aircraft programmes.
The French certainly subscribed to this view.
About 70 per cent of that country's aircraft industry
was owned by the state in any event. However, the
French Government forced the merger of its two airframe undertakings, Nord Aviation and Sud Aviation,
along with a rocket R & D establishment (SEREB, or
Société pour l'Étude et la Réalisation d'Engins Bal-
listiques), into a large, integrated concern, namely,
Aérospatiale.[26] The reasons put forward to justify
the enlarged corporation were three-fold: first, to
muster an increased resource base for launching new
projects, secondly, to streamline management, and
finally, to render the French industry more competitive in relation to the US aerospace giants. At the
same time, the Government promoted merger in the private sector (Figure 6.4). The outcome was the union
of Breguet and Dassault in the airframe sector and
the acquisition of Hispano-Suiza by state-owned
SNECMA in the aeroengine sector.[27] By the end of the
1970s the state-aeroengine enterprise had formed an
alliance with GE of the USA to muster the requisite
resources for large turbine development (CFM International).

The West Germans accomplished wholesale merger
only in 1980. Yet, the formation of MBB-VFW was the
outcome of a long process of government-induced
rationalisation (Figure 6.5). By the end of the
1960s, two airframe producers of consequence had
emerged in the Federal Republic: MBB and VFW. Unfor-
tunately from the point of view of the West German
Government, VFW had teamed up with Fokker of the
Netherlands in order to access airliner technology.
This, the pinnacle of foreign penetration of the German industry, was perceived by the Government as
detrimental to a national, state-sponsored aerospace
sector. Consequently, the Government made the separation of VFW-Fokker a precondition for subsidising
the merger of Bremen-based VFW and Munich-based
MBB.[28] It had already staved off bankruptcy for the
former in 1977 (the result of the failure of the
model 614) by advancing credits amounting to $250
million. However, by 1979 VFW was making sales in
excess of $575 million whereas MBB's sales were in
the order of $1 billion and the Government believed
that a merged company would be able to compete on
equal terms with BAe and Aérospatiale. In 1980
Fokker formally dissociated itself from VFW and the
US firm, UTC, agreed to sell its 26.4 per cent holding to Fried. Krupp GmbH. The threat of withholding
state funds for the Airbus programme was sufficient
incentive to bring together VFW and MBB in that year.

Figure 6.4 :   French State and Private-Sector Mergers

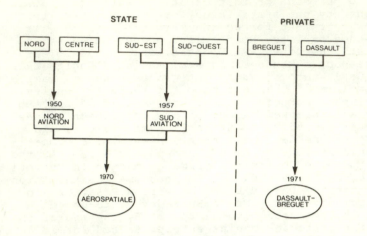

The unified corporation inherited a range of international programmes giving the German industry access
to the spectrum of aerospace technology, viz: the
Tornado MRCA (42.5 per cent share), Airbus (37.5 per
cent share), Euromissile (50 per cent share), PAH-2
helicopter (50 per cent share) and Eurosatellite (24
per cent share).[29]
     Emulation of the British-French mania for merg-
ers was not confined to West Germany. At the beginning of the 1970s, the Italian Government instituted
merger proceedings for the same reason: the need for
an entity large enough to participate in new-generation aircraft developments. An invigorated state
undertaking, Aeritalia, was created out of the aircraft interests of Fiat and Aerfer (Finmeccanica-
IRI), and was soon joined by Aermacchi. The helicop-
ter-producer Agusta also expanded by acquiring
SIAI-Marchetti.[30] A major rationalisation underway in
the 1980s consolidated the state's role in Italian
aerospace. In terms of the airframe sector, the
results included the take-over of Partenavia by Aeritalia and the partial acquisition of Aermacchi by
this dominant aircraft firm. In return, however,
Aeritalia transferred its Nerviano (Milan) factory to
Agusta, the state-owned helicopter and light aircraft
group. Comparable mergers in the aeroengine field in
both West Germany and Italy followed the precedent
set by R-R and SNECMA. Thus, as the 1980s unfolded,

Figure 6.5 :   West German Mergers

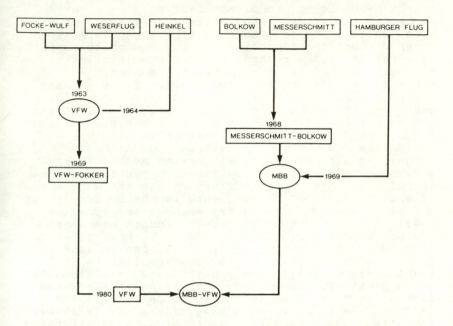

EEC Governments felt that their national industries were better placed to compete with US corporations in aircraft development.[31] To facilitate that competitiveness, they also fostered co-operative international aircraft projects with each other, but that topic deserves addressing from the viewpoint of technology transfer.

TECHNOLOGY TRANSFER

Technology transfer is a mechanism used by some industrial organisations in order to overcome the problems associated with innovating new aircraft or production technology. It involves the transfer of technology developed by one enterprise to another enterprise in return for a fee, royalty, or other kind of remuneration. The conduits for technology transfer are three in number: first, by way of interfirm co-production agreements, secondly, through the provision of licence-production agreements, and thirdly, by virtue of the operations of subsidiary companies established to utilise the R & D efforts of the parent firm.[32] Co-production occurs when two or more firms participate in roughly equal proportions in the development and/or manufacture of aircraft. It can be subdivided into fully-integrated co-production, which is to say, each participating firm is given production responsibility for a particular part or aircraft system regardless of the multiplicity of assembly lines (i.e. 'world product mandates'). If the agreement is international in scope (as in many EEC programmes), this means that one firm supplies the needs for a specific item for all the collaborating countries. Alternatively, the other subdivision, licence co-production, involves the manufacture of assemblies and systems by a variety of firms in roughly equal amounts but with prime authority for design, development and modification resting with the 'lead' firm which acts as licensor for the aircraft. Licence-production, per se, entails the production of a foreign design in a country without the licensee having any involvement in 'world product mandates' for particular assemblies or systems. More often than not, the licence-production reduces to assembly (and minimum fabrication) of subassemblies built in the country of origin and imported into the licensee's premises. Subsidiary operations may be established by enterprises in foreign countries in order to boost the technological base of the host's aerospace industry. As with licence-production, it tends to act as a mechanism for transferring technology from AICs and NICs.

Co-Production
In a nutshell, the fully integrated variant has been characteristic of European efforts whereas the licence variant has typified American ventures into the co-production arena. Frequently, European co-production initiatives have involved the creation of a holding company to act as focal organisation for the project: Airbus Industrie (initially for the A300) and Panavia (for the Tornado MRCA) are cases in point. Examples of prominent fully-integrated co-production projects are presented in Table 6.5 while some of the principal licence co-production programmes are proffered in Table 6.6.

The Europeans favour co-production not only because it reduces duplication in R & D and therefore cuts the unit costs of aircraft to the individual enterprise, but also because it offers the prospect of economies of scale with the longer production runs that follow from several guaranteed customers.

Table 6.5 :   Fully-Integrated European Co-Production
              Programmes

Project	Prime Airframe Contractor	Other Airframe Contractors
Atlantic patrol plane	Breguet (1959)	Dornier SABCA (Belgium) Fokker Aérospatiale Aeritalia (after 1968)
Transall transport	Aérospatiale (Nord) (1959) MBB (Hamburger Flug)	
G.91 tactical fighter	Aeritalia (Fiat) (1956)	Dornier Heinkel Messerschmitt
Alpha Jet trainer	Dassault-Breguet (1970) Dornier	SABCA
Jaguar strike fighter	SEPECAT holding company (1967) BAe (BAC) Dassault-Breguet	
Tornado MRCA	Panavia holding company (1969) BAe (BAC) MBB Aeritalia	

Moreover, some enterprises stand to gain from access
to technology developed by a partner organisation, a
major factor in West German involvement in Panavia
and Airbus as mentioned. One of the earliest co-production agreements, that for the Atlantic maritime-
patrol aircraft, was the outcome of a NATO competition of 1958.[33] Based on the winning design of
Breguet and funded by the USA, the machine was built
for France, West Germany, the Netherlands and Italy.
The Belgian ABAP group (Fairey SA, FN, SABCA) produced components, Aérospatiale (then Sud Aviation)
built the outer wings, Fokker was responsible for the
centre section and nacelles, Dornier for the rear
fuselage and tail, and Breguet for the forward fuselage and final assembly. Later Aeritalia was brought
into the programme as a reward for an order from the
Italian Air Force.[34] The aircraft's engines – R-R
Tyne Type 21s – were also the subject of collaborative production: R-R, SNECMA, FN and MTU all being
involved. A more recent illustration is provided by
the Tornado. This MRCA is managed by Panavia, a
Munich-based holding company which accommodates the
interests of the partners from the UK, West Germany

and Italy (divided in a ratio of 42.5 per cent each
to BAe and MBB, and the remaining 15 per cent to Aeritalia). A parallel holding company, Turbo-Union,
oversees development and manufacture of the RB.199
engine for the Tornado (shared 40 per cent each by
R-R and MTU and 20 per cent by Fiat). The compli-
cated allocation of work-sharing stemmed from the
commitment of each nation to purchase batches of aircraft: the larger the procurement, the greater the
weight in airframe and aeroengine work.[35]

The US licence co-production agreements listed
in Table 6.6 embrace foreign designs (UK, as it hap-
pens) built, after due modification, in the USA and
American designs built by NATO European consortia.
Under the proviso that all major items of equipment
for the US armed forces must be domestically produced, the general rule is for the DoD to purchase
American-designed and made aircraft. Exceptions
occur wherever US manaufacturers are tardy in innovating particular weapons systems, e.g., the light
jet bomber (causing the adoption of the British Canberra as the B-57) and the V/STOL tactical fighter
(filled by adaptation of the BAe Harrier). In 1949
the Martin XB-51 attack bomber failed to meet USAF
operational requirements and was scrapped in favour
of the Canberra to which Martin was entrusted with
redesigning to US standards. The initial model - the
B-57A - was virtually a copy of the 'B2' version of
English Electric's original Canberra; subsequent models, however, incorporated increasingly novel features. The engine incidentally, was a US Wright-
built version of the UK Armstrong-Siddeley (later
part of Bristol) Sapphire. A total of 403 B-57s
emerged from Martin's plant at Baltimore. With the
AV-8 project, licence-production of the British original followed the purchase of an initial batch of
Harriers (AV-8A) from HS in the UK. The US Marine
Corps purchased a dozen for $48 million and then
requested $96.2 million for another 18. A quarter of
the latter sum was required to provide for partial
assembly at St. Louis by MD - the surcharge, as it
were, of insisting on domestic production.[36] The
updated AV-8B was a true co-production venture with
60 per cent of the airframe work assigned to MD and
the residual to BAe. The British firm manufactures
the rear and centre fuselage as well as the fin and
rudder and ships them to the USA for completion.[37] By
the same token, the R-R Pegasus engine for the AV-8B
is jointly built by its designer in the UK and P & W
in the USA. Continuing the US-UK co-production for-
mula is the BAe Hawk, due to fulfil the US Navy jet
trainer role from 1987 onwards. Shared in a 55:45

164

Table 6.6 :   US Licence Co-Production Programmes

Project	US Prime Contractor	Other Airframe Contractors
B-57 bomber	Martin (1953)	English Electric
F-104G fighter	Lockheed (1959)	MBB VFW Fokker SABCA Aeritalia
F-16 fighter	GD (1975)	Fokker SABCA/SONACA
AV-8B V/STOL fighter	MD (1981)	BAe

ratio between MD and BAe, the former's Long Beach, California, plant will build the forward and rear fuselage sections and assemble the finished aircraft, leaving the latter's Kingston plant to make the wings, centre fuselage, canopy and empennage.[38]
   Both the F-104G and the F-16 were US designs widely adopted by NATO and built as collaborative efforts on both continents. Designed with West German needs in mind, the F-104G update of the USAF Starfighter was also adopted by Belgium, the Netherlands and Italy. Consequently, four production consortia were established (German, Dutch/German, Belgian, Italian) and produced 947 machines for the four air forces, added to which were a further 290 shipped direct from Lockheed. A vital spin-off of this project was the augmentation of the aerospace manufacturing capabilities of the European participants.[39] In 1975 the F-16 was adopted as a replacement by Belgium, the Netherlands, Denmark and Norway.[40] Regardless of a unit cost penalty ($4.55 million each if built entirely by GD, but $6.091 million each if co-produced), the Europeans opted to establish production facilities for co-producing the F-16.[41] One American engineer surmised that the higher unit costs entailed by such a move would be compensated by technology transfer. He averred that the Europeans "are really interested in procedures, quality control, configuration management – all practical things such as precise machining and close tolerances".[42] In other words, they wanted to gain

access to process innovations as much as the F-16 product innovation. Fokker, for instance, obtained new milling machines, SABCA got new plant for building wings, and Kongsberg Vapenfabrik (of Norway) was able to use F-16 technology in developing new lines of shipboard navigation systems.

Co-production is becoming increasingly popular outside of the NATO context. Both West Germany and Japan have used it to boost their respective aerospace capabilities. This is especially pertinent to helicopter technology, an area in which MBB has been prominent. Its BO105 was the world's first twin-turbine helicopter (flying in 1967) and also it pioneered the use of rigid titanium hubs with feathering blades in the rotor system, not to speak of rotor blades made of composites. Assembly of the BO105 began in the Philippines in 1974 and its manufacture was commenced in Indonesia in 1976. It was with Japan, however, that co-operation was to bear most fruit. In February 1977 MBB and Kawasaki agreed to develop the BK-117, a scaled-up version of the BO105 and having many interchangeable parts with the earlier aircraft. Development costs were to be shared equally between the two partners, with MBB retaining responsibility for the dynamic and hydraulic systems, tail boom and empennage, and power-amplified controls, while Kawasaki dealt with the airframe, landing gear and equipment. The innovating forte of MBB earned it the right to participate with Aérospatiale in the PAH-2 project to develop an Army helicopter for France and West Germany in the late 1980s, and has also given it design leadership in an agreement with India's HAL to develop a twin-turbine helicopter for the Indian military.[43] Before concluding the co-production section, the present trend in aeroengine development deserves mention. Since the agreement between GE and SNECMA leading to the CFM56 turbofan (referred to earlier), all large engines have tended to become collaborative efforts by virtue of their huge development costs.[44] R-R, for instance, engineered the establishment of International Aero Engines in 1983 to develop the V2500 (for the A320 Airbus) along with P & W, MTU, Fiat and a Japanese consortium.[45] P & W, for its part, has allowed MTU, Volvo and MHI a minority stake in its JT8D-200 turbofan which powers the MD-80 series of jetliners.[46]

Licence-Production
Table 6.7 lists the major US warplanes built under licence elsewhere. Notable among the AICs are Canada, Italy and Japan which repeatedly adopt American

designs and therefore circumvent the problems associated with innovating their own aircraft (Britain has followed suit with helicopters). Also present in the table are a scattering of NICs - Taiwan and South Korea in particular - and this pattern of licence-production typifies the classic way in which 'underdeveloped' aircraft industries acquire technological know-how.[47] Historically, the pattern of accumulating expertise progressively through licence-production until indigenous R & D comes of age is best exemplified by the postwar experience of Japan. Abetted by the Japanese Government which was willing to pay uneconomic prices for licence-built aircraft solely to enable the native producers to gain access to American know-how, Japanese companies started building light aircraft in the early 1950s (Fuji's contract for Beech T-34 piston-engined trainers and Kawasaki's for Bell 47 helicopters). However, after a remarkably brief learning period, they were capable of copying relatively advanced designs. From 1956 they built the Lockheed T-33 jet trainer (Kawasaki), North American F-86 jet fighter (MHI) and Lockheed P-2 patrol plane (Kawasaki).[48] By 1962, Japan could face the prospect of building the supersonic F-104 with equanimity. Experience derived from this programme and the replacement F-4, built under licence from MD, gave MHI the technological base to develop its own fighter and jet trainer. By the mid-1970s, Japan was interested less in licence-production than in partial co-production. As recounted elsewhere, it was a partner (albeit junior) in the Boeing 767 and had attained equal status with R-R in the development of the RJ500 engine. Nevertheless, it persisted in licence-building US designs in areas where its technological expertise was lacking. However, the current MD F-15 and Lockheed P-3C programmes are widely distributed among Japanese contractors in order to disseminate technological know-how. With respect to the F-15, the nose, forward and centre fuselages and final assembly are the province of MHI, whereas IHI produces the engine (under P & W licence) and Kawasaki the aft fuselage and wings. The P-3C programme is even wider dispersed: Kawasaki (centre fuselage and final assembly), Fuji (wing), Shin Meiwa (nose and tail), Nihon Hikohki (nacelles) and IHI (Allison T56 turboprops) all having a part to play.[49] The fact that Japan was prepared to find an extra $1.8 billion to domestically-produce the F-15s instead of buying them direct from the USA has caused some unease among American aviation circles which express dismay at the prospect of rising Japanese competition in the aerospace field fuelled, ironically, by the results of US

Table 6.7 :   US Aircraft Subject to Multiple Licensing
              Agreements

Type	US Licensor	Licensee Country (Year of agreement)
F-86 fighter	North American	Canada (1949) Australia (1952) Italy (1954) Japan (1955)
S-55 helicopter	Sikorsky	UK (1950) Japan (1958)
T-33 trainer	Lockheed	Canada (1951) Japan (1954)
47G helicopter	Bell	Italy (1952) Japan (1953) UK (1957)
T-34 trainer	Beech	Canada (1955) Japan (1957) Argentina (1958)
S-58 helicopter	Sikorsky	UK (1956) France (1960)
F-104 fighter	Lockheed	Canada (1959) Japan (1960)
UH-1 helicopter	Bell	Italy (1961) Japan (1964) Taiwan (1969)
S-61B helicopter	Sikorsky	Canada (1962) Japan (1962) Italy (1963) UK (1963)
F-5 fighter	Northrop	Canada (1965) Spain (1965) Taiwan (1973) Switzerland (1976) South Korea (1979)
OH-58 helicopter	Bell	Italy (1967) Japan (1971)
OH-6 helicopter	Hughes	Japan (1968) Italy (1969) Argentina (1973) South Korea (1976)

Source: Derived from M. Rich et al, _Multinational Corporation
        of Military Aerospace Systems_, Appendix A.

R & D.[50]

       Several countries insist on technology-transfer
as a return for ordering foreign aircraft, and this

usually entails a combination of process technology and the licence-production of some or all of the air-craft in question. Such offset agreements are now the order of the day. Thus, Australia was introduced to titanium hot forming and chemical milling and machining in return for its $2.75 billion order to MD for F-18 fighters. The engine manufacturer, GE, also allowed Australia to make 20 per cent of the air-craft's F404 high-performance engine.[51] The sheer extent of such technology-transfer can be gauged from the offsets dangled before Greece in an attempt to get that nation to buy the Panavia Tornado. In its final (unsuccessful) offer, Panavia was prepared to let Greece assemble the aircraft and engine for the Greek order and build components for all future Tornadoes regardless of customer. Additionally, the Greeks were to build the Mauser aircraft cannon under licence and co-produce the aircraft's missiles; they were to build a trainer aircraft selected by Panavia, obtain gas-turbine overhaul capacity, an aircraft tyre retread facility, and an ejection seat overhaul facility, and last but not least, to benefit from the repair and maintenance of Tornadoes sold to other countries.[52] The package of benefits clearly extended from Tier I to Tier III operations, of which airframe assembly was but one constituent.

Subsidiary Operations
Perhaps one of the more historically crucial examples of a subsidiary firm established to funnel the trans-fer of technology was the Junkers venture in the USSR of the 1920s. Founded in the wake of the Soviet-German Trade Agreement of 1921, this German enterprise erected a factory at Fili on the outskirts of Moscow and passed on metal-monoplane technology to the unin-itiated Soviet aircraft industry.[53] Since then, the use of subsidiaries to trigger national aircraft industries has not been uncommon. Canada is an obvi-ous example: its first supplier for a nascent RCAF was a subsidiary of British Vickers. Some contempo-rary NIC aerospace sectors are virtual subsidiary operations in spite of official state guardianship. Spain's CASA for instance, hides a minority foreign shareholding under the dominant 65.62 per cent stake held by the state. Northrop of the USA holds 20.8 per cent of CASA while MBB of West Germany and Das-sault-Breguet of France have nominal shares (2.25 and 1.47 per cent respectively) reflecting their techni-cal assistance.[54] To take another example, Israel's Bet-Shemesh aeroengine maker is also ostensibly a government enterprise, but the state's 49 per cent

holding was overshadowed by the majority stake of
Turboméca of France. In fact, the French company
built the Israeli plant to licence-produce Marboré
turbojets required for the Magister aircraft then
being manufactured under licence by IAI. In view of
Israel's desire to power the indigenously-designed
Lavi fighter with P & W engines, the engine-maker's
parent company, UTC, was intent on buying a 40 per
cent share of Bet-Shemesh in 1984 presumably with the
object of facilitating technology transfer.[55] Even
enterprises in AICs sometimes contain a foreign
shareholding. The generally successful Fokker organisation in the Netherlands is one-fifth owned by
Northrop Corporation.[56] The former holding of UTC in
West German VFW has already been mentioned and much
of the postwar revival of Italian aerospace depended
on American involvement.

    Often, foreign shareholding goes hand-in-hand
with licence-production. The licensor forms a pact
with a national concern - usually the government - in
order to set up from scratch the facilities for aircraft assembly. The peripatetic Northrop Corporation
was involved in the creation of an aircraft industry
in Iran. Under the auspices of Iran Aircraft Industries (IACI), a firm owned 49 per cent each by Northrop and the Iranian Government and two per cent by
the Imbdi Iranian Bank, the US enterprise embarked on
an ambitious plan at Mehrabad. Commencing with airframe and engine overhauls, IACI was to graduate to
aircraft assembly and, in due course, design its own
types.[57] Before disruption as a result of the Iranian
Revolution, IACI had completed two sites totalling
almost 32,000 m² and was underway with a personnel
training programme.

CONCLUSION

Technological change is the quintessence of evolution
for the aircraft industry and at its heart is the
commitment to R & D. Under the rubric of the structural contingency framework, the rationale for view-
ing technological change as the cornerstone of a particular firm soon becomes apparent. Both markets and
relations with the state depend, ultimately, on the
firm's technical initiatives. In turn, the manner in
which those 'environmental' forces respond to the
firm's technical initiatives reverberate to mould its
form of business organisation. Made specific by
Phillips, frameworks of this nature can accommodate
distinctions between exogenous and endogenous R & D
on the one hand, as well as allowing for interfirm

competition (manifest through the entry of new firms) on the other. Throughout, however, the key role of technological change remains sacrosanct.

The chapter summoned evidence to support the basic precepts of such a framework. It established the trend towards market concentration as a result of the inexorable rise in development costs of aircraft. Yet, even firm enlargement was no guarantee either of finding the necessary resources to innovate new aircraft types or innovating a saleable product should the resources be forthcoming. In other words, the risk burden associated with continual product innovation is tending to become untenable. Only massive backing by the state offers inducement to persevere. The Americans accomplish this aim through defence RDT & E and large aircraft contracts. The Europeans, conversely, call upon formal state involvement in the industrial organisations themselves.

Technology-transfer can lighten some of the burden of development costs for firms determined to maintain technical initiatives. Such firms resort to collaborative measures, apportioning the development load among the partners and thus dividing both the costs and risks. Large EEC firms, devoid of the security of the 'follow-on' system enjoyed by US companies, have been especially prominent in this respect. Alternatively, technology transfer can be used in its traditional sense; as a means of acquiring know-how when the donor firm is technologically superior to the receiver. Used by the smaller NATO countries to acquire American process technology, co-production has emerged as a major form of international warplane manufacture. Technology-transfer in the guise of licence-production remains the norm for instituting aircraft manufacture in NICs.

NOTES AND REFERENCES

1. P. McDermott and M. Taylor, Industrial Organisation and Location, (Cambridge University Press, Cambridge, 1982). Note, 'environment' is a deliberately vague concept here which can embrace everything outside the focal organisation.

2. For a review of the salient features of technical change, see: E. Mansfield, The Economics of Technical Change, (Longman, London, 1968); J. Schmookler, Invention and Economic Growth, (Harvard University Press, Cambridge, Mass., 1966).

3. Almarin Phillips, Technology and Market Structure: A Study of the Aircraft Industry (D. C. Heath, Lexington, Mass., 1971).

4. The adoption of passenger-carrying airships in the 1920s can be put forward to illustrate the idea of 'false-start' innovations: the product is either faulted or before its time and therefore is ultimately rejected by the market. The post-1945 attempt to resurrect flying-boat airline services is another case in point.

5. A. Phillips, Technology and Market Structure, p.127.

6. Ibid, p.90.

7. Ibid, pp.115-126.

8. R. Miller and D. Sawers, The Technical Development of Modern Aviation, (Routledge & Kegan Paul, London, 1968), p.246.

9. Ibid, pp.248-9.

10. Ibid, p.263.

11. K. M. Molson and H. A. Taylor, Canadian Aircraft since 1909, (Putnam, London, 1982), p.268.

12. The historical experience of the RAE supports this criticism. See P. Fearon, 'The British Airframe Industry and the State', Economic History Review, vol.27 (1974), pp.236-251, and especially p.247.

13. FI, 29 March 1962, p.489.

14. FI, 23 January 1975, p.83.

15. FI, 30 January 1975, p.122.

16. AW & ST, 1 November 1971, pp.18-19.

17. Air Pictorial, vol.44 (July 1982), pp.266-7.

18. AW & ST, 8 February 1971, p.25.

19. AW & ST, 1 December 1980, p.37.

20. Charles Gardner, British Aircraft Corporation: A History (B. T. Batsford, London, 1981), p.15.

21. Ibid, p.22.

22. The helicopter specialist, Westland, had emerged as an enlarged company in 1960 when the helicopter interests of Bristol, Fairey and Saro were merged into it. Note, the aeroengine companies were collapsed into two companies about this time also (i.e. R-R and Bristol Siddeley Engines Ltd).

23. C. Gardner, British Aircraft Corporation, p.63.

24. G. Williams, F. Gregory and J. Simpson, Crisis in Procurement: A Case Study of the TSR-2, (Royal United Services Institute, London, 1969), p.50.

25. Contemporaneous with the TSR-2 cancellation was the ending of the P.1154 supersonic V/STOL fighter and HS.681 STOL transport projects of HS. HS responded by closing its Whitworth-Gloster division and its accompanying airframe plant at Coventry.

26. More properly, Société Nationale Industrielle Aérospatiale.

27. AW & ST, 26 January 1970, p.21-2.
28. Prior to the merger, state interest in VFW was reflected through Bremen's 38.4 per cent holding, while MBB was owned by Bavaria (22.65 per cent) and Hamburg (20.25 per cent). Currently, MBB is about 50 per cent state owned.
29. The events leading up to the merger of MBB-VFW are dealt with in AW & ST, 18 February 1980, p.24; 6 October 1980, p.28; 20 October 1980, p.115 and 8 June 1981, p.94.
30. AW & ST, 9 March 1970, p.50 and 30 March 1970, p.11.
31. The UK experienced another bout of merger in 1977 leading to the formation of BAe, but that story is bound up with nationalisation and, as such, is reserved for Chapter 7.
32. There is a fourth possibility; namely, that firms purchase the specialised expertise from other organisations. Such technology transfer is akin to tapping specialist sub-contractors for a specific purpose within the overall project development. CASA, for example, invited MBB to produce the rear fuselage section for its prototype C-101 jet trainer in 1974. Similarly, Saab-Scania contracted BAe to design and develop the carbon-fibre composite wings for the JAS 39. See AW & ST, 27 March 1978, p.41 and 29 November 1982, p.28.
33. The programme, renamed 'Atlantique 2' was resuscitated in 1984 to provide for the needs of the French Navy into the 1990s.
34. AW & ST, 10 August 1970, p.51.
35. The combined orders for in excess of 800 aircraft allow for production economies despite the fragmented international input and enable unit costs of Tornado aircraft to match those of comparable US programmes. See Trevor Taylor, Defence, Technology and International Integration, (St Martin's Press, New York, 1982), p.89.
36. AW & ST, 5 January 1970, p.19 and 2 March 1970, p.17.
37. AW & ST, 31 August 1981, p.18.
38. FI, 28 November 1981, p.1604.
39. M. Rich et al, Multinational Coproduction of Military Aerospace Systems, (Rand Corporation, Santa Monica, October 1981), p.3.
40. Denmark and Norway were supplied with F-104s built by Canadair. This Canadian firm built 200 for the RCAF and then a batch of 140, paid for by DoD, to be distributed to NATO countries.
41. The first batch of 650 F-16s for the USAF (as opposed to 348 for the four NATO countries) are expected to be five per cent more expensive as a

result of European participation in the US domestic production system. The programme covers three assembly sites: GD in the USA, SABCA in Belgium, and Fokker in the Netherlands. See Rich et al, <u>Multinational Coproduction</u>, pp.82-104.

42. AW & ST, 2 May 1977, pp.47-9. Quote from p.47.

43. See <u>Air Pictorial</u>, vol.43 (April 1981), pp.128-133; AW & ST, 1 May 1978, p.15 and 20 August 1984, p.21. The BO105 is also to be built under licence in Canada.

44. FI, 17 January 1981, p.142.

45. AW & ST, 21 May 1984, p.33.

46. AW & ST, 18 June 1984, p.43.

47. This is not to say, of course, that advanced aerospace nations are not sometimes prone to undertake licence-production. The USA adopted Euromissile's (i.e. Aérospatiale and MBB) Roland 2 for manufacture under the auspices of Hughes. Fairchild also built a small number of Swiss Pilatus Turbo-Porters for the USAF and Thai air force.

48. AW & ST, 12 January 1970, pp.56-66.

49. AW & ST, 24 April 1978, p.16.

50. AW & ST, 19 April 1982, p.11.

51. AW & ST, 26 October 1981, pp.22-3.

52. AW & ST, 11 October 1982, p.22.

53. A. Boyd, <u>The Soviet Air Force since 1918</u>, (MacDonald and Jane's, London, 1977), p.9.

54. FI, 17 January 1981, p.173.

55. AW & ST, 18 June 1984, p.28.

56. AW & ST, 8 February 1982, p.55.

57. AW & ST, 21 May 1973, pp.60-1. Note, Bell-Helicopter-Textron was to undertake a similar project, this time for helicopter assembly, at Isfahan.

Chapter Seven

THE STATE AND THE AIRCRAFT INDUSTRY

Throughout this book the point has been repeatedly
made that the aircraft industry cannot be considered
independently of the actions of the state. The fact
that the industry relies for the bulk of its market
on military customers was brought out in Chapter 2
where the dependence of aircraft manufacturers on the
whims of government (as manifest through the wave-cycle) was affirmed. By the same token, the reliance
of aircraft firms on government financing schemes in
the civil market became apparent in Chapter 3. The
formal structure enabling state co-operation with
aircraft firms which functioned as defence contractors was evinced in Chapter 4 where the MIC was con-
strued, in the American context, as a government-pri-
vate enterprise partnership. The aircraft industry
was shown to be inordinately dependent on government
even in the selection of its plant locations and was,
indeed, a prime candidate for use in regional policy
(Chapter 5). Finally, Chapter 6 elicited the seeming
truism that innovation cannot be effective in aerospace enterprise unless bolstered by the state. The
object of this chapter is not to reiterate that
material, but instead to focus on the state's
involvement in the industry from its inception, that
is, the nurturing of aerospace as an 'infant' industry; to consider the state's maintenance of aircraft
enterprises on the grounds that they are national
assets; and to examine the attitude of European
states who foster joint aerospace ventures in the
name of enhanced competitiveness of their own
national aircraft industries.
    Before pursuing those themes, it will not go
amiss to remind ourselves of the ubiquitous interfer-
ence of the state in aerospace affairs. At one
extreme is the model of the communist bloc, followed,
wittingly or otherwise, by most NIC aircraft industries; namely, the state asserting the right to own

and operate the industry in its entirety. One need
only point to the Soviet Ministry of Aircraft Production which has under its jurisdiction about 400 Tier
I, II and III plants and which, moreover, designs,
manufactures and markets all the aircraft required by
the USSR.[1] This, the world's largest aerospace enterprise, is a far cry from the state sponsored fledgling aircraft industries of Chile or the Philippines:
but the essential ingredient of state intervention
remains common to all of them, and for the obvious
reason that, without it, the chances of a national
aircraft industry emerging at all are likely to be
very slim indeed. By way of contrast, the US approach
is fundamentally different. The state is, in truth,
the chief market (in the manifestation of the DoD)
and the chief supplier of R & D funds: it is not,
however, officially involved in the organisation of
the aircraft industry. None the less, even the US
Government feels obligated to sponsor the export
efforts of private US aerospace corporations. In 1974
the Department of Commerce singled out the industry
as one of fifteen 'target' industries eligible to
receive government support for staging displays and
trade shows around the world. Furthermore, the US
Government began to stand as official backer of offset warplane deals struck between US corporations and
foreign governments (e.g. the F-16 NATO venture).[2]
When it is recollected that US firms also benefit
from a de facto protected domestic market - the
effect of the 'Buy America Act' - then the ostensible
non-intervention of the US Government is seen to be
largely a chimera.[3]

Adopting a position mid-way between that of the
USSR and the USA is the array of EEC countries and
Japan. In most instances, state involvement in the
aerospace business is officially countenanced through
state-owned enterprises, although this pattern is
eschewed in Japan. That country, in marked contrast,
tolerates only private aircraft firms but it ensures,
for all that, a close regulation on the part of the
state. Notwithstanding the fact that Japan does not
allow export of arms nor officially maintains offen-
sive forces, and despite its firms having the highest
dependence of any upon warplane orders, the Japanese
Government has emphasised the need for its aerospace
sector to hinge on civil aircraft projects. Accordingly, MITI is prepared to advance 50 per cent of new
product development costs, insists that Japanese
firms are accorded full-partner rights in international programmes, and sets up holding companies
whenever appropriate.[4] The first of these - Nihon -
received passing mention in Chapter 1, but the latest

arrangement, the Civil Transport Aircraft Development
Corporation, is subsidised by MITI to fulfil Japan's
input into the Boeing 767 and the next-generation YXX
project.[5] Regardless of ideological outlook, all
states foment the creation of national aircraft
industries and it is to that theme that we now turn.

THE INFANT INDUSTRY CASE

The state's role in nurturing a domestic aircraft
industry is as old as the industry itself. The rudi-
mentary British aircraft designs of World War I were,
for the most part, pioneered by government establishments in Britain and, to a much lesser extent, built
in them too. Formation of the Royal Flying Corps in
1912 meant that along with the military air arm came
a joint R & D and production facility; namely, the
Royal Aircraft Factory at Farnborough. The hiving
off of a naval branch, the Royal Naval Air Service,
was not complete without the foundation of its Experimental Construction Depot at Port Victoria near
Chatham. A combination of ineffectual production
mobilisation, some poor designs, and jealousy from
the newly-ascendant private firms, led to the demise
of aircraft production at those two sites in 1918.
Instead, the pattern was set whereby the UK public
sector was to confine its attention to R & D; to
become the source, in fact, of exogenous R & D for
use by the private aircraft companies. Interestingly,
however, the UK Government had no qualms about establishing 'National Aircraft Factories' (albeit under
private management) at Aintree(Liverpool), Wad-
don(Croydon) and Heaton Chapel(Manchester) in that
same year when the supply of warplanes fell short of
requirements on the Western Front (they were precursors of the 'shadow factories' run by private firms
in World War II).[6] That bastion of private enterprise, the USA, also toyed with state airframe facilities in the formative era. The Naval Aircraft Factory was founded in 1916 at Philadelphia in order to
provide the plant, unavailable in private firms,
required to build large flying boats. It lingered on
through to the end of World War II designing some
aircraft (latterly, target drones), but mainly building standard aeroplanes under licence from Grumman
and other major private contractors. By then it was
an anomaly, as US practice had conformed to the British pattern, which is to say, the state provided the
firms with exogenous R & D through the likes of NASA
and its predecessors.
    Several other AICs emulated the British and

American experience in the years following World War
I. Unlike the precursors, however, they maintained
state enterprises throughout. One of the more constant in this respect is Switzerland. The Federal
Aircraft Factory at Emmen began by building foreign
combat aircraft under licence for the Swiss Flug-
waffe, but in 1934 shifted to indigenous design.
Curiously, an indigenous type, the C-36 dating from
World War II, was rebuilt in 1968-72 with US Lycoming
T53 turboprops rather than the original piston
engines.[7] True to minor aircraft industries, however,
most of Emmen's efforts were directed to building
foreign types (e.g. DH Vampire, Dassault Mirage and
Northrop F-5). Belgium, likewise, relied on the
state for the inception of its aircraft industry.
SABCA was founded in 1920 on the promise of a monopoly supply of all government aircraft. While engaging
in indigenous design from the outset, most of the
enterprise's energies have been expended on licence
production.[8] By the late 1970s its Haren factory was
busy with components manufacture for the F-104G and
Fokker F-27, whereas its airframe plant at Gosselies
was assembling Mirage 5 fighters and Alouette II helicopters for the Belgian forces. To facilitate technology transfer, the Belgian Government had connived
at minority participation by Fokker and Dassault.[9]
The other lodger at Gosselies, SONACA, had been set
up in 1931 as Avions Fairey and was to be integrated
with SABCA in the 1970s on the failure of its foreign
parent company. At government insistence, the UK
Fairey company had established the subsidiary in
order to build the Firefly and Fox aircraft for the
Belgian Air Force, providing, as it were, an alternative means of procuring an aircraft industry to the
state establishment.[10]

Infant Industries in NICs

Development of state aircraft industries in NICs has
had mixed results. While reasonably adept at licence-
production, they have, with few exceptions, been unable to formulate marketable indigenous designs. The
experience of Argentina is typical. Created at Cordoba in 1927, the Military Aircraft Factory (FMA or
Fabrica Militar de Aviones) is a constituent part of
the Argentine Air Force. Employing 8,000 and occupying factory space of 263,000m^2, FMA has built Cessna
light planes under licence and also undertakes 'in-
house' design; the latest product of which is the IA
63 jet trainer.[11] Two designs of merit warrant mention. The IA 50-G II is a twin-turboprop light transport (powered by French Turboméca Bastan engines) and

178

a total of 41 were built for the air force from the late 1960s. The IA 58 Pucara of Falklands War fame, is a twin-turboprop (i.e. Turboméca Astazou) counter-insurgency combat aircraft based on the IA 50. Deliveries began in 1975 for an initial air force requirement of 100 and it has subsequently been exported to other Latin American and African nations in modest numbers. The fact that it can operate from rough air-strips of about 700m in length, plus its turboprop power, makes it a cost-effective machine for cash-starved air forces.

Taiwan is another NIC whose aircraft industry is a branch of the air force. Commencing aircraft construction in 1968, the Taiwan enterprise (which became the AIDC in July 1969) built a slightly modified US Pazmany PL-1 light aeroplane in small numbers. This was followed in short order by licence-production of the Bell UH-1H helicopter and, since 1973, by the much more sophisticated Northrop F-5E. The Taichung airframe plant progressed through five phases in this fighter programme. The first of these merely entailed acceptance of shipments of major airframe structural components built in the USA and then assembled by AIDC. In the second phase, Northrop transferred more of the subassembly finishing work to Taiwan. By the third phase, AIDC was in a position to assume responsibility for manufacturing and assembling the forward fuselage. The fourth phase extended AIDC responsibility to the fabrication of the aircraft's rudder, leading edge extensions and nose landing gear doors. Before the programme culminated in 1980, AIDC fabrication also embraced fuselage dorsal covers, trailing edge flaps and ailerons.[12] The engines were beyond Taiwanese capability and this constraint has hindered development of the AT-3 indigenous jet light-attack aircraft (only the Avco Lycoming T53 turboprops are built under licence in Taiwan).[13] The much desired autonomy of warplane supply (in the manner of Israel) thus continues to elude the Taiwan Government.

As mentioned in Chapter 1, the Egyptian attempt at creating a fully-fledged aircraft industry highlighted the pitfalls associated with forced industrialisation. Dating from 5 July 1950 when the Defence Minister, El Ferik Muhammed Haydar Pasha, announced that an aircraft enterprise would be established at the cost of E£400,000, the General Aero Organisation was formed to make the German Bucker Bestmann trainer under licence. Emanating from 'Factory 72' at Helwan near Cairo, the Bestmann was restyled the Gomhouriya and remained in intermittent production up to the 1980s. Initially powered by Czech-made Walter Minor

engines, later batches of this primary trainer were
equipped with imported US Continental and Lycoming
piston engines. At the forefront during the Nasser
years, the aircraft industry extended its efforts to
the licence-production of jet trainers (the Spanish
Hispano Saeta, retitled the Ha-200 Al Kahiras) after
1960 and also embarked upon an ambitious scheme to
build a lightweight supersonic air-superiority
fighter. Importing a team from Spain led by Willi
Messerschmitt (the designer of the Ha-200), Egypt
built new plant at Helwan for the Ha-300 programme.
Simultaneously, it hired Austrian engineer Ferdinand
Brandner to develop the E-300A turbojet for mating
with the Ha-300 airframe. Difficulties with both the
airframe and engine resulted in the abandonment of
the programme in 1967 but not before 17 engines and
four aircraft had been assembled. At the same time,
development problems with the missiles designed by
'Factory 333' at Helwan meant that the small Kahir,
larger Zafir and two-stage Ared surface-to-air missiles were never put into production.[14] For well over
a decade, Egypt remained disillusioned with indigenous R & D and confined its aircraft enterprise to
overhaul of Soviet-built hardware. Only since the
rapprochement with the West has the industry been
retooled for assembly of French-designed machines
(Alpha Jets and Gazelles along with SNECMA engines)
and latterly, the Embraer Tucano from fellow NIC,
Brazil. Ultimately, the industry wishes to gear up
to co-production of the Mirage 2000 fighter.[15]

The problem of marshalling the correct resources
to produce viable aircraft designs is endemic to
infant aircraft industries notwithstanding the full
backing they receive as state enterprises. India is
salutary in this respect. Upon achieving independence, the Government of India authorised HAL to supply the needs of the air force. Licence-production of
light trainers (the UK Percival Prentice) began in
1948 and was followed in 1950 by assembly of the DH
Vampire light jet fighter, again of UK design. The
first indigenous design, the HT-2, appeared in 1953
and it was a satisfactory, if unsophisticated, primary trainer.[16] More sophisticated work stemmed from
modifications to the licence-built HS Gnat (the
Ajeet) and its various jet trainer derivatives in the
1960s and 1970s. However, Indian attempts to design a
supersonic combat aircraft were doomed to disappoint-
ment. The HF-24 Marut was ready (after a gestation
period of eight years) in its Mark 1 form in 1964,
but was found to be underpowered. The brainchild of
the German engineer Kurt Tank, the HF-24 was tried
with two R-R Orpheus engines (then being made under

licence for the Gnat) and about 100 were built by
1977. Scarcely capable of reaching Mach 1, let alone
the hoped-for Mach 2, the HF-24 was refitted with the
Egyptian E-300A prior to the abandonment of that
engine. A Mark 3 Marut has been projected, equipped
with the same engines as those powering the Panavia
Tornado (RB.199), and this machine should be capable
of realising the original performance requirements
specified thirty years ago. In the meantime, Indian
Air Force needs have been met through licence-production of Soviet and Western supersonic types (e.g.
Mig-21, Mig-27, SEPECAT Jaguar). Clearly, successive
experience of licence-production, no matter how
sophisticated the aircraft, is no guarantee that the
transition to indigenous design of high-performance
aircraft will be plain sailing. India continues to
subscribe to the classic NIC pattern as the Jaguar
programme attests, that is, a progression from the
initial phase where the aircraft are supplied by the
licensor (BAe) in kit form for assembly by the licensee (HAL) to a final (in this case, seventh) phase
when the complete aeroplane is manufactured in the
NIC.[17] Otherwise, production of indigenous designs is
limited to the Kiran 2 jet trainer and the HPT-32
piston-engined trainer: a situation not too far
removed from the 1950s when the Indian aircraft
industry was in its infancy. Nothing daunted, however, India intends to develop a new fighter for the
1990s from its own resources which includes design
and production of an appropriate engine.

Protected Markets
The proclivity of governments to protect their aircraft industries by reserving civil aircraft orders
for state airlines was commented upon in Chapter 3.
Air France and British Airways' predecessors, BEA and
BOAC, were all state owned and compelled, as a
result, to operate domestically-made transports. The
French carrier complied by introducing the Sud Caravelle jetliner, BEA was induced to pioneer the service life of the Vickers Viscount, while BOAC was
primary user of the DH Comet jetliner and Bristol
Britannia turboprop airliner. While providential for
the aircraft manufacturers, this policy had mixed
results for the airlines and, consequently, was abandoned in the 1960s. It has been estimated, for example, that BOAC suffered capital losses of $21 million
on its Comet fleet and $63 million on its Britannia
fleet, whereas the Vickers VC-10 jetliner inflicted
operating costs on BOAC variously estimated at ten to
fifteen per cent higher than the comparable Boeing

707.[18] With respect to military aviation, government
protected markets have become institutionalised
through the 'follow-on' system and, without it, the
US aerospace sector would most likely collapse. The
point to be made, however, is that protected markets
are part-and-parcel of the infant-industry approach
to the aircraft industry: in other words, establishment of a state airframe constructor demands government connivance in the provision of guaranteed markets. Historically, even where the state has eschewed
formal government-owned aircraft enterprises, it has
been obliged to maintain private aircraft firms as
informal national production and design facilities,
and contemporary American practice is not an aberra-
tion in this respect. The British post-World War I
record bears out this assertion as well.

The onset of demobilisational instability cut a
swath through the aircraft firms, so much so, that
the industry was in danger of disappearing. The UK
Government had no choice but to bolster the survivors
- even though it had officially disparaged state
involvement in aircraft manufacture - just to ensure
a reserve capacity in the national interest. In 1920
it decided to designate a number of firms as official
defence contractors, that is to say, they alone would
be allowed to tender for military aircraft contracts.
Furthermore, in order to ensure a degree of competition among suppliers, the state disbursed R & D contracts to the firms so that more than one could
respond to each operational specification issued by
the military. The resultant 'fly-off' of prototypes
would determine the best machine but would also,
incidentally, underwrite the survival of the losers
at least as design bureaux if not as recipients of
major production contracts. Holding to a 'ring' of
sixteen firms, the Air Ministry claimed that any
diminution in the number would reduce the technical
competitiveness among the warplane enterprises. Moreover, winning designs were contracted out to firms
other than the innovating enterprise just to maintain
their manufacturing plant in workable order and hoard
key workers.[19] One firm, Handley Page, was on the
verge of collapse in 1922 when the Air Ministry, in
response to a desperate letter from the firm's
founder, sent some RAF aircraft (DH-9A) to the plant
for reconditioning.[20] Production contracts, such as
they were, just sufficed to keep the 'ring' firms in
existence; but this accomplishment rested on the
willingness of the firms to cater to special RAF
needs. Table 7.1 identifies the firms comprising the
'ring' and notes their warplane specialisation in the
1920s and 1930s. Thus, whenever a fighter

Table 7.1 Protected Firms and their UK Warplane Specialisation

Firm	Location	Aircraft	Example
Armstrong Whitworth	Coventry	Fighter	Siskin IIIA
Boulton Paul	Wolverhampton	Bomber	Sidestrand
Bristol	Bristol	Fighter	Bulldog
Blackburn	Brough (Hull)	Marine aircraft	Perth
DH	Hatfield	Trainer	Gipsy Moth
Fairey	Hayes (London)	Carrier-borne aircraft	Seal
Handley Page	Cricklewood (London)	Transport/Bomber	Hinaidi
Hawker	Kingston (London)	Fighter	Fury
Gloster	Cheltenham	Fighter	Gamecock
A.V. Roe (Avro)	Manchester	Trainer	Tutor
Supermarine	Eastleigh (Southampton)	Marine aircraft	Southampton
Short	Rochester	Flying-boat	Rangoon
Saunders Roe (Saro)	Isle of Wight	Marine aircraft	Singapore
Vickers	Weybridge	Transport/Bomber	Valencia
Westland	Yeovil	Army co-operation aircraft	Wapiti
G. Parnell	Bristol	Carrier-borne aircraft	Plover

specification was formulated, Hawker and Gloster
would invariably tender a design, whereas Handley
Page and Vickers were generally forthcoming with
designs whenever a multi-engined aircraft (bomber or
transport) order was in the offing. Should the design
fail to win the contract, it might be revamped as a
private venture and offered for export.[21]
    Aircraft exports acted as 'bonuses' for the
firms, but they also served as direct competition to
the indigenous aircraft industries of the importing
countries. The extent of the competitive edge enjoyed
by AIC aircraft exports can be gauged from Table 7.2
which lists the additional costs required to build
comparable aircraft in the importing country (in this
case India). With the examples cited, domestic production of aircraft cost from half as much again as
equivalent imports to almost double the AIC amount.
Indeed, India's insistence on licence-production of
Jaguar strike fighters means that the country has to
absorb a cost penalty of 100 per cent over and above
what would have been the price if the machines had
been imported.[22] The cost differential arises out of
inefficiencies in the 'learning curve' experienced by
NIC constructors, but it is equally attributable to
the costs of purchasing engines, avionics and parts
which are generally beyond the manufacturing capabilities of NIC aerospace sectors. Consequently, governments must assimilate excessive costs and attempt to
partially recoup them through extended production
runs for state air arms and airlines. This is the
route adopted by India. Production contracts for the
Mig-21 have run to over 500 while, at 69 aircraft in
the initial batch, HAL's production of the BAe 748
has amounted to about one-third of the effort devoted
to the programme in Britain. As noted elsewhere, such
'protected markets' have enabled NIC enterprises in
Brazil and Indonesia to overcome initial start-up
problems.

PERMANENT RECEIVERSHIP

An integral part of being a defence contractor in the
USA is the guarantee of government support whenever
certain circumstances arise; namely, a financial crisis visited upon the organisation in the first place
and an indispensable position within the DoD procurement system in the second. Known as the 'bail-out
imperative', the government commitment is to ensure
the ongoing viability of the enterprise as a supplier
entity, regardless of whether that entails organisational restructuring or simply the revitalising of

the firm through state subsidies. In fact, this process can be generalised to apply to most non-commu-
nist nations and is best subsumed under the guise of
'permanent receivership'. Coined by Lowi, the term
refers to those organisations, be they officially
private or public enterprises, which are the recipients of state attention in order to guarantee their
continued stability and success.[23] In vouching for
organisational stability through the underwriting and
socialisation of risk, the "government maintains a
steadfast position that any institution large enough
to be a significant factor in the community" shall
not be permitted to founder.[24] As vital elements of
national defence, aircraft firms of any stature are
automatically accorded the status of permanent
receivership.

This condition pertains in the USA as elsewhere,
but the American version of permanent receivership is
stripped of any public enterprise connotations. An
obvious indirect way of underwriting risk for the
companies is to provide them with plant and premises
on 'loan'. While common practice in periods of rearmamental instability and wartime equilibrium, the
phenomenon of government-owned, company-operated
plants is still widespread in the US aerospace sector. Table 7.3 elicits the amount of fixed capital
made available in this way. Evidently, some firms
rely on government premises to a much greater extent
than average (e.g. GD), whereas others (e.g. UTC)
make use of no government plant at all.[25] However,
the US Government has directly intervened to rescue
ailing aircraft companies. The most notable venture
was the 1971 decision of President Nixon to provide
$250 million in loan guarantees to Lockheed Corpora-
tion in a successful attempt to prevent its bankruptcy. Overextended on the L-1011 Tristar airliner,
Lockheed had invested $1.4 billion ($400 million in
bank loans, $240 million in advance payments from
airlines, $350 million from sub-contractors and the
balance from its own resources) and had still been
unable to bring the project to fruition. At the same
time, it was faced with a $200 million loss on the
C-5A cargo transport for the USAF. Collapse of the
company would have meant the loss of 10,000 jobs (not
to speak of 7,000 R-R workers in the UK who were also
adversely affected by the L-1011) and a negative
spill-over cutting another 14,000 employed by sub-
contractors in 25 states. Under pressure from the UK
Government, disturbed at the prospect of the demise
of R-R, the Nixon administration felt obligated to
keep the Tristar programme operational virtually at
any cost - ideological as much as pecuniary.[26]

Table 7.2 Costs of Indigenous Designs versus Imported Aircraft as Exemplified by HAL

HAL Production	Total production cost ($'000)	Cost of importing comparable aircraft ($'000)	Indigenous-Import ratio
Kiran basic trainer	340	200	1.7:1
Mig-21 (Soviet licence) fighter	1,520	830	1.8:1
HF-24 Marut fighter	940	600	1.6:1
Alouette (French licence) helicopter	270	170	1.6:1
BAe.748 (UK licence) transport	1,490	1,000	1.5:1
Gnat (UK licence) fighter	380	200	1.9:1

Source: H. Tuomi and R. Väyrynen, Transnational Corporations, Armaments and Development, (Gower, Aldershot, 1982), p. 204.

The State and the Aircraft Industry

Table 7.3 : Plant Leased by Aircraft Companies from
the US Government

Company/main site	Total Factory Area ('000 m²)	Proportion leased from Government (%)
Boeing/Kent, Wa.	3,404.6	1.1
GD/Fort Worth, Texas	1,199.1	54.9
Grumman/Bethpage, N.Y.	932.2	24.3
Lockheed/Burbank, Calif.	2,278.6	31.8
MD/St. Louis, Mo. and Long Beach, Calif.	2,409.0	13.4
RI/El Segundo, Calif. and Columbus, Ohio	4,509.0	13.0

Source: Derived from G. Adams, The Politics of Defense Contracting:
The Iran Triangle, (Transaction Books, New Brunswick, 1982).

Despite the furore at the time, the Lockheed subsidy was not unprecedented. The company itself pointed out that in the immediate postwar years the Reconstruction Finance Corporation had provided the Glenn L. Martin Company with credits of $26.6 million after that firm had almost gone bankrupt over a disastrous venture into civil aviation (the Martin 2-0-2 airliner, a departure from Martin's previous experience with USAF bombers and US Navy flying-boats). Similarly, Lockheed justified its own federal support on the strength of the $75 million provided by the US Government to Douglas Aircraft in 1967 when that firm was in financial trouble as a result of development problems associated with the DC-8 and DC-9. Last but not least, Lockheed hinted that airliner manufacturers such as Boeing were persistently receiving subsidies by virtue of the $600 million in loan guarantees provided, up to that time, by the government-owned Export-Import Bank which induced foreign airlines to purchase US products.[27] Availability of civil aircraft orders enabled firms such as Boeing to survive regardless of cutbacks in military programmes.

Nationalisation
Unlike the US variant, European approaches to permanent receivership have been characterised by state acquisition of industrial organisations. The French

187

have been particularly prominent in this respect, for, the country's aircraft industry has experienced piecemeal acquisition over more than four decades. The first foray into nationalisation occurred in 1936 and, in the years prior to World War II, about 70 per cent of the industry was acquired by the state. Effected in order to maintain a viable defence industry, this initial nationalisation did not result in a monolithic state enterprise: rather, organisations centred in distinct regions were established. Initially numbering six, the Sociétes Nationales de Constructions Aéronautiques (SNCA) were reduced to four in 1941 when the Vichy regime forced the merger of SNCA de l'Ouest with SNCA de Sud-Ouest (assuming the latter title) and SNCA du Midi with SNCA de Sud-Est (under the mantle of Sud-Est).[28]

A second nationalisation spree came on the heels of Liberation when private firms accused of collaborating with the Germans were summarily taken into public ownership. The better known of those firms were Amiot, Caudron and Farman; the first being retitled Ateliers Aéronautiques de Colombes. State ownership did not prevent liquidation of enterprises, it should be noted, for SNCA du Centre collapsed in 1949. A typical state aircraft manufacturer of the 1950s, SNCA du Nord ('Nord'), was constituted from the original 1936 acquisitions (Potez, CAMS, Les Mureaux, and part of Breguet), a forcible 1945 acquisition (Caudron-Renault), the SNCA du Centre assets transferred in 1949, and the SFECMAS (Arsenal de l'Aéronautique) assimilated in 1954.[29] In 1957 the state decided to 'rationalise' its aircraft enterprises, that is to say, to consolidate them into larger focal organisations. Sud-Ouest (the former Bloch and Bleriot concerns) and Sud-Est (centred on the former Potez firm) were combined into Sud Aviation in that year. Yet it was not until 1970 that rationalisation was taken to its logical conclusion: the formation of Aérospatiale with the merger of Sud and Nord airframe manufacturers and other aerospace elements (recall Figure 6.4). Interestingly, the state had felt obliged to take over Morane-Saulnier when it had failed in 1966: the former Sud subsidiary becoming the SOCATA light aircraft branch of Aérospatiale in the consolidation exercise of 1970. In so doing, the French Government was ensuring a domestically-owned competitor to the country's only other significant light aircraft manufacturer, Reims Aviation, which concentrated on Cessna licence-production and was, to boot, 49 per cent owned by that US firm.

The final phase in the nationalisation of the

aircraft industry in France began in 1978 when the government took 21 per cent of the shares of Dassault-Breguet, the only sizeable private aircraft company remaining in operation. That company is, of course, esteemed for its export success with warplanes (Mirages), and the state's acquisition of part of it was actuated by a desire to be "better able to co-ordinate all French aerospace efforts".[30] Spurred on by ideological commitment, the new Socialist Government effectively nationalised Dassault along with the Matra missile firm in 1981.[31] Officially, the state boosted its holding of Dassault stock to 46 per cent, but by virtue of double-voting rights accorded to some shares, it obtained majority control of the company.[32] The 1981 acquisitions, however, have not been incorporated within the Aérospatiale structure. The distribution of the main aircraft plants in France is shown in Figure 7.1.

The French record of nationalisation renders it possible to discern various catalysts to permanent receivership. The first is associated with the desire to augment national defence capability, the reason why the industry was partly nationalised in 1936 and also, incidentally, the grounds upon which the US Government subsidises 'surge capacity' among its defence contractors. Secondly, the state has intervened as a 'punitive' measure, acquiring those firms that defy the national interest (by analogy, communist states have also commandeered private firms in the name of the public interest) and this rationale accounts for the 1945 acquisitions. The nationalisation of foreign-owned DHC (an HS subsidiary) in 1974 and Canadair (a GD subsidiary) in 1976 by the Canadian Government can perhaps be viewed in the same light, that is, as a sign of the displeasure of the state at the strategies adopted by private industrial organisations. Thirdly, the state intervenes to rationalise capacity under the supposition that the international competitiveness of the industry will not otherwise be forthcoming. It was on this count that Aérospatiale was created in 1970 and the industry 'co-ordinated' in 1981. Finally, firms may be acquired by the state simply to ensure their survival, as the acquisition of SOCATA amply testifies. This last is, of course, a pure expression of the bail-out imperative at work and is resorted to whenever private interests cannot be shored up (à la Lockheed) or have shied away from further investment owing to the excessive risk burden. The Belgian Government, for example, was forced to nationalise the bankrupt UK-owned Fairey SA at Gosselies and reconstitute it as SONACA because insufficient private

Figure 7.1 : French Aircraft Plants

investors were willing to continue the firm's commitment to the F-16 co-production programme.[33]
    The UK nationalisation experience reflects some
of these symptoms. In short, it has been motivated,
by and large, through a desire to combine rationalisation with the bail-out imperative. As a result,
government involvement has proved to be somewhat con-
tradictory. On the one hand, firms have been taken
into public ownership in order to vouchsafe their
survival - and the communities that depend upon them

- most notably the state's take-over of Shorts in
Northern Ireland. But, on the other, the government
has not demurred at the decisions of state enterprises to close aircraft factories which, inevitably,
exacerbate local unemployment (e.g. the decision of
BAe to axe its Bournemouth/Hurn airframe facility in
the early 1980s). Indeed, a lack of clear purpose in
UK nationalisation is all too evident. The intent of
the Labour Government to acquire the bulk of the
industry in the mid-1970s was surrounded by contro-
versy. For one thing, the principal airframe manufacturers were profitable entities: BAC, for instance,
consistently recorded profits throughout the 1970s.[34]
'Inside' opinion was convinced that nationalisation
was the outcome of the ideological bent of the government of the day. In answering its opponents, the
UK Government claimed that the industry must be taken
into public ownership bacause of its overwhelming
reliance on the public purse. State control would
provide greater public accountability and, by dint of
fresh management, lead to a restructuring of the
industry along more effective lines, and incidentally, centralise the firms' chaotic missiles divisions. More specifically, the aims of the new state
enterprise were: (1) the securing of long-term
viability, (2) the 'unification' of production units,
(3) integration of the industry's interests with
those of the country, (4) the furthering of flexible
operations, (5) the development of worker participation and (6) the pushing ahead with diversification.[35] All companies with turnover in excess of £20
million were to be incorporated in British Aerospace.
Curiously, the helicopter sub-sector was excluded
(i.e. the Westland firm) and the existing state firm
in Northern Ireland (Shorts) remained outside the
mainland conglomerate. Consequently, when it finally
appeared in 1977, BAe was the product of merging BAC,
HS Aviation, HS Dynamics (the missiles branch of HS)
and Scottish Aviation. At that juncture, therefore,
the UK Government controlled most of the airframe
industry and, through its Rolls-Royce interests, the
aeroengine industry as well.
    The argument that state ownership would facili-
tate 'viability', 'unification', 'flexibility' and
'diversification' as variously proffered, was seen as
promoting rationalisation in all but name. It will
be recollected that it was under this banner that the
UK Government had urged the private-enterprise mergers of 1960. Yet, the merits of rationalisation
seemed inconclusive in theory and turned out to be
somewhat elusive in practice. Some doubted the argument that increasing size of enterprise was conducive

to economies of scale. Referring to the earlier
merger episode, one commentator stated that the case
for rationalisation was not proven despite the size
advantages enjoyed by competing US enterprises.

> On the assumption that size was, in fact, synon-
> ymous with efficiency and (the second basic fal-
> lacy of rationalisation) that size in itself
> would be sufficient to attract new orders to the
> industry from overseas, which meant, of course,
> that Government expenditure need not be
> increased, the reshaping of the industry was
> enforced by the stick-and-carrot process of mak-
> ing contracts conditional upon amalgamation.[36]

In other words, the state had realised a degree of
success (as manifest through profitable merged private firms) in forcing rationalisation on the aircraft industry of 1960, but had also imposed costs on
those firms which flowed directly from unwieldy organisational units; to be blunt, organisations too
large to be efficient. The prospect of further economies of scale from an even larger organisation was,
therefore, very questionable. Besides, US firms were
large owing to their organisation around large DoD
contracts, something which could not be replicated in
Britain which had a defence effort amounting to only
a fraction of the US effort.

American critics were even more scathing of the
move to acquire profitable HS and BAC, claiming that
"the Labour Government's chief motive in grabbing
control of a thriving and prosperous industry is to
solidify its role as a job source for the government's union supporters".[37] This view must be tempered, however, by the thought that rationalisation
also carries with it the prospect of plant closure; a
condition scarcely compatible with the maintenance of
jobs (sinecures or otherwise). In any event, BAe
became a modestly profitable enterprise which, with a
change in government and ideological complexion, was
partially denationalised in 1980 (the state retaining
a 49 per cent holding) and offered for almost complete 'privatisation' in 1985. It made pretax profits
of £52.8 million in the year prior to this volte-
face, and £70.6 million in the year immediately following it (its main plants are distributed as in Figure 7.2). Regardless of formal ownership, BAe is
still heavily incumbent on the state for development
monies, as indeed is Westland which had never been
taken into state ownership during the rationalisation
mania (in 1984, for example, this latter was promised
£60 million in state aid to develop the EH-101

Figure 7.2 : Distribution of UK Aircraft Plants

anti-submarine helicopter with Agusta of Italy).
    Contrasting with the ambiguity surrounding the
rationale for nationalising the UK airframe industry,
the reasons for taking R-R into public ownership owed
much more to the bail-out imperative. Reconstituted
out of the gas-turbine interests of the old private
company which had gone bankrupt with the Lockheed
Tristar venture, Rolls-Royce (1971) Ltd had the UK
Government as its sole shareholder. At its inception,
it employed 62,000 at factories located, in the main,

at Derby, Glasgow, Bristol, Coventry and Leaves-
den(Watford).[38] In addition to the large RB.211
engine designed for the Tristar, R-R had major programmes for powering the Concorde (based on the Olym-
pus two-shaft turbojet jointly developed with
SNECMA), the Tornado (using the RB.199 under the
aegis of Turbo-Union), the Vought A-7 for the USAF
and Navy (in co-operation with the Allison Division
of General Motors on the TF41 version of the Spey
engine) and the Jaguar (for which it produces the
Adour in collaboration with Turboméca). Table 7.4
lists the engine programmes underway at R-R in the
1970s. To them must be added the collaborative ventures initiated with the Japanese to develop the
experimental RJ500 in 1979 and the 1983-formed International Aero Engines, set up to offer an alternative
powerplant for the A320 Airbus.[39] Such a diverse
effort was monumentally expensive and R-R was repeatedly turning to its government paymaster for extra
funds, for example, the £364 million for the ongoing
development of the RB.211 between 1979 and 1984, and
£60 million for the V2500 that R-R is designing in
co-operation with International Aero Engines.[40] Notwithstanding subsidies of this magnitude, the enterprise continued to make losses: £134 million in 1982
and £193 million in 1983.[41] The state persisted, however, in wholeheartedly backing R-R on the score that
it was a national asset. By the same token, it had
stepped in to inject £15 million into the Ferranti
avionics firm in 1974 (in return for 62.5 per cent of
the equity) using a similar rationale; namely, that
the firm possessed invaluable technical capabilities
and, besides, was an important source of employment
in job-scarce Scotland.[42] State commitment of this
kind is instrumental in fomenting the multinational
'mega-projects' which characterise much of European
aerospace initiative in the 1980s. Those ventures
are, in effect, the culmination of permanent receivership as conceived by national governments.

GOVERNMENT-INDUCED INTERNATIONAL CO-OPERATION

The inspiration for state-sponsored European-wide
aircraft projects came out of the crisis facing individual European industries in the early 1960s. On the
one hand, they were effectively denied access to the
crucial US civil aviation market as a result of the
protection afforded US manufacturers by the 'Buy
America Act'. On the other hand, they were having
difficulties competing with large, efficient US aircraft enterprises cushioned by lucrative defence R &

Table 7.4 :   R-R Engine Programmes

Engine	Type	Representative User Aircraft	Production/Development Centre
TF41	turbofan	A-7	Indianapolis (Allison), Derby (R-R)
M45	turbofan	VFW-614	Bristol (R-R), Paris (SNECMA)
Olympus	turbojet	Concorde	Bristol (R-R), Paris (SNECMA)
Adour	turbofan	Jaguar	Derby (R-R), Tarnus (Turboméca)
RB.199	turbofan	Tornado	Bristol (R-R), Munich (MTU), Turin (Fiat)
RB.162	turbojet	Trident 3B	Derby
RB.211	turbofan	L-1011	Derby
Spey	turbofan	BAe.111	Derby
Dart	turboprop	Fokker F-27	Derby
Tyne	turboprop	Atlantic	Derby
Viper	turbojet	Soko Jastreb	Bristol
Pegasus	turbofan	Harrier	Bristol
BS.360	turboshaft	Lynx	Leavesden

Source: Jane's All the World's Aircraft, various editions.

D and production contracts. Even with state-induced mergers creating larger organisations, the average European firm was not comparable in size to the giant US aerospace companies (Table 7.5). Furthermore, structural problems unique to Europe exacerbated matters. In the first place, Britain and France were curtailing their military commitments as a consequence of reduced imperial responsibilities: the resultant "cancellation of major defence projects; the increase in project cost to the point where the relative smallness of the home market became a limiting factor" compelled some form of drastic state action to save industries inordinately dependent upon defence contracts of which aerospace was the prime example.[43] Secondly, employment policies, in insisting on retaining underemployed labour, made European plants less productive than their US competitors who showed much less reluctance in dismissing unwanted labour (witness the violent fluctuations in Boeing's workforce).[44] Thirdly, European civil aircraft were accused of being tailor-made for national airlines which were, in any event, obliged to buy them; but

Table 7.5 :   Contrasts in Enterprise Sizes,
              Europe and America

Europe: Company	Employment[1]	Turnover[2]	USA: Company	Employment	Turnover
BAe	75,000	2,260	Boeing	98,300	8,130
R-R	56,600	1,680	MD	82,700	5,280
Aérospatiale	37,200	2,710	GD	81,600	4,060
Dassault-Breguet	15,600	1,700	Lockheed	66,500	4,060
SNECMA	10,700[3]	540[3]			
Turboméca	4,500	220			
MBB	26,500[4]	1,450			
VFW	12,000[4]	560			
Dornier	8,000	480			
MTU	6,200	280			

Notes: a. 1979 figures
        b. Millions of 1979 dollars
        c. 1978 figures
        d. 1980 figures

Source: M. Rich, et al, Multinational Co-production of Military Aerospace
         Systems, (Rand, Santa Monica, 1981), p. 19.

the machines were, in consequence, ill-fitted to compete in international markets.[45]
     To directly confront these problems, European
Governments attacked on two fronts: inducing merger
of their domestic firms often under the rubric of
state acquisition (as recounted above), and forcing
the restructured enterprises to co-operate with each
other across international lines. The latter strategy
was adopted largely to prevent American dominance of
European civil and military aviation markets. It
would, moreover, have specific political and technical advantages; not least of which were a reduction
in national contributions to joint R & D projects as
the share of the overall cost (admittedly, boosted as
a result of the duplication inherent in collaboration) would be spread among several partners, and a
larger guaranteed market - the outcome of several
states committing themselves to buying the product -
enabling economies of scale in production costs
(which, in turn, would lower the unit cost of aircraft and enhance their marketability elsewhere).[46]

The State and the Aircraft Industry

As the worst affected by the structural problems coming to a head, the British were the first to formally embrace international collaboration as an escape route for a purely national aircraft industry. According to the Plowden Report of 1965, salvation was to be sought in collaborating with other European aircraft industries because the UK Government was simply in too straitened circumstances to continue the level of support which it had hitherto provided the industry. It foresaw, in addition, a direct government stake in the recently-merged BAC and HS undertakings.[47] In certain respects, the official report – accepted without demur by the Government – was merely endorsing existing trends as manifest through the Concorde programme.

Concorde

The Anglo-French SST was the progenitor of a string of collaborative aircraft programmes that dominate European aerospace today. In the 1960s, it led to a series of European airliner projects (Table 7.6), some successful and others less so. Without doubt, however, Concorde was the most momentous of them all, not only for the technical innovation entailed in developing a supersonic airliner, but also in terms of the sheer size of the capitalisation involved. At £2.2 billion, the level of public funding was not matched in a civil aviation project until the A320 Airbus of the mid-1980s. Agreement on Concorde was reached in 1962 on two levels: between the manufacturers, BAC (inherited by BAe) and Sud Aviation (as it then was), and between their respective governments. In detail, the agreements called for an equal division of work between the airframe companies and an even split in development costs between the two countries. Six RDT & E aircraft were covered under the agreement: two prototypes, two pre-production models, and two complete airframes for static and fatigue testing. Co-production guaranteed the absence of any duplication in production jigs, but two assembly lines were set up: Toulouse and Bristol(Filton). Similarly, the aeroengines were to be the outcome of joint enterprise, R-R and SNECMA, and production was to be, once again, equally divided between the partners.[48]

Flight testing of Concorde was begun in 1969 and the first production machine was ready at the end of 1971. BAC's Weybridge plant was responsible for manufacturing the nose and forward fuselage of the production aircraft which were then sent to Toulouse or Filton for final assembly. Other BAC works undertook

Table 7.6 :   State-Backing of International Programmes

Aircraft	Development Cost (millions of pounds)	Participating Countries (State enterprise in parentheses)	Government support (%)
Concorde	2,200	France (Aérospatiale)	100
		UK (ultimately BAe)	100
A300	595	France (Aérospatiale)	100
		West Germany	90
		UK (ultimately BAe)	100
		Spain (CASA)	-
		Netherlands	90
Mercure	171	France	80
		Italy, Spain, Belgium, Switzerland	-
VFW-614	69	West Germany	80
		Netherlands	100
		Belgium, UK	-
F-28	50	Netherlands	100
		West Germany	40
		UK	-

Source: Derived from Flight International, 20 November 1982, p. 1522.

to build the rear fuselage, vertical tail surfaces, engine nacelles, electrical system, fuel system and engine installation. Aérospatiale (the erstwhile Sud) was responsible for the rear cabin section, wings and wing control surfaces, hydraulic system, flying controls, navigation system, radio and air conditioning systems. The finished product was capable of 2,300 km/h, had a passenger capacity of 100 over a range of 4,900 km, and cruised at a service ceiling of 18,200 m. The aircraft entered service with Air France and British Airways in 1976 but only 16 production models were built: all the provisional orders (originally 74) evaporating when escalating fuel costs made the aeroplane an uneconomic proposition.

Airbus
It was in the spirit of the Plowden Report that Britain and France entered negotiations in 1965 into the desirability of producing a 250-300 seat jetliner as a collaborative effort. Conceived as a European answer to the American DC-10 and L-1011 'wide-bodies',the 'Airbus' was intended to be a major innovation in the Concorde tradition. From the outset, however, British attitudes were clouded by the priority accorded to Rolls-Royce as the prime medium for

advancing aeroengine technology. The company's new, heavy turbofan had been thwarted in the bid to have it accepted as the engine for Boeing's 747 and, accordingly, pressure was placed on the UK Government to have it diverted to the Airbus.[49] Under a Memorandum of Understanding of September 1967, aeroengine leadership for the Airbus would be assigned to R-R while airframe leadership would be the province of Aérospatiale, and the Germans would contribute a secondary input. Airframe costs would be shared equally by the UK and France, but the former would assume responsibility for the lion's share (75 per cent) of aeroengine costs. However, in May 1968 R-R scored a triumph in winning the contract to supply the engines for Lockheed's L-1011 and soon ran into capacity constraints. As the 1971 collapse was to illustrate so graphically, R-R was in no position to simultaneously develop two advanced-technology engines. At UK Government connivance, it opted to develop the RB.211 for the L-1011, and the RB.207 for the Airbus was allowed to wither. Official UK Government involvement in the first-phase of Airbus was thereby curtailed.

Rebounding, the European partners in Airbus Industrie redesigned the A300 jetliner round the CF6-50 engine, a product of GE which was manufactured under licence by SNECMA and MTU. Construction of the first aircraft began in 1969 by a consortium of aircraft constructors. The main contributor was Aérospatiale, which apart from design leadership, manufactured the nose, lower centre fuselage and engine pylons, and undertook final assembly at Toulouse. Deutsche Airbus (centred on MBB) built the forward and rear fuselage as well as the vertical tail surfaces, CASA manufactured the horizontal tail surfaces, fuselage main doors and landing gear doors; while HS Aviation was entrusted with the wing. After a series of delays (the aircraft did not enter service until 1975), the success of the project was assured and no fewer than 246 A300s were on order or had been delivered by mid-1984. Market breakthrough (notably by US major airline, Eastern) encouraged the French Government to redirect resources into the programme in 1978, "including an immediate order from Air France for 24 A300s".[50] Moreover, the UK Government had second thoughts and, at the cost of some $600 million, bought itself a 20 per cent share of the A300 programme.

From this point onwards, Airbus Industrie committed itself to producing a family of jetliners, of which the A310 and A320 have so far materialised from the A300 stable (Table 7.7). The A310 is a smaller version of the A300 (with 210 to 234 passengers rather than the 300 or so of the earlier machine) which made its first flight in 1982. At its roll-out, it had already accumulated 90 orders and 90 options: a better record than the A300 when at a comparable stage of development (on the eve of the A300's first flight it had only achieved 14 sales). In view of formal British participation, the A310 workload was apportioned as follows: Aérospatiale and Deutsche Airbus (37.9 per cent each), BAe (20 per cent), CASA (4.2 per cent); while Fokker, along with Belairbus, enjoyed subcontractor status as 'associate' members of Airbus Industrie. As before, final assembly takes place at Toulouse but minor changes have been made to the A300 consortium arrangements with, for example, the Aérospatiale plant at Les Mureaux being called in to produce the A310's flight deck, and more fitting-out work being undertaken at MBB's Bremen facility.[51] A major order from Pan American World Airways in 1984 confirmed the viability of the type in global markets.

The A320, meanwhile, is a 150-180 passenger airliner, launched with much fanfare in 1984. Intended to fly in 1988, a production rate of 60 aircraft per year is planned. Costing in excess of £2 billion for development, BAe's contribution is put at £637 million.[52] In many respects an innovative machine, the A320 will, for example, be the first airliner with fly-by-wire primary flying controls (i.e. the ailerons and elevators respond to electrical signals rather than being activated by mechanical cables and pulleys). What is more, extensive use will be made of CFRP and aluminium-lithium in its construction: the latter is not only lighter, stronger and stiffer than conventional aluminium but is far less corrosive. Initial aircraft will be powered by the CFM 56-5, jointly developed by GE and SNECMA, and later aircraft may be fitted with the V2500 of International Aero Engines (e.g. those on order for Pan Am). At launch date, 51 A320s had been ordered with another 45 held on option.[53] Table 7.8 lists the financial and production responsibilities of each of the participating enterprises.

As Table 7.7 evinces, there is no shortage of planned successors to the A300, 310 and 320. The first of these, envisaged to enter service in 1992, is the four-engined 230 seat TA-11. It will occupy the long-range slot omitted from the present Airbus offerings. Replacement for the A300 will take two forms: the TA-9 which is a stretched, rewinged variant of the A300 for the short-range high-density (up to 400 passenger) market, and the TA-12 which will be a hybrid aircraft combining the A310/TA-11 fuselage

Table 7.7 : Family of Airbus Industrie Jetliners

Aircraft Size	Aircraft Range:	Short	Type Designator Medium	Long
Small		A320	A310	TA-11
Medium		A310	A300	modified TA-11
Long		TA-9	enlarged TA-9	-

Source: Derived from Flight International, 1 September 1984, p. 391.

Table 7.8 : A320 Programme Breakdown

Enterprise	Share (%)	Responsibility
(Production)		
Aérospatiale	36.0	front fuselage, lower centre fuselage, pylons, nacelles, power plant integration, final assembly (at Toulouse)
Deutsche Airbus	31.0	upper centre fuselage, rear fuselage, fin and flaps
BAe	27.0	wing (at Chester), slats, flaps, ailerons, spoilers (at Hatfield)
CASA	6.0	CFRP tailplane
Belairbus	associate	slats
(Financial)		
Aérospatiale	37.6	
Deutsche Airbus	37.6	
BAe	20.0	
CASA	4.8	

Source: Flight International, 24 March 1984, p. 738.

with the wing and engine of the TA-9 and be optimised for routes of up to 4,500 nautical miles. These projects are being designed around fuel consumption targets one-quarter less than is the case with the

A300.[54] Eventually, modified versions of the new designs will cater for all size/range categories with the single exception of the large, long-haul class.

Tornado

The two aforementioned programmes are civil aviation initiatives, but the monumental Tornado tri-national programme is military inspired. Born out of the disarray created in the UK aircraft industry with the cancellation of the TSR-2 strike aircraft in 1965, the MRCA project was finalised as a collaborative effort between Britain, West Germany and Italy. Panavia Aircraft GmbH formulated a design which received government approval in 1970 and production authorisation in 1974. The MRCA (i.e. Tornado) was conceived as a twin-engined, two-seat supersonic strike fighter equipped with a variable-geometry wing having a sweep of 25° in the fully forward position and 66° when swept fully backward. It is powered by the RB.199 turbofan made by Turbo-Union, a consortium of R-R, MTU and Fiat formed in 1969. Panavia itself uses facilities provided by BAe, MBB and Aeritalia, with work-sharing apportioned according to the size of order from each government. Planned procurement called for nine prototypes, four from the UK (Preston/Warton), three from Germany (Manching) and two from Italy (Caselle). They would be followed by 809 production machines - 385 for Britain, 324 for West Germany and 100 for Italy - with final assembly of each nation's consignment at the appropriate one of the three international Panavia sites.[55] At £11.25 million a copy (1981 prices), the scale of the programme is truly staggering and has been frequently slowed to prevent the over-taxing of national defence budgets. By August 1984, the programme was less than half complete with 349 Tornadoes issued.[56] The sheer expense of such a complex aircraft has deterred export orders.

CONCLUSION

This chapter has stressed the pervasive nature of state involvement in the aircraft industry, not merely as an interested on-looker, but as an active ingredient in the formation of many aircraft enterprises and a guarantor of their continuance. Political ideologies are obviously of crucial import in determining the form of direct government involvement. Nationalisation has been a gambit of both capitalist and communist states, but its record of

continuity has been much more discordant in the liberal democracies. Britain and France, for example,
have tolerated at various times mixed public and private sector influence in the aircraft business, state
monopoly control, and (in the British case) retrench-
ment of direct state involvement. The USA, for its
part, is consistent in rejecting a direct role for
the state in aircraft manufacture (apart from the
'infant' industry phase). The American alternative
is, of course, the 'Iron Triangle', an indirect
approach to government supervision of the aircraft
industry.

   All governments lay great store on the inception
of domestic aircraft manufacture and the nurturing of
aerospace as a classic infant industry goes on apace.
To give but one example, the Philippines established
the National Aero Manufacturing Corporation at Manila
in 1973. On the strength of orders from the military,
this enterprise is engaged in assembling MBB BO105
helicopters (44 by 1983) and PBN Islander light
transports (57 by 1983) under licence from West Germany and the UK respectively. In accordance with the
usual route to indigenous design, it is building a
prototype light piston-engined trainer; in this
instance strongly influenced by the Italian SIAI-Marchetti SF-260 aircraft.[57] Continuance of the trainer
programme depends upon state generosity both in subsidising its development and in creating a protected
market through military orders. The process whereby
states furnish the means for aircraft industry expansion within the greater context of national industrial development is the subject of the next chapter.

NOTES AND REFERENCES

   1. A. Boyd, The Soviet Air Force since 1918,
(MacDonald and Jane's, London, 1977), p.227.
   2. AW & ST, 2 September 1974, p.19 and 14 October 1974, p.7.
   3. Two instances bear out the basic protectionist mentality prevailing in the USA. The first concerns the protest of New York Senator Alfonso D'Amato
who felt aggrieved at the loss by Grumman (of Bethpage, New York) of a US Navy trainer contract to BAe.
On the evocative cry that 43 per cent of the work on
the T-45 Hawk would go to the UK and thus deny 16,000
jobs to Americans, D'Amato almost succeeded in block-
ing the MD/BAe contract (see FI, 26 December 1981,
p.1880). The second, mentioned in Chapter 4, revolves
around British protests at American bad faith when
their Martin-Baker ejection seat was rejected by

Congress after winning the competition to fulfil the requirements of the F/A-18.

4. FI, 10 October 1981, p.1065.
5. AW & ST, 9 November 1981, p.164.
6. Peter Fearon, 'The Formative Years of the British Aircraft Industry, 1913-1924', Business History Review, vol. 43 (1969), pp.476-495.
7. Jane's All The World's Aircraft 1972-73, (Jane's Yearbooks, London, 1972), p.181.
8. Air-Britain Digest, vol. 32 (November-December 1980), pp.127-131.
9. FI, 10 April 1969, p.603.
10. Air-Britain Digest, vol. 33 (May-June 1981), pp.63-7.
11. Jane's, pp.3-4.
12. AW & ST, 5 June 1978, pp,14-16.
13. AW & ST, 21 May 1984, p.24.
14. Air Pictorial, vol. 38 (January 1976), pp.26-9.
15. FI, 9 January 1982, p.46.
16. Pushpindar Singh, Aircraft of the Indian Air Force, 1933-73, (The English Book Store, New Delhi, 1974).
17. FI, 18 December 1982, pp.1771-4.
18. Mahlon R. Straszheim, The International Airline Industry, (The Brookings Institution, Washington, D.C., 1969), pp.22-3.
19. Peter Fearon, 'The Vicissitudes of a British Aircraft Company: Handley Page Ltd Between the Wars', Business History, vol. 20 (1978), pp.63-86.
20. Ibid, p.71.
21. Peter Lewis, The British Fighter since 1912, (Putnam, London, 1979), p.165.
22. H. Tuomi and R. Vayrynen, Transnational Corporations, Armaments and Development, (Gower, Aldershot, 1982), p.205.
23. T. J. Lowi, 'Towards a Politics of Economics: The State of Permanent Receivership', in L. N. Lindberg et al (eds.), Stress and Contradiction in Modern Capitalism: Public Policy and the Theory of the State, (Lexington Books, Toronto, 1975), pp.115-24.
24. Ibid, p.117.
25. Some California aircraft firms realised 'windfall' subsidies as an outcome of the Watts race riots in 1965 and 1967. The Economic Resources Corporation used US Department of Commerce funds to set up factories in Los Angeles for employing unskilled, 'minority' labour. Lockheed made use of a $2.5 million factory to produce L-1011 parts while MD had one for making wire harnesses, bulkheads, floor beams, ash trays and pulley brackets for installation in its

airliners. See AW & ST, 18 May 1970, p.65 and 9 November 1970, p.61.
26. AW & ST, 10 May 1971, p.26.
27. AW & ST, 24 May 1971, pp.15-16.
28. Air Pictorial, vol. 39 (June 1977), pp.212-13.
29. Air-Britain Digest, vol. 36 (May-June 1984), p.59.
30. H. Tuomi and R. Vayrynen, Transnational Corporations, p.36.
31. E. A. Kolodziej, 'France', in N. Ball and M. Leitenberg (eds.), The Structure of the Defense Industry, (St. Martin's Press, New York, 1983), pp.81-110.
32. Jane's All The World's Aircraft 1983-84, (Jane's Publishing Company, London, 1983), p.59.
33. AW & ST, 1 September 1980, p.99.
34. In detail, the profits were (in millions of pounds): 4.1, 6.5, 13.7, 24.2, 30.0 and 40.0 for 1971-6. See H. Evans, Vickers: Against the Odds 1956-1977, (Hodder and Stoughton, London, 1978), p.185.
35. Air Pictorial, vol. 37 (March 1975), pp.92-3.
36. M. Hardy, 'Rationalise and Forget?', FI, 11 January 1962, pp.48-50.
37. AW & ST, 6 September 1976, p.23.
38. Jane's 1972-73, p.684.
39. AW & ST, 21 May 1984, p.33.
40. FI, 25 August 1984, p.178.
41. FI, 5 May 1984, p.1223.
42. FI, 22 May 1975, p.812.
43. R. L. Nobbs, 'A Note on Aerospace Collaboration', Journal of Common Market Studies, vol. 14 (1976), pp.368-71. Quote from p.368.
44. The stark contrast between Dassault which kept its workforce between 14,693 and 15,161 throughout most of the 1970s and Boeing which cut its payroll by about 60 per cent from 1968 to 1971 is indicative of transatlantic differences. See M. Rich et al, Multinational Coproduction of Military Aerospace Systems, (Rand, Santa Monica, California, 1981), p.15.
45. Joseph Rallo, 'The European Community's Industrial Policy Revisited: The Case of Aerospace', Journal of Common Market Studies, vol. 22 (1984), pp.245-67.
46. Keith Hayward, 'Politics and European Aerospace Collaboration: The A300 Airbus', Journal of Common Market Studies, vol. 14 (1976), pp.354-67.
47. Plowden Report, 'Report of the Committee of Inquiry into the Aircraft Industry', (HMSO, London,

Cmnd. 2853, 1965).
    48. Jane's 1972-73, pp.104-106.
    49. K. Hayward, 'Politics and European Aerospace Collaboration', p.359.
    50. J. Rallo, 'The European Community's Industrial Policy Revisited', p.254.
    51. Air Pictorial, vol. 44 (May 1982), pp.172-8.
    52. FI, 10 March 1984, p.615.
    53. Air Pictorial, vol. 46 (September 1984), pp.332-3.
    54. FI, 1 September 1984, pp.391-3 and 8 September 1984, p.520.
    55. Air Pictorial, vol. 38 (January 1976), pp.11-16.
    56. Air Pictorial, vol. 46 (October 1984), pp.364-5.
    57. Ibid, p.385. See also Jane's 1983-84, p.168. Note, the Philippines Aerospace Development Corporation - the holding company into which NAM was merged - manufactures the glass reinforced plastic parts for both types.

Chapter Eight

AEROSPACE AND DEVELOPMENT

The purpose of this chapter is simply to provide a
broad overview of the general relationship between
the aircraft industry and national economic development. The preceding chapter has loosely categorised
the variety of relationships extant between the state
and the major airframe manufacturers. These relationships, ranging from the classic infant industry
case to the permanent receivership case and incorpo-
rating a number of institutional forms, must be set
within the broader political-economic context of
their emergence. In other words, the policy instruments utilised to cultivate the variety of state-industry links and the relationship of these to
national development strategies warrant special
attention. This chapter, then, will briefly highlight the general theoretical setting in which
national aircraft industries are nurtured, and secondly, will examine a number of national examples
deemed representative of the forms in which the
industry may occur. Since much of the discussion
hitherto has focused on the already established aircraft industries of the world, especially those of
the USA and EEC; by way of contrast, the following
examples will be drawn from those countries attempting to initiate aircraft industries.

THE THEORETICAL SETTING

The international economic system may be conceptualised as a hierarchical structure based on the division of labour, and is made manifest in the form of
uneven accumulation among nation-states (ranging from
the advanced industrial economies through to the low-
income countries). The structure is not static, but
rather is characterised by at least three important
tendencies: concentration of political and economic

power; 'transnationalisation' of markets, production
and finance; and the importance of control over technology since, "Control over technology is an instrument to accumulate economic and political power and
to steer transnational relations. Technological
power is an important factor in determining the
nature of the international hierarchy".[1] The unfold-
ing of these general tendencies is plagued with
crises, which frequently results in structural
change, and necessitates an expanding state role (in
capitalist economies). In the wake of poor economic
performance during much of the 1970s coupled with
changing international economic relationships centr-
ing on the concerns of technological change and the
labour process, virtually all governments have turned
towards industrial policies and strategies as means
to foster industrial expansion and international competitiveness.[2]

In general, and along with fiscal and monetary
policies, industrial policies constitute one element
of a nation's basic economic policy framework. Simply, "industrial policy may be generally defined as
any government measure or set of measures, to promote
or prevent structural change" and in contrast to earlier experiences, "modern industrial policy aims at
more than merely setting a general framework";
rather, "it descends increasingly into the microeco-
nomic sphere of economic decision-taking that was
formerly left to the price mechanism".[3] Two broad
types of industrial policy may be discerned; namely,
negative policies which are designed to slow down
structural change and positive policies which are
designed to facilitate the expansion of industries
and firms at the forefront of technological development and/on experiencing rapid growth.[4] A number of
types of industrial policy may be identified depending on their scope, time and intensity dimensions.[5]
For example, policies may be broad based and apply
across-the-board to all industries, albeit with differential impacts. The objective of this type of
general industrial policy is to enhance the aggregate
resource allocation of the economy. Frequently in
conjunction with these broad based policies are a
variety of selective policies aimed at realising specific objectives, as is the case with R & D policies.
Similarly, sector-, industry-, and firm-specific policies may be formulated to achieve industrial development objectives. In practice, a number of industrial policy types are usually enacted at any given
moment.

A prominent industrial strategy adopted by many
developing and developed nations is import

substitution.[6] Basically, this strategy calls for the
domestic production of goods that were previously
imported. The strategy depends, for the most part,
on protection, principally through tariffs or quotas
on competing imports; and often on the transfer of
technology from established industries as well. In
so far as a logical extension of import substitution
strategies is to penetrate export markets for these
goods, and thus diversify exports, the desire to
produce goods experiencing growing demand inevitably
follows. Moreover, given the paramount importance
generally accorded technology, a salient feature of
these industrial strategies has been to 'target' specific high technology industries and firms as recipients of special state attention and largesse. The
aircraft industry is one such 'target' industry. As
outlined in the foregoing chapters, there are a number of features of this industry which invariably
make it a part of many national industrial programmes. Specifically, it is an important industry
in the major industrial economies, it is a technologically-intensive industry which generates substantial multiplier effects and offers sizeable balance
of payment gains, and furthermore, is potentially
capable of bestowing important external economies on
the national industrial environment as a whole. Of
perhaps equal importance, the desire to develop an
indigenous aircraft capability emanates from the
strategic importance for national sovereignty allot-
ted to it by virtue of its military function. Perhaps ironically, however, it is the military function
which circumscribes the possibilities of developing a
domestic aircraft industry. The defence market, as
Chapter 4 made clear, is pivotal to virtually all
aircraft firms. Thus a nation's defence policy, and
in particular its procurement procedures, has important ramifications for fostering an indigenous aircraft industry. At the same time, since the control
of aircraft technology (particularly with military
applications) is highly concentrated in a few countries, and since the transfer of military technology
is tantamount to foreign policy statements, a
nation's geopolitical position in the world order
conditions the direction of the development of its
aircraft industry. Finally, whereas the realisation
of industrial policy objectives may be attained
through private sector initiatives and/or direct
state involvement, the nature of aircraft production
(substantial barriers to entry, especially in terms
of front-end capital) has, in most cases, precluded
the former option, and overwhelmingly favoured direct
state participation.

JAPAN

Among the AICs, Japan's economic performance has
stood second to none for much of the postwar period.
Growth of GDP over the 1960s and 1970s exceeded that
of all other AICs while, simultaneously, Japanese
exports grew at an average annual rate of 17.5 per
cent between 1960 and 1970 and 9.1 per cent over the
following decade.[7] Manufacturing sector growth
exceeded that of the economy as a whole and averaged
10.9 and 6 per cent respectively throughout the 1960s
and 1970s.[8] In light of the country's limited endowment of natural resources, the Japanese Government
has, since the 1950s, promoted industrial development
as a means to sustained national accumulation. At
the heart of Japan's industrial policy is MITI; the
provider of administrative guidance in terms of the
allocation of resources. In consultation with the
private sector, it offers 'visions' which serve as
general policy targets for the direction of industrial growth.[9] A salient feature of these so-called
visions has been the choice of strategic industries
as harbingers of long-run industrial expansion. The
selection of specific priority industries is generally based on four key criteria: an industry's potential international competitiveness; the propensity of
the industry to benefit from economies of scale and
technological change (the efficiency of capital criteria); the nature of the industry's income-elastic-
ity in terms of export demand and world real income;
and the ability of the industry to generate linkages.[10] As a result, the government rejected the dic-
tates of static comparative advantage as a guidepost
to industrialisation; rather, MITI:

> Decided to establish in Japan industries which
> require intensive employment of capital and
> technology, industries that in consideration of
> comparative cost of production should be the
> most inappropriate for Japan, industries such as
> ... aircraft ... From a short-run, static view-
> point, encouragement of such industries would
> seem to conflict with economic rationalism.
> But, from a long-range viewpoint, these are pre-
> cisely the industries where income elasticity of
> demand is high, technological progress is rapid,
> and labour productivity rises fast.[11]

In 1945, the once formidable Japanese aircraft
industry was dissolved under the American occupation.
However, with the outbreak of the Korean War and the
signing of the 1952 Peace Treaty, the Japanese

aircraft industry was again revived under a government decree, the Aircraft Manufacturing Law (later
revised as the Aircraft Manufacturing Industry Law)
which was designed to provide a foundation for future
aircraft development and production.[12] Stimulated by
demand for repair and overhaul work on USAF aircraft,
the decree distributed airframe production contracts
to seven factories, component-supply contracts to 41
factories and overhaul contracts to an additional 12
factories. Subsequently, characteristic of the economy as a whole, the Japanese Government has played a
critical role in fostering the development of the
industry.

First and foremost, this support has come by way
of state procurement, and especially through the Japanese Defence Agency (JDA). Prior to 1954, Japan was
prohibited from maintaining national armed forces; a
provision which did not augur well for the promotion
of an aircraft industry.[13] However, in 1954, the Diet
assented to the Self-Defence Law which provided for
the re-establishment of the armed forces and, moreover, served as an important catalyst in the development of Japan's aircraft industry. The need to equip
the Self-Defence Forces (SDF) with aircraft provided
the requisite demand to expand the industry's manufacturing capacity. The desire to develop a broad
industrial base was entrusted to MITI which allocated
JDA contracts among the principal aircraft producers.[14] In concert with Japan's propensity to rely
upon foreign technology transfer, the lead programmes
at the key manufacturers tended to be licensed production of US designs. Frequently building on prior
overhaul experience, technology transfer generally
proceeded in a phased process beginning with the
licensee assembling 'knock-down' aircraft followed by
the incorporation of locally-manufactured parts as
production tooling was completed, and finally leading
to the assumption of full manufacturing responsibility.[15] As recounted in Chapter 6, licence production
of warplanes embraced Kawasaki's responsibility for
Lockheed T-33 and P-2 aircraft, and Bell 47 helicopters; Fuji's manufacture of Beech T-34s and Cessna
L-19s; and, in particular, the entrusting of F-86F
jet fighter production to MHI. By 1969, MHI had
delivered 300 F-86s to the armed forces (with domestic content finally reaching about 77 per cent of
airframe components).[16] Although virtually all of the
production technology (e.g. production data and tooling) associated with F-86F manufacture was imported,
the programme (as was the case with the other licensing arrangements mentioned) proved invaluable in
terms of elevating the firm's (and industry's) basic

technological capabilities.

In order to facilitate production continuity, the phase-out of F-86F manufacture was co-ordinated with the phase-in of production of the more sophisticated Lockheed F-104 Starfighter at MHI. With Kawasaki as the major subcontractor, the JDA and MHI signed an agreement in March 1961 calling for the purchase of 200 F-104s (with the Japanese designation F-104J), including 20 trainer versions, (F-104DJs), at an estimated cost of $269 million (of which the US Government agreed to contribute $75 million). Typical of previous licensing arrangements, technology transfer progressed in a phased fashion: after the delivery of three complete airframes from the USA, 17 F-104J and 20 F-104DJ knock-down kits were supplied by Lockheed to MHI, with 160 F-104Js assembled and increasingly manufactured in Japan.[17] A follow-on order for 30 additional F-104Js in 1966 also increased the proportion of Japanese involvement. Similar to the F-86F experience, the F-104J avionics systems had to be imported from the USA owing to their complexity and high cost of transfer. Besides, a myriad of other parts were imported because the limited production run precluded economic manufacture (in contrast to the various European F-104 programmes). Complementing the transfer of product technology, Japanese industry was also exposed to important process technology, including chemical milling techniques, the spray-mat process to control icing, and improved techniques to form and handle high-heat treatment steel.[18] In addition to acquiring airframe technology, the F-104J programme also augmented Japan's aeroengine manufacturing capabilities, as IHI acquired the licence to produce the GE J-79 jet engine. Overall, it was estimated that Japanese-made F-104 airframes were cheaper to produce than US ones ($620,000 instead of $789,000), but Japanese aeroengines were more expensive ($232,000 as opposed to $184,000).[19]

The propensity to engage in licence production of front-line combat aircraft has since remained unabated. As a follow-on programme to the F-104J, licensed production of the MD F-4EJ fighter again witnessed MHI selected as the prime contractor and Kawasaki as the main subcontractor, with IHI responsible for the manufacture of the powerplant, an upgraded J-79. As was the case with previous co-production arrangements, technology transfer evolved in a step-wise format, with initial delivery of two F-4EJs from St. Louis being followed by Japanese production. Improved capabilities, however, ensured that almost 100 per cent of the F-4EJ airframe, avionics

212

and engine were manufactured in Japan (in contrast to
the F-104J, where main avionics systems were
imported).[20] Analogous to the follow-on imperative
discussed in Chapter 4, the JDA and MITI ensured Japanese production continuity with the decision to
produce 100 MD F-15 air-superiority fighters at a
projected cost of $3.3 billion.[21] A second memorandum
of understanding, signed in December 1983, called for
the purchase of an additional 55 F-15s scheduled for
delivery over the 1986-90 period. Paralleling earlier programmes, MITI distributed production contracts among the three manufacturers with MHI as
prime contractor and responsible for final assembly
and production of the nose and forward and centre
fuselage sections, Kawasaki overseeing aft fuselage
and wing manufacture, and IHI again building the aeroengine (the P & W F100 in this instance). Following
delivery of the last F-4EJ in May 1981, the first
Japanese assembled F-15J (from a knock-down kit)
rolled off MHI's Komaki South production line in
August 1981.[22] Prior to Japanese assembly, the first
eight F-15s were procured through US Foreign Military
Sales credits while the remaining aircraft are to be
progressively manufactured in Japan, with local content expected to reach 55 per cent.[23]
     A second major military programme designed to
carry the Japanese aircraft industry through the
1980s is the licensed production of the Lockheed P-3C
patrol aircraft. By way of a technical assistance
agreement struck between Lockheed and Kawasaki in
1973, the latter acquired the rights (through an initial payment of $16.5 million and a $270,000 per aircraft royalty fee thereafter) to produce the P-3C to
meet an SDF requirement.[24] On the basis of a JDA order
for 45 aircraft (since raised to 75), and consistent
with its ambitions to develop a broad industrial
base, MITI allocated production contracts to the
major firms; namely, Kawasaki (as prime contractor),
MHI, Fuji, Shin Meiwa, Japan Aircraft Corporation,
and Sumitoma Precision Products.[25]
     Although the majority of defence output is
attributable to licensed-production programmes,
experience and technology gained through these
projects have spurred indigenous design efforts in
the military field. These efforts have proceeded in
two directions: on the one hand, Japanese firms have
designed derivatives of aircraft produced under
licence, and on the other, Japanese firms have undertaken more extensive design efforts which have led to
new aircraft. In terms of the former, Fuji developed
a modified version of the Beech T-34 trainer, the
LM-1 Nikko liaison aircraft, of which 27 were

delivered to the SDF.[26] Similarly, Kawasaki, designed
the P-2J derivative of the Lockheed P2V-7 Neptune
patrol aircraft.[27] With respect to truly indigenous
designs, most Japanese efforts have focused on
trainer aircraft (a characteristic which typifies
many contemporary NIC aircraft efforts). To this
end, the first postwar jet aircraft entirely of Japanese design was the Fuji T1F1 (T-1B) trainer powered
by an imported UK engine initially, and then by an
IHI designed J3-IHI-3 turbojet engine.[28] Built to a
JDA requirement to replace US North American T-6s,
some 60 T1F1s and T1F2s were procured for use by the
SDF. A second trainer programme sponsored by the JDA
was the Mitsubishi T-2. Initiated in the late 1960s,
the T-2 was the first supersonic aircraft developed
by the Japanese aircraft industry. Powered by two
R-R Turboméca Adour turbofans, T-2 production began
in the mid 1970s, with MHI receiving orders for 92
aircraft.[29] The T-2 programme subsequently spawned
two offshoot projects. In the first of these, the
T-2 was redesigned as a close-air-support fighter and
restyled the F-1. After completion of design work
and flight testing in 1976, deliveries of F-1s began
in 1977, with orders numbering 74 by mid-1984. A
second spin-off arose in 1978, when the JDA's Technical Research and Development Institute selected the
T-2 as a testbed with which to develop active flight
control technologies, and subsequently redesigned the
T-2 to control configured vehicle (ccv) configuration. Finally, the JDA initiated a third trainer
programme (XT-4/T-4) to replace Lockheed T-33As and
Fuji T-1A/Bs. Based on Kawasaki's KA-850 design, the
programme is a joint development/production project
shared by Kawasaki (prime contractor and a 40 per
cent share), Fuji (30 per cent) and MHI (30 per
cent), with the SDF expected to procure 200 T-4s into
the 1990s.[30] In addition to the foregoing, notable
indigenous designs destined for the military market
include: the Shin Meiwa PS-1 patrol flying boat and
its air-sea-rescue derivative the SS-2A, of which 23
and 8 respectively were procured by the SDF; and the
C-1 twin-jet transport which was designed under the
auspices of the Nihon Aeroplane Manufacturing Company (NAMC), with Kawasaki, Fuji, MHI, Shin Meiwa,
and Nihon Hikoki assuming production responsibility.
    The government's prime policy measure for sup-
porting the development of the aircraft industry has
been military procurement. The JDA and MITI have
utilised defence expenditure, in a manner reminiscent
of the American follow-on system, as a means to sponsor licence-production programmes virtually irrespective of their economic feasibility. Indeed, "The

government has been willing to support licenced production programs of clearly uneconomical projects
simple to gain the technological know-how for reviv-
ing its industry."[31] Thus, the Japanese Government
procured only 24 Fuji-built Cessna L-19 observation
aircraft, when a production run of at least 120 aircraft was required to provide a minimum economic
basis for the programme. Similarly, the Japanese
Government was willing to pay $1.8 billion more for
90 F-15s in order to build the aircraft in Japan and
gain access to the most sophisticated aircraft technology in use.[32] Clearly, the liberal expenditure of
defence monies serves not only to secure markets for
Japanese firms, but also acts as an outright subsidy
to the industry. However, the acute dependence on
defence contracts, which in 1977 accounted for 88.6
per cent of total aircraft production, presents serious challenges to the industry.[33] Specifically, the
industry is not allowed to export military hardware
and domestic defence expenditure is limited to
approximately one per cent of GNP.[34] In view of these
restrictions, continued reliance on defence contracts
would appear inconsistent with MITI's strategy of
developing strong export industries. Not surprisingly, therefore, the Japanese Government has
attempted to foster civil programmes in tandem with
the more extensive military ones.
     In contrast to military projects, state support
of civil programmes has not relied upon direct procurement; rather, the Japanese Government has tended
to socialise risks through the underwriting of R & D
costs. In terms of civil projects, MITI has set its
sights on penetrating the commercial airliner market.
The first effort in this direction was initiated in
the late 1950s under the auspices of NAMC. Created
under the Aircraft Industry Promotion Law (1959),
NAMC was established as a consortium of major Japanese aircraft producers (consisting of MHI, Kawasaki,
Fuji, Shin Meiwa, Showa, and Nihon) and tasked with
the design and development of a medium-range airliner.[35] MITI and NAMC member firms jointly subscribed the necessary capital requirement, with the
former contributing $11.6 million in start-up costs
along with a commitment to underwrite debentures of
$74.1 million. The outcome of this effort was the
YS-11 twin-turboprop 60-passenger airliner. While
NAMC was responsible for design and development work,
production of the YS-11 was farmed out to the member
firms with MHI handling final assembly and fuselage
and equipment production, Fuji producing tail sections, Kawasaki building wings and engine nacelles,
Shin Meiwa overseeing rear fuselage work; Nihon

manufacturing the ailerons and flaps, and Showa responsible for honeycomb structures.[36] From the flight of the first production aircraft in October 1964 to the termination of production in 1974, 182 YS-11s had been delivered.[37] Although recording a loss of some $35 million over the course of the project, the YS-11 programme did realise a number of important benefits in terms of technological capabilities and, to a lesser extent, export market penetration. Whereas, industry exports in 1968 (the best year of the YS-11 programme) amounted to a meagre 18.8 per cent, approximately half of the YS-11s delivered were destined for the US market.[38] At the same time, however, the YS-11 experience also exposed the industry's weak marketing and support network. Commenting on the YS-11 programme, Kenji Uchino (an executive of Japan's Commercial Airplane Company) lamented, "To make the airplane is not that tough. Selling it is the real challenge."[39]

Cognisant of the importance of developing civil lines of business and given the institutional restrictions extant in the defence sector, NAMC began design work on the F-X commercial transport in the late 1960s. As a result, the YS-33 short-haul trijet was designed as a planned successor to the YS-11.[40] However, the YS-33 project was soon terminated as key elements of the Japanese aircraft industry preferred to concentrate their efforts on military contracts which provide a "relatively low risk haven" in comparison with commercial projects.[41] With the obvious need to generate civil activity, Japanese industry decided not to pursue the risky business of designing a complete airframe and instead opted to participate as a subcontractor and risk-sharing partner with established commercial transport manufacturers. Consequently, Kawasaki produced entry doors for Lockheed L-1011s, outer trailing-edge flaps for Boeing 747s, actuator transmissions for 727s, and inner flaps and wing ribs for the 737; while MHI built engine transport kits for 757s, inner trailing-edge flaps for 747SPs and assembled tail cones for DC-10s; and Fuji manufactured rudders for 747SPs.[42]

Meanwhile, the aforementioned F-X programme eventually evolved into a risk-sharing partnership with Boeing on its 767 transport. To this end, the Civil Transport Development Corporation (CTDC) was established (in much the same fashion as the NAMC) to manage Japan's 17 per cent interest in the 767 programme. MITI provided CTDC with an initial endowment of $87 million to undertake the project, and as a risk-sharing partner, CTDC was obliged to contribute $170 million towards 767 development costs.[43] In addition, MITI has pledged to underwrite production costs in order to allow Japanese firms to reduce their prices by 5-10 per cent and thereby make the 767 more competitive with the Airbus.[44] Production of fuselage panels, wing and fuselage fairings, cargo and entry doors as well as other airframe components is apportioned among member firms. Building on this experience, a consortium of Japanese firms under the aegis of the Japan Airplane Development Corporation (JADC) - an offshoot of the CTDC - entered into a second risk-sharing partnership with Boeing for the planned development of a 150-passenger airliner, the 7-7 (or alternatively the YXX in Japan).[45] Along with a 25 per cent share in the estimated $2 billion development cost, JADC is seeking a larger role in design, production, and marketing of the 7-7, relative to its status in the 767 programme.[46] As with other programmes, the Japanese effort is sponsored by MITI, which will underwrite the majority of R & D costs.

While MITI and industry ambitions in the civil market have been primarily focused on the airliner market, a number of important programmes have been undertaken in the business aircraft and helicopter markets. In terms of the former, MHI began basic design work on the MU-2 twin-turboprop in 1960, and the first aircraft flew in September 1963. By early 1971, roughly 85 per cent of the first 200 aircraft were destined for export markets, primarily the USA.[47] To further US market penetration, and following a decision by the Nixon administration to "permit government purchases of the MU-2 on the grounds that 65 per cent of the manufacturer's cost of production is spent in the US", MHI established an American subsidiary, Mitsubishi Aircraft International (MAI), to handle world-wide marketing as well as final assembly.[48] By March 1984 the firm had received orders for 745 MU-2s, of which 689 were exports.[49] MHI diversified its business aircraft product line in the early 1980s with the introduction of the MU-300 (Diamond I) turbofan. Like the MU-2, the MU-300 is shipped to San Angelo, Texas, for final assembly and the installation of engines and systems at MAI. As of July 1983, MHI had received orders for 61 Diamond I aircraft, of which North American sales numbered 48.[50] Japanese efforts in the area of rotary wing aircraft, though decidedly less pronounced than those in fixed-wing areas, have also been pursued. In typical fashion, initial efforts to familiarise the industry with the manufacture of helicopters were centred on licensed production of US designs, principally for JDA requirements. The only firm to undertake the

development of an all new helicopter is Kawasaki.
Following licensed production of Bell 47s, Boeing-
Vertol KV-107s and Hughes OH-6s, Kawasaki entered
into an agreement in 1972 with MBB for the joint
development of a twin-engined multi-purpose helicopter in the 8-10 seat class. The resultant aircraft,
the BK-117, entered the market in 1982 with orders
reaching well over a 100. Production of the BK-117
is split between the two firms and sees Kawasaki
responsible for airframe and landing gear manufacture, with both firms undertaking final assembly.

All told, the Japanese aircraft industry has
grown rapidly since its rebirth in 1952. In large
measure this growth has been spurred by state industrial policy and, in particular, through the use of
military procurement. The JDA and MITI have integrated defence and industry requirements such as to
ensure industrial growth in a pattern reminiscent of
the American follow-on imperative. To facilitate
technological development, the Japanese Government
has sponsored licensed production programmes with
established aircraft manufacturers. Building on
product and process technology acquired and adapted
from these programmes, Japanese firms have undertaken
a variety of indigenous projects in the civil and
military markets. At the same time, participation in
licence and co-production programmes has slowly stimulated the development of important linkages. The
fact that parts, component and equipment production
accounted for $1.15 billion (or 51 per cent) of the
industry's output in 1984 is ample testimony to that
effort.[51] On the basis of the above, industry sales
totalled $2.2 billion in 1984, a far cry from the
$309.33 million recorded in 1971 (although employment
growth has slowed considerably). Despite this laudable performance, the fact remains that the industry
is overwhelmingly dependent on domestic military
work, which has been increasing since the early 1970s
and has generally exceeded 75 per cent during the
recent period. Given the constraints on defence production in Japan, the dependence on defence work has
meant that the industry's export mandate has remained
largely unfulfilled. While low-risk defence production will carry the industry through the 1980s (on
the strength of the P-3C, F-15, T-4, and a new
fighter, the FXX), the Japanese aircraft industry
does possess two important advantages which can
potentially allow it to penetrate the more risky commercial export markets. On the one hand, the Japanese Government has firmly committed itself to supporting the industry into the future, and on the
other, the major Japanese manufacturers are not

inordinately dependent on aircraft production (with
aircraft sales accounting for only 10-15 per cent of
total sales).[52] In any event, industry growth will
still rely on imports of foreign technology.

CANADA

The Canadian aircraft industry consists of approximately 100 firms and in 1982 accounted for $2.8 bil-
lion in sales (seventh in the world) and employed
some 36,320 workers.[53] Approximately 77 per cent of
these sales were exports, and the ratio of industry
exports to imports was 3.11.[54] In terms of complete
airframes and aeroengines, fully 88 and 69 per cent
respectively of total sales were exports, the majority of which were destined for the USA, the country's
major trading partner.[55] While most firms undertake
Tier II and Tier III activities, there are three main
Tier I firms. In particular, there are two airframe
manufacturers, Canadair and DHC, which are nationalised enterprises held by the Canada Development
Investment Corporation (CDIC). Both Canadair and DHC
were foreign subsidiaries prior to the government's
decision to take them over in the mid-1970s. The
remaining Tier I firm is P & WC; a wholly-owned subsidiary of UTC of Hartford, Connecticut, and the
nation's only aeroengine producer. In fact, P & WC
is representative of the industry in Canada in as
much as foreign firms tend to predominate. Indeed,
more than half of the Tier II enterprise are subsidiaries of foreign corporations. Arguably, this structural characteristic has contributed to the rather
dubious R & D record of the industry and its basically 'built-to-print' status, and directly led to
the nationalisation of DHC in 1974 and Canadair in
1976. Another salient feature of the Canadian aircraft industry is the general absence of defence
production among the Tier I firms.[56] In contradis-
tinction to virtually all other aircraft industries,
Canada's industry has had to evolve without the benefit of a relatively independent national defence
procurement policy, a void which has had significant
implications for the industry's development. In
large measure, the industry's lacklustre R & D performance, and the abrogation of the independent Canadian defence policy are manifestations of the historical evolution of the North American
political economy. The division of labour emerging
out of this evolution sees Canada's primary role as a
supplier of resources to the USA and, as a result,
the nation's manufacturing sector remains dependent

and under-developed. The aerospace industry, however, is one area where the Canadian Government has
ostensibly pledged to forge a new division of labour.
The evolution of the Canadian aircraft industry
may be divided into roughly three broad phases. The
initial or formative phase ran from around 1915 to
the onset of mobilisation for World War II. From the
outset, and consistent with import substitution, foreign manufacturers established a marked presence in
Canada. The first venture into aircraft production
was the US Curtiss Company which, in 1915, established a subsidiary for the purpose of capturing
British Admiralty orders. Boeing (US), Fairchild
(US), Consolidated (US), Vickers (UK), and DH (UK)
all established subsidiaries in Canada prior to World
War II, and thus, "The aircraft industry ... evolved
on a derivative basis with most research and design
located elsewhere."[57] At the same time, Canada's traditional UK ties were giving way to continental ones.
The preparation for war signalled the transition to
the second phase of the industry's evolution, which
extended to the early 1970s.

This phase was characterised first and foremost
by the gradual erosion of Canadian production of complete airframes for defence markets. The need for
additional aircraft production capacity prompted the
Canadian Government to establish several new manufacturing operations. More importantly, however, the
exigencies of war stimulated the crystalisation of a
US-Canada defence pact along the precepts of a continental alliance. The initial step in this direction
was the signing of the Ogdensburgh Declaration in
1940, which created the Permanent Joint Board of
Defence (PJBD), and was closely followed by the Hyde
Park Declaration (1941) which extended continental
defence strategy into the realm of production and
articulated the position that, "in mobilising the
resources of this continent each country would provide the other with the defence articles which it is
best able to produce".[58] In terms of aircraft production, the result reflected the industry's established
dependence on foreign inputs, as of the 16,000 aircraft made in Canada for the war effort, only one of
the dozen principal types produced was an indigenous
design, and all the aeroengines were imported. With
the cessation of hostilities, the Canadian Government
divested itself of its aeronautical ventures. The
industry, however, continued to direct most of its
output towards defence markets throughout the 1950s
and 1960s. Not surprisingly, given the industry's
technological status, licensed production of US aircraft was its trademark: the F-86 fighter (1949),

T-33 trainer (1951), T-34 trainer (1955) and F-104
fighter (1959) leading the way.[59] Despite this propensity, Canadian industry did maintain local design
and production capabilities and this was best exemplified by the CF-100 produced by HS subsidiary, Avro
Canada.) All the while, Canada-US defence links were
moving towards formal integration. By 1957 this
trend was formalised with the creation of the North
American Air Defence Command (NORAD) held responsible
for continental air defence. Concurrent with the
integration of air defence, and arguably a result of
it, Canada withdrew from autonomous military aircraft
development. Thus the cancellation of the Avro Arrow
supersonic fighter programme led not only to the demise of the last military aerospace design team in
Canada, but to the purchase of all Canada's future
combat aircraft from American sources. In recom-
pense, and in order to maintain at least a semblance
of Canadian military aircraft manufacturing (though
not necessarily design) capability, the Canadian Government negotiated the Defence Production Sharing
Agreement (DPSA) in 1959.

Under the DPSA, Canadian aerospace firms are
able to direct their output to the needs of the Pentagon by way of free market access to US defence contracts, and thus receive reprieve from the 'Buy America Act'. In 1963, the two nations agreed to keep
trade covered by the DPSA in a rough balance, and
thereby, linked Canadian aerospace exports to the USA
to sustained Canadian procurement of American military equipment. The ensuing period witnessed the
continuation of licensed production (e.g. the CF-5
version of Northrop's F-5A), and the lucrative participation in the US Vietnam War effort. As indicated in Table 8.1, the peak of Canadian aerospace
industry output and employment coincided with the
peak of the Vietnam War in 1967-68. However, the
acute dependence on US defence markets left the
industry vulnerable, especially since much of its R &
D had been abrogated under the DPSA. As Vietnam production wound down from the late 1960s, Canadian
aerospace employment fell from 48,000 in 1967 to
25,000 in 1976. The composition of the industry's
output told the story; whereas in the 1960s from
50-60 per cent of output was destined for defence
markets, by the 1970s the proportion had dropped to
below 40 per cent. Even licensed production of US
aircraft ceased, as Canadair's (then a subsidiary of
GD) CF-5 programme came to a close. Dwindling activity levels in the warplane field, coupled with difficulties encountered by the airframe firms in diversifying into civil markets, compelled state acquisition

and, in so doing, ushered in the third and current
phase of the industry's evolution.
   The nationalisation of DHC and Canadair in many
respects adopts the semblance of an industrial strategy in Canada. It arose not so much as part of a
dirigiste industrial strategy, but rather, to secure
manufacturing jobs and to maintain a Canadian presence in an important global industry. In terms of
the latter, aerospace was viewed as a useful instrument for diversifying an otherwise largely resource-
dependent economy. However, the government's ability
to foster an indigenous industry was severely circum-
scribed as a consequence of its historical ties to
the USA. In view of the importance of defence procurement to aerospace, the nationalisation and subsequent course of development of the industry emerged
as a logical outcome of Canadian defence policy.
Yet, as defence policy was subservient to US policy,
so too became Canadian defence industry - and not
least the aircraft industry. Thus, the subsequent
development of the industry, under state auspices,
would proceed along two basic lines: first, in the
area of defence, the remaining policy instrument
available to the Canadian Government was the negotiation of compensatory industrial offset agreements in
exchange for the procurement of US military aircraft
(and these will be discussed in the following section); and secondly, to concentrate indigenous aircraft production in the area of civil and commercial
markets. This latter option is best exemplified by
the strategy adopted by DHC; namely, that of
strengthening its established lines of expertise in
the STOL transport market. To this end, DHC fur-
nishes a range of STOL types: the highly succcessful
Twin Otter (19 passenger category), the recently
developed DASH 8 (36 passenger class), and the DASH 7
(50 passenger class). In the case of Canadair, the
Canadian Government saw the key to this firm's fortunes in the bizjet market. Paradoxically, while the
government ostensibly promised to maintain a domestic
design capability, it none the less saw fit to import
a US design, that of William P. Lear's Learstar 600,
as the basis for the Canadair Challenger programme.[60]
   The industry's problems steadily mounted notwithstanding state ownership. In fact, the state's
disenchantment became evident in its vacillating
desire to, alternately, sell and retain its flounder-
ing enterprises. In 1981, however, the then Liberal
Government seemingly issued a vote of confidence in
the industry through its strategy document, which
explicitly acknowledged aerospace as a leading industry in the nation's future;

Table 8.1 : Canadian Aerospace Industry Statistics

Year	Sales ($m)	Defence (%)	Exports (%)	Employment ('000)
1963	550	66.0	40.5	
1964	589	61.9	48.2	37.5
1965	541	61.9	43.6	37.9
1966	594	50.0	50.5	45.9
1967	680	54.0	59.1	48.1
1968	750	54.9	74.5	47.8
1969	695	52.7	71.5	44.4
1970	659	52.2	73.1	35.8
1971	596	48.0	71.0	28.7
1972	625	35.0	81.6	28.8
1973	662	32.9	77.9	31.7
1974	729	32.0	80.1	28.4
1975	785	32.0	79.6	27.3
1976[1]	800	36.0	77.5	25.3
1977[1]	872	39.0	73.6	27.4

Note: 1. Estimated figures.
Source: Canada, A Report by the Sector Task Force on the
        Canadian Aerospace Industry, (Department of Industry,
        Trade and Commerce, Ottawa, 1978).

The third direction of growth is ... the innovative resources of Canadians in the development
and exploitation of advanced technology and high
productivity goods and services ... in manufacturing, engineering and service areas such as
... aerospace ... [that] can place ourselves
[Canadians] at the forefront of technological
change in selected world markets.[61]

The pronouncement could hardly have come at a more
inopportune time as the global economy was amidst
recession, interest rates were high, and civil aircraft markets were flat. Canadair alone lost $1.4
billion (largely attributable to the Challenger programme) on sales of $429 million in 1982.[62] DHC, for
its part, did not fare much better, losing $226 mil-
lion in the last seven months of 1982. While assuming responsibility for the losses, the Canadian Government has been pressed to inject a further $310
million and $240 million in new investment into Cana-
dair and DHC.[63] Moreover, the Canadian Government was

compelled to restructure Canadair and thus relieve
the firm of its debt burden in order to instil confidence in the market so that the Challenger programme could at least continue.[64] All told, the government subsidised the two firms to the tune of
$823.3 million per year (average figure) through the
1981-83 period.[65] In addition, under a Special Capital Recovery Program, the government conjured up, at
a cost of $147 million, an order for 20 Canadair
CL-215 water bombers in order to keep the production
line active.[66] None the less, employment at Canadair
dropped to a low of 4,200 in 1983, down from 7,000 in
June 1982.[67] Obviously, the distinction between backing 'high-tech' winners and undertaking corporate
bail-outs remains dubious, especially in view of the
opportunity costs foregone.

Seemingly undaunted however, the Canadian Government again chased aerospace employment. This
time, the government canvassed a number of foreign
helicopter firms to locate a production (assembly)
facility in Canada in order to capture a share of the
country's large domestic market - and at the same
time reduce the nation's import bill. Offering
lucrative subsidies, the government successfully
attracted Bell-Helicopter-Textron to Mirabel, Quebec
(with the prospect of 3,700 jobs). In exchange for
$275 million in state support (from the federal and
provincial governments), Bell is to initially produce
the Model 400 Twin Ranger. More importantly, the
agreement calls for the establishment of a domestic
design and production capability, initially through
transfer of 'state-of-the-art' technology, which is
to be followed by a Canadian designed and produced
derivative of the 400, the 440. Concomitant with the
development of the Model 440, the government has
extended some $468 million (over ten years) to P & WC
for the development and production of a new series of
gas-turbines to power the aircraft (the PW 200
series).[68] In addition to the Bell venture, MBB was
induced to locate an assembly facility in Fort Erie,
Ontario (by way of $34.9 million in government sup-
port) to enable it to produce its BO105. Interestingly, both ventures are destined to produce civil
products, thus making all complete airframe production in Canada dependent on civil markets. If the
experience of Canadair and DHC is any indication, the
result may be costly.

INDUSTRIAL OFFSET AGREEMENTS

In the past decade, major foreign defence sales have
shown a marked propensity to involve compensatory
co-production (as noted in Chapter 6) or 'offset'
agreements. A US Treasury Department survey revealed
that 144 contracts negotiated between American firms
and foreign customers between 1975-81, were valued
at $14.8 billion, but yet required $13.7 billion
(91.9 per cent) worth of compensatory offsets.[69] Of
these, aircraft contracts totalled $10.84 billion and
were accompanied by $7.02 billion in offsets. More-
over, where co-production and offset agreements were
primarily the preserve of AICs, the developing countries are beginning to demand industrial offsets in
exchange for procurement of major warplanes. The
recent acquisitions of F-16s by Turkey and Greece and
F-18s by Spain are indicative of these new expecta-
tions. Relatively poor economic conditions, increasing financial constraints, and industrialisation
desires have increased the pressure on governments to
negotiate deals with ever increasing percentages of
offset commitments, at times in excess of the cost of
the purchase.[70] For example, in the Greek fighter
competition, an official from a competing airframe
manufacturer noted, "The Greeks have never asked for
more than 100 per cent offset, but they have said they
would not settle for less".[71] In the case of the
four-nation NATO fighter replacement programme, Saab-
Scania's proposal for its Viggen included direct and
indirect industrial compensation in the neighbourhood
of 200 per cent of the aircraft purchase costs.[72] In
effect, compensatory industrial offset agreements
have become a way of life for exporters of most major
military aircraft.
    Basically, co-production and/or offset agree-
ments are struck between prime aircraft contractors
and foreign governments, with the contractor's government also heavily involved. These agreements
involve the specific geographic placement of work on
contracts by prime aircraft manufacturers in exchange
for major purchases of aircraft. The work allocated
may be directly associated with the production of the
aircraft being procured, or completely unrelated. In
practice, the range of offset commitments extends
across the spectrum of economic activity, including
aerospace work, tourism promotion, and export marketing. From the buyer's perspective, co-production
agreements are usually set within the nation's
broader political-economic relationships with participating countries. If need be, the seller's government may support the sale through agreed purchases of

goods from the purchasing nation or through the provision of preferential financing arrangements. From
the selling firm's perspective, industrial offsets
are concessions necessary to successfully compete for
foreign aircraft sales. Finally, the rationale
underpinning the negotiation of co-production agreements from the purchasing government's perspective
may be loosely divided into two categories: economic
and political. In terms of economic considerations,
short and long term objectives may be discerned. In
the short term, the expenditure of large sums of public funds provides an important and visible economic
stimulus to the economy, particularly in terms of job
creation and subsequent multiplier effects. When
these funds are spent on foreign goods, such effects
are lost on the local economy. Consequently, purchasing governments attempt to internalise these benefits to the domestic economy through offset demands.
Of equal importance, compensatory offsets provide a
means to overcome foreign exchange losses associated
with the procurement of expensive weapons systems.
In the medium to longer term, industrial offset packages are generally conceptualised within the framework of import substitution strategies. In this
sense, budgetary allocations for major defence purchases are utilised as a policy instrument to foster
industrial expansion. This is especially so with
aerospace in view of its 'high tech' status. As
such, these arrangements lean heavily towards facilitating transfer of advanced technology, promoting an
indigenous design and development capability and creating a skilled labour force, all of which are
expected to provide a base for future industrial
strength. Finally at the political level, offsets
are a means to generate public support for political
initiatives (through employment creation) as well as
to develop economic and political linkages to supplier nations. More ambitiously, these agreements
are seen frequently as stepping-stones in furthering
national sovereignty. To this end, Turkish President
Kenan Evren exclaimed of the F-16 offset package, "It
is impossible to defend this country by begging others for arms or purchasing weapons through credit.
To overcome these problems it has become essential
that we produce our own weapons.".[73] It should be
pointed out, however, that the demand for offset participation imposes additional costs on the price paid
for aircraft (relative to the off-the-shelf "fly
away" cost), and thus diverts additional resources
away from potentially productive uses. These
increases arise (as indicated in Chapter 6) from
additional transaction costs, transfer of technology

costs (e.g. learning curve considerations), duplication of capital investment, the involvement of less
efficient firms (to satisfy national objectives) and
reduced economies of scale on the prime assembly
line. The decision to demand offsets, therefore,
must be weighed against the additional costs incurred
in selecting this course of action. In the case of
the NATO co-production of F-16s, the four nations
involved incurred a 34 per cent cost penalty relative
to a direct purchase.[74] In so far as defence spending
is seen as a burden on the domestic economy, these
penalties may be unacceptable.

In the aforementioned US Treasury Department
survey, Canada had received the most offsets negotiated between the sampled US firms and foreign pur-
chasers. Specifically, Canada had received industrial offsets valued at $4.66 billion on the 28
contracts included in the survey.[75] In Canada's two
most recent purchases of military aircraft – the
CP-140 (the Lockheed P-3 Orion) and CF-18 (the MD
F/A-18) – significant offset industrial agreements
have been involved. In large measure, Canada's propensity to engage in offset agreements with US corporations, and the tenor of those agreements, is a
product of the country's political-economic evolution. Since the interwar years the country's economy
has become heavily dependent on the United States, as
manifest through trade patterns, large cross flows of
foreign investment and an integrated defence structure.[76] By virtue of the latter consideration, Canada's aerospace industry has evolved on a derivative
basis; largely (though not entirely) dependent on
American R & D, and licensed producer of US combat
aircraft. The tendency for licensed production of US
designs was reversed, however, with the decision to
procure 18 CP-140 maritime patrol aircraft "off-the-
shelf" and promote Canadian industry through offset
subcontract work rather than through airframe assembly. The offset benefit package was to extend from
1975 to 1994. It was conceived as follows:[77]

Phase 1 1975-1981: $213.2 million to be placed in
         Canada, including $94 million in direct
         orders, and $119.2 million in indirect
         offsets principally through arrangements
         with other Canadian companies for sales
         from Canada. Subject to a 10 per cent
         penalty if schedule not maintained.
Phase 2 1982-December 1993: $201.4 million to be
         placed in Canada, of which, $66 million in
         direct orders, and $135 million in indi-
         rect offsets arranged as above. Subject

to a 5 per cent penalty if the schedule is
not maintained.
Lockheed to place $168 million in subcontracts to
Canadian companies if the company sells an
additional 150 P-3 aircraft over the programme period. No penalty for non-per-
formance.

The Canadian Government returned to the offset
bargaining table a few years later with its New
Fighter Aircraft (NFA) programme to replace its age-
ing fleet of CF-101s, CF-104s and CF-5s. The earlier
CP-140 experience raised concerns about the distribution of offset work among the nation's provinces, as
Quebec and Ontario received the majority of the 'targeted' work, although no regional breakdowns were
specified in the contract. The regional dimension
was elevated to priority status in the NFA programme
and, in particular, the distribution of work between
Ontario and Quebec was stressed. The NFA request for
proposals was responded to by a number of firms
including MD (F-18), GD (F-16), and Panavia (Tornado). The last entry really stood little chance,
since Canada had been one of the original participants of the MRCA and subsequently dropped out, and
because the country was so tightly integrated into
the North American economy. Thus, the F-18 and the
F-16 emerged as the front-runners and the chances of
landing the contract rested on the size of offsets.
Ostensibly, the MD and GD proposals shared a
number of similarities. For its part, MD presented a
wide ranging $2.6 billion package to the Canadian
Government based on an estimated sale of $2.34 bil-
lion, of which approximately $700 million was in the
form of direct offsets to Canada (with possible final
assembly and test of aircraft) and an additional $1.9
billion was manifested in indirect offsets covering
aerospace-related programmes as well as non-industry
benefits such as promoting Canadian tourism.[78] The GD
offset package was valued at $2.84 billion.[79] Of
this, $2.4 billion was to be in the form of offset
benefits to Canadian industry (and expected to provide more than 20,000 jobs) while the remaining $500
million was to be in the form of Canadian industrial
exports, generated through GD assistance. Significantly, the NFA programme was influenced by important
national questions, including a government defeat, a
federal election (1980) and the Quebec referendum on
the independence option for that province. As the
federal government's electoral fortunes were wholly
dependent on Quebec and moreover, the Federal cabinet
(and the Prime Minister himself) was dominated by

Quebecers, the issue then, was not only the nominal
value of compensatory offsets, but where those were
to be placed. GD read the political winds carefully
and played up the regional distribution, implying in
the Quebec press that the MD proposal was of limited
benefit to that province.[80] Not to the outdone, and
also sensitive to the Quebec question, MD astutely
shifted the location of a proposed $60 million GE
(F-18 engine manufacturer) blade and vane plant from
Ontario to a part of Quebec experiencing economic
hardship.[81] The move was an "11th-hour attempt to
sweeten the offset pot" with MD adding an extra $300
million to its NFA offset package.[82] The operational
principle guiding the Canadian Government through
this process was an equitable distribution of offset
benefits throughout Canada, largely based on the
existing distribution of aerospace activity in Canada
- Quebec and Ontario comprising 48 per cent and 41
per cent respectively. From the government's perspective the proposed offset packages broke down as
follows:[83]

    GD: total offset package $2.62 billion, of which
                      Quebec was to receive $1.47
                      billion (56 per cent) over a 15
                      year period.
    MD: total offset package $3.26 billion, of which
                      Quebec was to receive $1.57
                      billion (48 per cent).

The MD proposal, therefore, benefited Quebec to a
greater extent than the GD offer, was consistent with
the government's operational principle, and potentially offered a better bargain to the country as a
whole. Thus, the MD aircraft was selected, and Canada contracted for 137 of them at a cost of $3 bil-
lion. Yet MD's marketing acumen was evident not so
much by what the company was proposing, but rather,
by what it was not saying. Because no explicit
regional quotas were specified, relative offset
shares were largely contingent upon Quebec and
Ontario firms bidding on potential contract work.
The government position was that since Quebec had
historically accounted for about 48 per cent of the
Canadian aircraft industry it was reasonable to suppose that, other things being equal, its firms would
capture a similar share of Canadian offset work.
Ottawa's folly was to overlook the fact that two-
thirds of Quebec's aerospace industry is accounted
for by two firms - Canadair (a former GD subsidiary)
and P & WC (a subsidiary of UTC). Canadair's preoc-
cupation with civil work effectively precluded its

ability to bid on major offset work. P & WC, on the other hand, was stymied owing to the fact that its parent was supplying the F-16 powerplant.[84] Hence, two-thirds of Quebec's aerospace industry was effectively removed from bidding on F-18 work, though seemingly neither Ottawa nor GD detected this. All told, the offset package had a potential value of $3.3 billion (or about 110 per cent of the contract value) over a fifteen year period and called for 60 per cent to be committed to the aerospace and electronic sectors (of which $545 million was for the supply of navigational systems for MD cruise missiles, and a further $654 million was derived from MD purchases of Canadian-built jetliner wings from the company's Toronto subsidiary). A further ten per cent ($300 million) was to be in the form of high technology business, and the balance was to occur in the establishment of a blade and vane plant in Quebec ($60 million), an NC machining centre ($225 million) and in tourism promotion.[85]

Consistent with events elsewhere, the Turkish Government has utilised industrial offset agreements as a policy instrument to foster domestic development and expansion. As a means of enacting a long-range programme to create a national aerospace (and defence) industry, the Turkish Government has recently used its military purchasing power as a vehicle to acquire aircraft manufacturing technology from 'export hungry' aircraft producers. As a first step, the Turkish Government negotiated a comprehensive offset package in its recent $4 billion purchase of 160 GD F-16s.[86] With the expressed intent of creating a national aircraft and armaments production capability, the government and GD arrived at an arrangement which will enable Turkey to licence-build 152 F-16 C/Ds. Tusas Aerospace Industries Inc will be established as a joint "turn-key" operation by Turkey and US firms. Turkish Aircraft Industries Inc (along with other Turkish interests) will control 51 per cent of the new firm, while GD will maintain a 42 per cent interest and the aeroengine supplier will likely assume the remaining seven per cent.[87] For their part, the US firms are to provide $67 million in equity, equipment and technical assistance towards the scheduled $137 million investment.[88] As noted, the agreement calls for the licensed assembly of 152 aircraft with Tusas eventually responsible for aft and centre fuselage and wing production, sheet metal forming, structural bonding, tube assembly and plumbing, wire harness assembly and machining of selected parts, as well as final assembly of complete aircraft. The actual production programme calls for the

phased build-up of Turkish participation, with the
first aircraft assembled from knock-down kits supplied by GD, to be followed by the progressive expansion of manufacturing activity as Tusas proceeds down
the learning curve. To accommodate production, a new
69,700 m² plant is to be constructed at an air base
near Ankara, with the first aircraft expected to roll
off the assembly line in 1988 and full production
expected in 1990. Employment at peak production is
set at about 1,500.

The second phase in the Turkish programme is
tied to the scheduled replacement of Turkey's fleet
of Douglas C-47 transport aircraft. Vying for the
estimated $500 million contract to supply 52 aircraft
are Spain's CASA (in co-operation with Nurtanio of
Indonesia) with its CN-235, Aeritalia with the G.222,
and DHC with its DHC-5D Buffalo.[89] In early 1985
while the decision was still pending, DHC had offered
to transfer the entire Buffalo production line to
Turkey, while Aeritalia had proposed an extensive
co-production programme, a soft financing package
including US Foreign Military Sales credits on US
supplied inputs, and Italian assistance in getting
Turkey into the EEC. Whether the Turkish Government's efforts are successful in nurturing a domestic
aerospace industry remains to be seen. However, the
Turkish case demonstrates the relative effectiveness
of utilising state purchasing power to induce technology transfer and establish at least a nominal
industrial capacity in a short period of time. In
addition, savings in foreign exchange are also
expected to ensue.

Whereas Turkey conceived of its industrial offset package as a means to establish its aircraft
industry virtually from scratch, Spain's industrial
offset package associated with the $3 billion pur-
chase of 72 MD F-18s is seen as a means to expand its
existing aircraft design, development and production
capacity.[90] To this end, the proposed $1.8 billion
offset package emphasises technology transfer to augment Spain's own efforts (through CASA) and calls for
some co-production of F-18 parts, as well as important process technology transfer including carbon
fibre epoxy bonding, aluminium honeycomb core carv-
ing, NC machining and ion-vapour deposition pro-
cesses. By using MD and its F-18 as the vehicle for
gaining process technology under the mantle of offsets, Spain is emulating the Australian example
(recall Chapter 6).

ROMANIA

In 1968, the Romanian Government targeted the aircraft industry as high-priority economic activity,
and established the Centrul National al Industriei
Aeronautice Romane (CNIAR) as an umbrella organisation under the auspices of the Ministry of Machine
Building Industry.[91] As a result, the nation's five
aircraft manufacturing facilities: Craiova, Bacau,
Brasov and two in Bucharest, were placed under the
control of CNIAR. The restructuring was undertaken
during Romania's fourth five-year plan of 1966-70,
and was envisaged as a concerted part of the nation's
postwar industrialisation drive, which, "has shifted
in emphasis from the creation of a wide foundation of
basic industries toward the development of technologically advanced secondary industries ...".[92] Upon
entering World War II the Romanian economy was one of
the least developed in Eastern Europe. In 1950,
agriculture accounted for nearly 75 per cent of total
employment, and 26 and 28 per cent of social product
and national income.[93] Through a series of successive
five-year plans beginning in 1950, the Romanian Communist Party (RCP) embarked on a long-term programme
to transform the country into a highly industrialised
economy. Underpinned by high rates of saving and
investment, average annual growth of gross industrial
production was 13 per cent over the entire 1951-75
period and, as a result, industry accounted in 1975
for 64.7, 56.2, and 30.6 per cent of social product,
national income, and employment respectively.[94] To
facilitate the transition to an advanced industrial
economy, the RCP has undertaken to intensify research
and technological development activities, concentrating on three themes; namely, improving the existing
technologies and developing new production technologies and the associated equipment; improving the
quality and diversification of production; and establishing export competitiveness.[95] To augment indigenous capacity, the RCP has made a deliberate effort
to cultivate international economic and technical
co-operation, particularly through licensing and
technical assistance agreements. Consequently, Romania's external links began to veer towards developed
market economies, "Further development of Romania's
leading sectors - chemicals and machine building -
required advanced technology, which could not be
obtained from socialist countries".[96] It is in this
context that Romania's aircraft industry has been
nurtured since its targeting in 1968.
    The selection of aircraft manufacture as a part
of Romania's industrialisation drive did not arise

232

simply as an ad hoc choice, rather the country's
courtship with the industry dates back to the earliest days of aviation. Since that time, the Romanian
Aircraft Industry (IAR) has produced some 90 different types of land planes, 80 of which were of indigenous design.[97] In fact, prior to World War II Romania
was one of Europe's leading aircraft producers and
was capable of military aircraft designs which were
second to none in Europe. With the onset of war, the
Romanian aircraft industry began extensive licence-
production of Messerschmitt Bf-109G aircraft as well
as production of indigenous IAR-80 and -81 high performance combat aircraft.[98] However, at the conclusion of the war, the Brasov factory was converted
into a farm-implement production facility, with most
aircraft manufacturing machinery and equipment transferred to the Soviet Union as the country's economic
priorities shifted to the development of heavy industry and modernisation of the agricultural sector.
Aircraft production for much of the post-war period
was confined to gliders and light aircraft. While
inheriting the semblance of an aircraft industry in
1968, much of its former prowess had eroded and Romania turned to the West to recoup its technological
capabilities. Therefore, the desire to develop an
industry capable of indigenous design and, ultimately, of promoting export-led development was
expressed through contracts established after 1968
with Western aerospace firms.
     As a point of departure, Romania signed an
agreement with Britten-Norman to licence-produce the
latter's Islander, a piston-engined light transport.
Faced with capacity constraints, the agreement
enabled Britten-Norman to meet its growing demand for
Islanders while, at the same time, providing Romania
with a launch project for its newly formed CNIAR as
well as a means to acquire Western production technology. Islander production began at the Baneasa
factory in 1969. The initial licence to produce 215
aircraft was subsequently extended in 1975, and by
September 1984, 400 aircraft had been manufactured,
of which 380 had been delivered to PBN.[99] As Islander
sales have slowed, CNIAR had indicated its intention
to build on the programme's experience, and begin
design work on its own 20-40 passenger commuter
transport/utility aircraft as a replacement for the
Islander.[100] In actuality, the Britten-Norman agreement was facilitated through fellow UK firm, BAC,
which arranged the deal as part of a compensatory
offset package tied to the Romanian Government's purchase of BAC-111 airliners.[101]
     A second set of licensing agreements aimed at

expanding CNIAR's product and technological base were
signed with Aérospatiale. In the first of these
agreements, beginning in 1971, Romania was granted a
licence to produce the Alouette III helicopter (with
the Romanian designation IAR-316B).[102] While providing for Romanian manufacture of various components,
the Brasov plant is still required to import a fair
amount of the aircraft's equipment, including its
engine. As a follow-on agreement, Romania acquired
the licence to produce 100 SA.330 (IAR-330) Puma helicopters in 1976. In contrast to the Alouette III
programme, the Puma project extended Romanian participation in the aircraft's production, including the
licence-production of the Puma's (Turboméca) Turmo IV
engine and transmission at Turbomecanica, the Bucha-
rest-based aeroengine manufacturer.[103] While originally conceived as an import substitution measure
aimed at supplying the domestic market and Romanian
Air Force requirements, the helicopter programmes are
being promoted for export markets. This latter shift
has been possible with the termination of Aérospatiale production of Alouette IIIs, thus enabling
Romania to gain export exposure. Some 190 Alouettes
and more than 100 Pumas had been produced at the Brasov plant by 1984, most of which were destined for
the Air Force. In addition to forging links to Western aerospace industries, CNIAR has also maintained
its COMECON ties in the aircraft industry with the
licensed-production of the Soviet Yak-52 aerobatic
trainer, some 500 of which have already been produced
at the Bacau plant for distribution throughout the
Warsaw Pact countries.

Arising out of Romania's business dealings with
BAC has been the licence-production of the BAC-111,
restyled the ROMBAC 1-11, production of which has
since been terminated by the UK firm in favour of its
new BAe 146 airliner. By way of offset commitments,
ten per cent of 1-11 airframe components were manufactured in Romania for transfer to the UK assembly
line. Subsequently, Romania struck an agreement in
May 1979 with BAe for the series 475 version (under
the Romanian designation 495) and the series 500
(redesignated the 560). Manufacture of the aircraft
in Romania is to proceed through a phased seven-stage
technology transfer process at the end of which,
expected to be 1987, the complete aircraft will be
almost entirely Romanian-made. To accommodate production of the ROMBAC 1-11, the Baneasa facility is
being expanded to cover about 200,000 m² of floor
space, and thereafter will concentrate its activities
primarily on transport aircraft. The first of a
scheduled production run of 22 aircraft rolled out in

September 1982 and was promptly delivered to the
national airline, Tarom. As a part of the licensing
agreement, BAe granted CNIAR exclusive worldwide marketing rights (with the exception of the UK) to the
BAe 111. However, marketing of the 1-11 has proved
difficult. On the one hand, the R-R Spey Mk.512 powered ROMBAC 1-11 is an old aircraft which is noisy
and relatively fuel inefficient. Moreover, Romanian
efforts to modernise the aircraft have been con-
strained by the country's economic crisis which is
placing financial constraints on the technological
upgrading of the aircraft. To this end, CNIAR is
looking to replace the current R-R Spey engine with
the quieter, improved thrust R-R Tay and is looking
for Western partners to participate in a modernisation programme. On the other hand, Romania has no
marketing experience in selling an aircraft as complex as the ROMBAC in a highly competitive environment. There are in fact a number of interrelated
problems in this respect. First, the BAe 111 has
been out of production for some time and the airlines
are reluctant to acquire an aircraft which is not
manufactured by an established firm which has proven
its capability to provide global support. Secondly,
there is concern over operating in the parochial
atmosphere of a planned economy which is largely
devoid of the discipline of Western markets. As one
industry official commented, "We have been spoiled by
having a planned economy domestically. When something is produced here, the consumer must purchase
it. But this isn't true on the Western-style open
airline aircraft market".[104] To overcome this marketing problem, CNIAR has conceded marketing tasks to
the British aircraft broking company, DK Aviation,
which will sell the 1-11 in Western Europe and Africa
on a commission basis.[105]

   Consistent with the pattern of development
extant in the airframe sector of the industry, Romania has relied heavily on the transfer of Western
aeroengine technology to establish an indigenous
technology base, again principally through licensing
arrangements. Turbomecanica began production in
1975, and since that time has produced several hundred powerplants. In order to augment the plant's
production capabilities, Romania has imported new NC
machines from Japan, West Germany and Switzerland to
supplement home-produced equipment. With the objective of developing an independent aeroengine design
and development capability, Turbomecanica has
acquired its existing technological capability and
quality control and assurance system through agreements with R-R, Turboméca and Aérospatiale.[106] In the

235

first of these, Romania acquired the licence to produce the R-R Viper 632-41 which serves as the powerplant for the Romanian/Yugoslavian IAR-93A combat fighter. Following this agreement, Turbomecanica entered into agreements with the French for the production of main and secondary gearboxes and rotor heads for the Alouette III and Puma helicopters, as well as the Turmo 4C turboshaft engine. As an offshoot of the ROMBAC 1-11 programme, Romania acquired the licence to produce and assemble R-R Spey Mk.512 turbofan engines in 1980. Specifically, the agreement calls for the progressive expansion of engine component manufacture leading to full Romanian production by 1987, and provides for immediate final assembly and testing. Moving beyond licensed production, Turbomecanica has entered into a co-production agreement with R-R and Yugoslavia, which will see the firm responsible for the development of variable nozzle and burner sections of a planned afterburning version of the Viper.

While the thrust of Romania's aircraft industry development strategy has relied on licensed production programmes centred on the ROMBAC 1-11 project, the country has demonstrated an indigenous design capability. Thus complementing the spate of licensed production programmes are the production of Romanian developed airframes including: the IAR-825 Triumf turboprop aircraft (also available as the IAR-831 Pelican in a piston version) which is initially targeted for the Romanian Air Force (for about 100 aircraft) and is to be powered by P & WC PT6 and/or (Czech) Walter M601B engines; and the IAR-827 piston, and IAR-828 turboprop, powered agricultural aircraft which fulfil both domestic and export requirements. Further testimony to the existence of a domestic airframe design capability is Romania's recent development of the IAR-99 Soim jet trainer powered with the same version of the Viper as the IAR-93A.[107] Finally, as a means to maintain a balanced product base and to move away from complete dependence on Soviet-designed combat aircraft, Romania entered into a joint development/production programme with Yugoslavia. Originated in 1970, the agreement has led to the production of IAR-93 (or Orao in Yugoslavia) twinjet strike-fighters - the first combat aircraft adopted in Romania since World War II that is not a Soviet design. The Romanian production line is building 20 of the Viper 632-powered IAR-93As and 165 of the Viper 633-powered IAR-93Bs.[108]

Since the 1968 reorganisation, Romania's aircraft industry has built up a diversified product base and has correspondingly expanded its

236

technological capabilities. The judicious selection of airframe and aeroengine licensing arrangements with BAe, R-R, Aérospatiale, Turboméca and Britten-Norman has considerably accelerated this process. Thus, in the space of 15 years employment has reached a respectable 25,000, and the industry maintains five firmly-established production facilities.[109] Over the course of the development of the industry, planners have looked to it as a leader in enhancing the country's industrial capabilities, in terms of quality control techniques, marketing in the world economy, and project management; as well as in stimulating important backward linkages in the economy – all with important balance of payment and employment implications. None the less, and common to virtually all nascent aircraft industries, technological dependence seemingly remains the order of the day. The country's recent economic problems have clearly demonstrated the constraints placed on the industry's development. Yet, one can hardly expect a country to establish itself in such a complex industry in such a short period of time. However, if Romania chooses to continue as a producer of complete airframe and aeroengines, it will inevitably have to ween itself away from its dependence on licensed production, and maintain a firm R & D commitment in its stead.

INDONESIA

Another NIC which has 'targeted' aircraft production as a part of its national industrial strategy is Indonesia. Following a decade of relatively slow growth during the 1960s, gross domestic product expanded at an average annual rate of 7.6 per cent throughout the 1970s, well in excess of other low-income countries.[110] In the 1970s growth of manufacturing output, averaging 12.5 per cent per year, provided an important impetus to industrial growth as a whole. None the less, the contribution of manufacturing to the nation's economy remained relatively small, constituting only nine per cent of GDP in 1978. Furthermore 98 per cent of Indonesia's exports were accounted for by fuels, minerals, metals and other primary commodities, while manufactured exports constituted a lowly two per cent.[111] By way of contrast, manufactured exports comprised 70 and 34 per cent of Romanian and Brazilian exports at that time.[112] To improve the situation, the Indonesian Government embarked on a programme to establish a national aircraft industry in the mid-1970s. Typical of the cases outlined so far, the industry was

established with the intent of facilitating import
substitution and diversifying the composition of
national exports, while at the same time serving as a
lead industry in a country with 'high-tech' ambitions. Although committed to private accumulation,
the Indonesian Government (like Brazil) is not averse
to direct participation in key national industries,
as is the case for example in oil production.
Indeed, on the basis of the investment of rents generated in the oil industry and appropriated by the
state-owned oil company, Pertamina, the Indonesian
Government established Pesawat Terbang Nurtanio (PT
Nurtanio) as the aircraft manufacturer. By a government decree of 5 April 1976, PT Nurtanio was created
out of the merger of LIPNUR (previously set up to
prepare for the development of the industry) and the
aviation activities of Pertamina. Created with the
mandate to set up a fully-fledged and commercially
viable aircraft industry, PT Nurtanio was placed
under the tutelage of Dr. B. J. Habibie, an Indonesian who gained extensive aerospace experience as a
vice-president at MBB.[113] Perhaps indicative of the
industry's importance to national development plans,
Habibie was subsequently appointed to the post of
Minister of State for Research and Technology, as
well as President of the Indonesian Agency for the
Development and Application of Technology. In terms
of industrial policy, the government has generously
underwritten the costs of production, initially providing $170 million for the construction of a new
manufacturing facility in 1975, and subsequently
allocating approximately $100 million per year for
working capital.[114] In addition, the government has
attempted to underwrite the risks of production by
requiring that Indonesian airlines and other aircraft
operators purchase PT Nurtanio-built aircraft when
these products fulfil user requirements. Furthermore, the government has not hesitated to use state
procurement to ensure a minimum level of demand.[115]
    At the time of its creation, PT Nurtanio's
development was set within a ten-year plan, at the
end of which the firm was to have significantly
enhanced its design, development and production capabilities. Ostensibly, a number of development phases
were discerned: Phase I called for the transfer of
technology for the assembly and partial manufacture
of established products as a means to move along the
'learning curve'; Phase II took the process a step
further with the application of existing technology
to the design and manufacturing of new products, as
well as continuing to acquire foreign product and
process technology through co-operative agreements;

and finally, a third phase envisaged the indigenous development of new aerospace technology.

While aircraft production was not completely alien to Indonesia, PT Nurtanio was essentially established without the benefit of any meaningful aeronautical production experience.[116] Hence, to gain familiarity with the production of aircraft the industry relied exclusively upon the transfer of foreign product and process technology in the formative phase. To launch production at its 500-employee Bandung facility, PT Nurtanio acquired the licences to produce the MBB BO105 helicopter and the CASA C-212 Aviocar turboprop commuter aircraft.[117] The selection of the BO105 (renamed NBO105) and C-212 (designated NC-212) was based on two general considerations. In the first place, the products met domestic transportation requirements and thus could displace imports. Secondly, the aircraft were of relatively simple design; an important consideration given the industry's technological and labour constraints. In order to augment PT Nurtanio's capabilities, the agreements were structured to allow the firm to take an increasing role in production. In both programmes, initial participation began with the simple assembly of knock-down kits provided by CASA and MBB, and a minimal level of local content.[118] On a step-by-step basis, locally manufactured airframe components accounted for a greater share of the total airframe, reaching approximately 80-90 per cent. Moreover, PT Nurtanio has since secured a contract to supply C-212 wings for CASA's main production line.[119] Behind import barriers, PT Nurtanio has sold 133 NC-212s and 130 NBO105s since production began in late 1976. Of perhaps greater significance, the firm has managed to realise 42 export sales (to Thailand, Bangladesh and Burma) for its NC-212. Consistent with its import substitution objectives, Nurtanio quickly signed a third licensing agreement in 1977 with Aérospatiale for the assembly of Puma and Super Puma helicopters with the purpose of supplying Indonesian military requirements from local sources.[120] As with the previous agreements, the deal called for the stepwise transfer of production technology so as to enhance the firm's capabilities while concomitantly diversifying its product base. Subsequently, PT Nurtanio has continued to maintain its cautious path of licensed production of established designs in order to expand its helicopter production capabilities. Stimulated by state orders for 36 helicopters, it entered into an agreement with Bell of the USA for the licence-production of Model 412s with initial deliveries expected in 1986.[121] Similarly, MBB and PT

Nurtanio extended their close ties; firstly, with the latter acquiring the licence for the manufacture of 100 BK-117 helicopters, principally destined to meet local demand, and secondly, through the joint participation in the development of a new light helicopter, the BN-109.[122] The BN-109 project appears well suited to launch PT Nurtanio's initial development helicopter programme, in as much as it demands minimal technological capabilities (in fact it utilises an automobile engine) and is relatively inexpensive.

Confident that it had accumulated sufficient production experience, PT Nurtanio began in 1979 the second phase of its ten-year plan, that is, the design and development of a new aircraft. In order to reduce programme risk, it combined with Spain's CASA to form Air Tech Industries, and the new enterprise was tasked with developing a 30-40 seat commuter/transport aircraft, the CN-235. As equal partners in the venture, the Indonesians assumed responsibility for the design and development of the aircraft's outer wing, rear and rear centre fuselage, empennage and cabin interior, as well as involvement with the hydraulic and flight control systems.[123] In addition, the agreement called for twin production lines in Spain and Indonesia and the establishment of a joint certification board. With limited experience in advanced development work, PT Nurtanio asked MBB for assistance with the flight-testing programme. In order to instil confidence in the project, the Indonesian Government made a commitment to purchase 100 CN-235s while the project was still in the design stage.[124] By March 1984, 110 firm orders had been received for the CN-235, with 22 destined for the Spanish airline Aviaco and four for the Royal Saudi Air Force.[125] What is more, well over half the options received were exports including aircraft for Thailand (20), Pakistan (10), Australia (9), Japan (6) and Burma (2).[126]

Although PT Nurtanio's airframe products are the backbone of its development, they are in fact only one aspect of a comprehensive strategy to develop the industry as a whole. Given the relatively weak state of the Indonesian manufacturing sector and PT Nurtanio's limited experience, the industry is confronted with technological and manpower (human capital) constraints. A number of programmes have been formulated to ameliorate these. Thus to meet growing demands for skilled labour, the firm established a training centre adjacent to its main production facilities, and is graduating about 300-350 persons per year (and is to increase this to 1,500 per annum).[127] To augment domestic capabilities, the

company has formulated agreements with foreign concerns for personnel training and sends employees
overseas to acquire needed skills.[128] Similarly, PT
Nurtanio has utilised co-operative agreements with
foreign producers to acquire process technology.
Thus, for example, it signed a five year technical
co-operation contract with Boeing. Under this agreement, the US firm is transferring CAD/CAM production
technology to Indonesia, and is assisting with the
improvement of production and quality control techniques.[129] In fact, the Boeing agreement was conceptualised as a means to qualify PT Nurtanio as a cer-
tified FAA (US) manufacturer and thereby allowing it
to perform Boeing subcontract work (while at the same
time allowing Boeing to capitalise on Indonesia's low
wage rates, which are about 80 per cent less than
those in the USA). Paralleling PT Nurtanio's
efforts, the Indonesian Government has continued its
support of the industry, investing $200 million for
the construction of a new 380,000 m² integrated production facility which will house the company's
expanded operations, and provide state-of-the-art
machinery.

On the basis of a firm state commitment to
develop an indigenous aircraft industry, PT Nurtanio
has progressed steadily since its creation in 1976.
Relative to its original objectives, company performance has been reasonably successful; contributing to
the expansion of the nation's industrial base, providing 12,000 industrial jobs, manufacturing products
consistent with import substitution, and is slowly
evolving into an export industry. Rather than place
heavy reliance on domestic military procurement to
nurture its aircraft industry in the Brazilian and
Romanian fashion, Indonesia is dependent on a protected domestic market which is largely civil in orientation. Its cautious dependence on foreign co-operation has minimised risks and facilitated the
transfer of technology. Yet, while company performance has been laudable as a capital-intensive enterprise in an economy plagued by low incomes and high
unemployment, its overall contribution to national
development remains to be proven.

BRAZIL

The chapter will conclude with a review of the most
promising case of NIC aircraft enterprise, that of
Brazil. Prior to the Revolution in 1964, Brazil
engaged in an extended programme (1947-63) of
import-substitution-industrialisation. With the

single-minded objective of promoting industrialisation, growth was rapid, averaging about eight per
cent per year during the 1950s, and by 1962, Brazil's
industrial base was capable of producing relatively
sophisticated consumer goods and capital equipment.
Following 1964, the political-economic foundations
for Brazilian state capitalism and renewed expansion
were being laid in the form of political stability
through military state control over the political
instruments and institutions, relative continuity in
the economic policy environment, and the effective
combination of a market-oriented economic philosophy
with an active state role in terms of economic planning and management. In respect of the last point,

> While encompassing a myriad of specific policy
> measures, the overall economic philosophy has
> been twofold: (1) strengthening markets and
> employing the price mechanism to more effi-
> ciently allocate economic resources, and (2)
> engaging in active government intervention to
> improve policy effectiveness in meeting basic
> objectives and to stimulate growth where markets
> were judged to operate ineffectively.[130]

Indicative of this tendency is that, in 1969, the
public sector accounted for about 61 per cent of
total investment, while in the manufacturing sector,
the state's market share had risen from 3.9 per cent
in 1956, to 11.3 per cent in 1971. Brazilian federal
and state governments have directly participated in
industries deemed important to national industrial
vitality. Accordingly, industrial expansion again
became the leading edge of Brazil's development
drive, with average annual industrial growth over the
1970-79 period reaching 9.6 per cent, while growth in
manufacturing averaged 10.9 per cent (versus 8.7 per
cent for GDP) per year over the same period.
   Given the nature of aircraft production and its
political-economic basis, Brazil's state capitalist
commitment lent itself favourably to the establishment of a national aircraft industry. Begun in ear-
nest in August 1969 with the creation of Empresa Bra-
sileira de Aeronáutica SA (Embraer), the Brazilian
aircraft industry was set up as an instrument of
national policy. Specifically, Embraer was created
with the intention of expanding Brazil's technological and industrial base, and as a means to ameliorate the nation's balance of payments position by
way of displacing expensive imports and generating
foreign exchange earnings through exports. Of equal
importance, Embraer, as an outgrowth of the air force

ministry, is a logical extension of the military's
long term objective (dating as far back as the early
1900s) to develop an indigenous armaments production
capability. The desire to obtain this capability
emanates from the elite's geopolitical vision of Brazil as an intermediate (regional) power.

In nurturing its aircraft industry, the Brazilian Government has utilised the conventional array of
industrial policy instruments including: the direct
support of R & D and production initiatives; the
judicious use of discretionary government expenditure, principally military procurement, to support
production; the provision of sales support by way of
liberal financing schemes; and the erection of trade
barriers to create a captive domestic market and
induce technology transfer. In terms of technology
transfer, Baranson notes, "Its strategy of effectively closing entry to its markets for all but the
foreign firm prepared to share front-end technology,
to impart sophisticated design and engineering capabilities, and to instruct Brazilian nationals in
managerial skills has been extremely successful."[131]
With reference to state support, Brazil's dual commitment to a formidable state role in the economy and
a respect for market forces is graphically illustrated in the case of Embraer, which was instituted
to reflect both these concerns. On the one hand, the
Brazilian Government supplied 23 per cent of the initial $19.5 million investment but retained control of
the voting stock in order to direct the firm along
state policy lines. On the other hand, the government relied upon the private sector to supply the
lion's share of the capital investment, and provided
tax concessions to stimulate support of the undertaking. The reliance on private capital has increased
since this time, with 94.23 per cent of the subscribed capital held by private shareholders,
although the government has retained its 51 per cent
control of the voting shares.

With the aforementioned objectives in mind, the
Brazilian aircraft industry has developed along three
general lines: first, there has been an adamant commitment to indigenous designs; secondly, co-operative
arrangements with foreign manufacturers have been
used to acquire and expand technological capabilities
and thirdly, industry output has been balanced
between military and civil markets. From the outset,
these themes have coloured the industry's evolution.
The immediate impetus behind the creation of Embraer
in 1969 was to bring into production the Bandeirante
twin-turboprop light transport. The Bandeirante
project began some years earlier at the Centro

Técnico de Aeronáutica (CTA) to fulfil a Ministry of Aeronautics specification calling for a general purpose aircraft. Under the design leadership of Max Holste, an established French designer, the first prototype flew in October 1968, and the first production aircraft flew in August 1972. As the lead programme at Embraer, the Bandeirante (designated the EMB-110 in its civil role and the C-95 for the Brazilian Air Force) was an unequivocal success, realising a number of important objectives. With some 428 aircraft delivered as of January 1984, the Bandeirante has provided Embraer with a long-term project, thus contributing to design (through successive derivatives) and production experience and the development of a skilled labour force. Catering to both civil and military markets, the EMB-110 has displaced Brazilian imports in both markets, serving initially as a replacement for US-made Beech C-45s used by the Brazilian Air Force and extending to other aircraft as well. In the civil commuter market, Brazil's 'law of similars', which blocks imports of products where similar domestic substitutes are available, has ensured Embraer with a captive market. Not entirely dependent on protectionist measures, the Bandeirante has scored admirably in export markets, with roughly 52 per cent of the aircraft destined for export to some 21 countries. Significantly, the Bandeirante increased its US market share from seven per cent in 1978 to 35 per cent in 1981, with some 115 aircraft delivered.[132] In a country burdened by a heavy foreign debt, such foreign exchange benefits are a valued commodity. Building on the Bandeirante programme, Embraer began design work on a second twin-turboprop transport in 1979, and had invested in excess of $200 million to bring the aircraft into the production phase.[133] Complementing Embraer's 19 passenger class Bandeirante, the 30 passenger class Brasilia (EMB-120) had secured 118 options by mid-1984, and is scheduled to enter the market in 1985. Export market penetration for the Bandeirante and the Brasilia has been facilitated by selling the aircraft with an attractive state-sponsored financing package: 15 per cent down and an extended low interest loan for the balance. Aside from the lead Bandeirante programme, a second project undertaken during the formative phase of the industry was the design and development of the Ipanema (EMB-200/210A) agricultural aircraft. The Ipanema project was initiated in 1969 in response to a Ministry of Agriculture proposal intended to meet domestic market requirements. Following its maiden flight in 1970, Ipanema sales totalled 484 as of December 1983.[134] Finally,

rounding out the array of domestic designs aimed at
meeting local requirements were the Embraer Urupema
sailplane, and the Aerotec 122 Uirapuru and Neiva
Universal Trainers, both of which were procured by
the Air Force to replace foreign designs. Subsequently, Brazil diversified its civil product base
with the design and development of the EMB-121 Xingu
twin-turboprop general purpose transport (9 passengers) and advanced trainer. Intended to be the first
in a series of pressurised turboprop twins, Xingu
sales have been modest, numbering about 110
(mid-1984) since its introduction in 1977. Significantly however, the Xingu outcompeted the US Beech
King Air C90 and Cessna 425 Corsair to capture a
French Government order for 41 trainers for the Air
Force and Navy.

While the thrust of Embraer's civil projects are
centred on local designs, foreign exchange pressures
and a desire to increase industrial capabilities led
to a comprehensive licensing agreement with US based
Piper Aircraft Corporation. On the heels of the 1973
oil shock, Brazil, representing the largest single
export market for US general aviation manufacturers
with 1974 sales of $600 million, sought to displace
costly imports through import substitution.[135] Effectively closing the Brazilian market on the basis of
the law of similars and through the imposition (in
1975) of a 50 per cent tax on imported light aircraft, Embraer acquired the licences to produce a
series of single and twin-engined Piper aircraft.
Production at Embraer's Neiva subsidiary is by way of
a three-stage technology transfer process. Beginning
with nominal assembly of completed structures and
systems, and proceeding to systematically substitute
locally-manufactured components, by the end of Phase-
III, approximately 66 to 70 per cent of the aircraft
will be of Brazilian origin – excepting those components which cannot be economically produced in Brazil. In addition to developing Tier I activities,
the Piper programme is aimed at expanding Brazil's
subcontractor base. After a decade of production
(between 1975-85), the Brazilian aircraft industry
manufactured greater than 1,800 Piper aircraft under
licence, with important balance of payments implications.

Whereas indigenous design efforts were the focus
of civil projects, Embraer looked towards a foreign
design to familiarise itself in the production of
military aircraft. Thus, Embraer acquired the
licence to assemble the Aermacchi MB.326 Trainer and
ground attack aircraft in May 1970. Renamed the
Xavante (EMB-326), Embraer has since delivered 166 of

the aircraft to the Brazilian Air Force, and even managed a number of export sales, including six to Togo and a further ten to Paraguay. On the basis of the production experience gained during the Xavante programme, Embraer began diversifying the military side of its operations relying on both domestic designs and co-operative and licensed production agreements. In terms of the former, independent efforts under the sponsorship of the Air Force have concentrated on the development of relatively simple trainer aircraft. Embraer began design and development work on a new basic trainer, the EMB-312 Tucano turboprop as a follow-on project to the Xavante. With an eye on both domestic and export markets, the Tucano gained initial support by way of an Air Force order for 118 aircraft with options for an additional 50. Brazilian sales were subsequently matched by an export coup whereby Egypt would manufacture 120 aircraft for its own and Iraqi use. Indicative of Brazil's ascendency in the world trainer market, the joint Egyptian/Iraqi purchase includes an extensive technology transfer programme with the Arab Organisation for Industrialisation responsible for final assembly as well as an increasing share of the aircraft's manufacture. The machine is also the subject of a licence-production pact with Shorts of the UK. In addition to the Tucano, the Air Force is also sponsoring the development of a cheaper piston-engined trainer, the Aerotec A-132 Tangará. Following funding of the prototype, the Air Force has indicated its intention to procure about a hundred of the aircraft which will provide sufficient impetus to launch production.

Aside from the independent design efforts for trainer aircraft, further development of Brazil's military aircraft production has been facilitated through co-operative efforts with foreign firms. To this end, since 1976 Embraer has been manufacturing components for the Northrop F-5E combat aircraft. However, "Since the early 1970s, Brazil has been trying to adopt a highly independent foreign policy, to defend its own interests rather than tying its international positions to those of the United States".[136] Thus, Brazil has looked largely to France and Italy for technology since these countries tend to impose fewer restrictions on recipient firms. As an extention of its earlier co-operation, Embraer entered into an agreement with Aeritalia/Aermacchi for the co-production of the AM-X light attack aircraft. The agreement calls for Brazil to underwrite about one third of the project's $420 million R & D costs (at a rate of $20 million annually) and will

see Embraer assume responsibility for approximately
30 per cent of the aircraft's production, including
development of the wing as well as undertaking final
assembly. As a relatively inexpensive multimission
aircraft, the AM-X is designed to meet stringent
budget requirements in both countries with the Brazilian Air Force expected to procure an initial 79
machines. At the same time, the AM-X would appear
well suited to Brazil's foreign policy objective;
that of becoming a reliable supplier of inexpensive
weapons within the Third World. In terms of technological development, the project will expand
Embraer's exposure to the use of composite materials
and NC machining. In respect to the former, Embraer
has entered into a technology transfer agreement with
the US Sikorsky firm involving the design and manufacture of composite material components for the AM-X
and the Brasilia.

The agreement with Sikorsky is also intended as
a building block for the development of a new lightweight helicopter. Brazil's initial entry into helicopter production was through the licence-production
of established French designs. Specifically, the
state government of Minas Gerais (with a holding of
52 per cent) and Aérospatiale (45 per cent) formed
Helibras in 1977 as a part of a ten-year programme
involving the assembly of SA-315B Lama (renamed the
HB-315B Gaviao) and AS-350B Ecureuil (HB-350B
Esquilo) helicopters. Again, aircraft production was
initially tied to military procurement with the Brazilian Navy providing the initial launch order, while
Brazil furthered its regional ties with subsequent
sales to Chile, Bolivia and Venezuela. However, Brazilian ambitions extend well beyond simple licensed
production of existing designs, as Ozires Silva
(Embraer's managing director) emphasises,

> Embraer is not interested in assembling somebody
> else's helicopters in Brazil either under
> license or with a duplicate production line.
> What we are interested in doing is to build a
> new-generation helicopter that will not be com-
> petitive with the Sikorsky line and can be mar-
> keted not only in Brazil, but internation-
> ally.[137]

Financial and technological constraints, however,
will necessarily demand co-operative programmes with
foreign manufacturers if Brazil hopes to link military procurement and domestic production.

All told, the Brazilian aircraft industry has
performed well in the years since the formation of

Embraer in 1969. Whereas the industry's output in
1969 amounted to a scant 30 aircraft, industry sales
in 1979 reached $142.8 million with Embraer deliver-
ing 436 aircraft.[138] Moreover, nearly 50 per cent of
these sales were in the form of exports, while the
remainder reduced imports. Factory floor space has
increased from 117,820 m² in 1978 to 238,000 m² by
mid-1984, with employment increasing over the same
period by nearly 70 per cent and totalling 7,300. On
the basis of protecting the domestic market and inte-
grating defence procurement with aircraft development, the Brazilian Government has successfully nurtured the industry. As a result, a number of
objectives have been realised including the expansion
of the economy's technological and industrial base,
the reduction of the reliance on imported aircraft,
and the development of an export industry. In addition, the expansion of Embraer's military aircraft
production capabilities has furthered Brazil's geopolitical aims, as is evidenced by the destination of
export sales. By the same token, Brazil is coming to
depend on military programmes. To the extent that
defence spending has negative consequences for
national development, this course of development will
impose political and economic pressures on the Brazilian Government. With intense competition in
international markets and given the increasing tendency for export sales to be tied to offset agreements, returns on foreign sales will be diluted and
therein will place additional onus on state support
for the industry. Furthermore, continued export success will no doubt place increasing pressures on the
government to decrease trade barriers, and thus open
up the Brazilian market. Finally, despite the sizeable inroads made in the development of the industry,
production is still highly dependent on foreign technology, especially in terms of aeroengines, avionics
and advanced design.

NOTES AND REFERENCES

1. Raimo Vayrynen, 'Semiperipheral Countries in
the Global Economic and Military Order', in Helena
Tuomi and Raimo Vayrynen, (eds.), Militarization and
Arms Production, (Croom Helm, London, 1983),
pp.163-192. Quote is from p.167.
2. Concerning the structural changes emanating
from technological change and the changing labour
process see for example: I. M. Clarke, 'The Changing
International Division of Labour Within ICI', in M.
Taylor and N. Thrift (eds.), The Geography of

Multinationals, (Croom Helm, London, 1982),
pp.90-116, A. Lipietz, 'Towards Global Fordism?', New
Left Review, 132 (March/April, 1982), pp.33-47 and
OECD, The Impact of the Newly-Industrialising Countries on Production and Trade in Manufacturing,
(OECD, Paris, 1979). In respect to industrial policies, see F. Gerard Adams and Lawrence R. Klein
(eds.), Industrial Policies for Growth and Competitiveness, (Lexington Books, Toronto, 1983).
     3. Victoria Curzon Price, Industrial Policies in
the European Community, (St. Martin's Press, New
York, 1981).
     4. Ibid, and Dennis Swann, Competition and
Industrial Policy in the European Community,
(Methuen, London, 1983).
     5. F. Gerard Adams and C. Andrea Bollino, 'Mean-
ing of Industrial Policy', in Adams and Klein
(eds.), Industrial Policies for Growth and Competitiveness, 1983, pp.13-20.
     6. See Gerald M. Meier, Leading Issues in Eco-
nomic Development, (Oxford University Press, New
York, 3rd edition,1976), and Michael Roemer 'Dependence and Industrialization Strategies', World Development, 9 (1981), pp.429-434.
     7. World Bank, World Development Report, 1981.
     8. Ibid, p.149.
     9. F. Gerard Adams and Shinichi Ichimura, 'In-
dustrial Policy in Japan', in Adams and Klein
(eds.), Industrial Policies, pp.307-330.
     10. Ibid, p.316.
     11. OECD, The Industrial Policy of Japan, (OECD,
Paris, 1972), p.15.
     12. Interavia, 10, 1971, p.1151.
     13. The absence of national armed forces ema-
nated from the country's postwar 'peace' Constitu-
tion, which in Article 9 reads:
     Aspiring sincerely to an international peace
     based on justice and order the Japanese forever
     renounce war as a sovereign right of the nation
     and the threat of force as a means of settling
     international disputes.
     In order to accomplish the aim of the preceding
     paragraph, land, sea, and air forces, as well as
     other war potential, will never be maintained.
     The right of belligerency of the State will not
     be recognized.
Cited in Daniel I. Okimoto, 'The Economics of
National Defense' in Daniel I. Okimoto (ed.), Japan's
Economy: Coping with Change in the International
Environment, (Westview Press, Boulder, Colorado,
1982), p.235.
     14. The JDA makes decisions on the procurement

of aircraft based on mission requirements of the SDF. These procurement decisions are then passed on to MITI which then decides which firms will build JDA aircraft.

15. G. R. Hall and R. E. Johnson, 'Transfers of United States Aerospace Technology to Japan', in Raymond Vernon (ed.), <u>The Technology Factor in International Trade</u>, (NBER, New York, 1970), pp.305-358.
16. <u>Jane's 1961-62</u>.
17. G. R. Hall and R. E. Johnson, 'Transfers', p.325.
18. Ibid, pp.326-328.
19. Ibid, pp.352-3.
20. AW & ST, 4 February 1980, p.47.
21. AW & ST, 24 April 1978, p.16.
22. <u>Jane's 1984-85</u>.
23. AW & ST, 4 February 1980, p.47.
24. AW & ST, 12 June 1973, p.23.
25. AW & ST, 4 February 1980, p.42-43.
26. <u>Jane's 1961-62</u>. In addition to the LM-1 derivative, Fuji also developed the KM-2 two-seat primary trainer version under a SDF contract for 10 aircraft. Similarly, Fuji produced a STOL version of the L-19, which was previously produced under a Cessna licence.
27. <u>Jane's 1971-72</u>. The basic differences between the P2V-7 and P-2J is that the latter has a longer fuselage, as well as redesigned landing gear and turboprop (as opposed to piston) engines.
28. <u>Interavia</u>, 6, 1966, p.906.
29. <u>Jane's 1984-85</u>.
30. AW & ST, 18 March 1985, p.72.
31. AW & ST, 12 January 1970, p.59.
32. AW & ST, 19 April 1982, p.11.
33. AW & ST, 4 February 1980, p.53.
34. Both of the conditions have arisen from Japan's renouncement of the use of force to solve international disputes (see footnote 13). The one per cent ceiling on defence expenditure, while not constitutionally entrenched, has emerged through interplay of domestic political forces to such an extent that Diet attempts to exceed this level are considered tantamount to constitutional breach.
35. <u>Jane's 1961-62</u>. The YS-11 project was originally advocated by MITI in 1956, and placed under the Transport Aircraft Development Association in 1957.
36. <u>Interavia</u>, 6, 1966, p.906.
37. <u>Interavia</u>, 10, 1983, p.1094.
38. <u>Interavia</u>, 10, 1976, p.967.
39. <u>Aerospace America</u>, March 1985, p.61. Similar problems have confronted Romania's young aircraft

industry in its efforts to sell the Rombac 1-11 airliner.

40. Interavia, 18, 1970, p.974.
41. AW & ST, 19 January 1970, pp.69, 71, 73.
42. AW & ST, 1 September 1980, p.125; Interavia, 10, 1976, p.967.
43. AW & ST, 9 November 1981, p.164.
44. FI, 1 December 1984, p.1435.
45. Interavia, 10, 1983, p.1095. JADC was formed out of the CTDC to manage the YXX programme, while existing 767 work was taken over by the Commercial Airplane Company.
46. AW & ST, 23 January 1983, p.30; 19 March 1984, p.32.
47. Interavia, 10, 1971, p.1152.
48. AW & ST, 5 March 1973, p.9.
49. Jane's 1984-85. Since its introduction in the early 1960s 15 versions of the MU-2 have been offered, the most recent of which are the Marquise (6-11 passengers) and the Solitaire (6-9 passengers).
50. Interavia, 10, 1983, p.1096. In September 1983 MAI announced the development of a more powerful Diamond II using two P & WC JT15D-5 turbofans.
51. AW & ST, 25 March 1985, p.81.
52. For example, aerospace sales accounted for 12, 18.2, 4.4, 11.7 and 8.5 per cent of MHI, Kawasaki, Fuji, Shin Meiwa and IHI respectively for the fiscal year ending 31 March 1983. AW & ST, 20 June 1983, p.52.
53. Canada, Aerospace in Canada - Outlook and Strategy, 1983, p.1-1.
54. Ibid, p.3-2.
55. Ibid, p.3-7.
56. While DHC, Canadair, and P & WC tailor most of their output to civil markets, there are none the less military applications of their products, for example, P & WC supplies the engine for Brazil's Tucano military trainer.
57. W. McAndrew, 'The Early Days of Aircraft Acquisition in Canadian Military Aviation', Canadian Defence Quarterly, 12 (1982), p.42.
58. Cited in R. D. Cuff and J. L. Granastein, Ties That Bind: Canadian-American Relations in Wartime From the Great War to the Cold War, (Hakkert, Toronto, 1977), p.69.
59. Michael Rich et al, Multinational Coproduction of Military Aerospace Systems, 1981, Appendix A.
60. AW & ST, 12 April 1975, p.17.
61. Canada, Economic Development for Canada in the 1980s, (November 1981), p.2.
62. AW & ST, 20 June 1983, p.25.
63. Financial Post of Toronto, 17 March 1984.

64. AW & ST, 7 May 1984, p.95.
65. AW & ST, 3 September 1984, p.226.
66. Canada, Aerospace in Canada, p.4-8.
67. AW & ST, 7 May 1984, p.98.
68. Financial Post, 3 December 1983.
69. AW & ST, 9 August 1982, p.17.
70. AW & ST, 30 May 1983, p.111.
71. AW & ST, 25 October 1982, p.16.
72. AW & ST, 31 March 1975, p.20.
73. AW & ST, 12 November 1984, p.19. The Greek decision to split its procurement between the French Mirage 2000 and the US F-16 (in order to give the country greater political flexibility should the nation become involved in a conflict with Turkey) would also appear to vindicate the validity of sovereignty concerns in offset agreements. See Interavia, 9,1984, p.853.
74. Michael Rich et al, Multinational Coproduction, p.vii.
75. AW & ST, 9 August 1982, p.17.
76. Financial Post, 4 June 1983, p.18.
77. Financial Post, 15 April 1978 (supplement), p.20.
78. AW & ST, 26 November 1979, p.34.
79. AW & ST, 5 November 1979, p.48.
80. Financial Post, 17 May 1980, p.52.
81. Financial Post, 19 April 1980, p.12; 17 May 1980, p.51.
82. AW & ST, 31 December 1979, p.11.
83. Financial Post, 19 April 1980, p.12.
84. Financial Post, 4 June 1983, p.18.
85. Financial Post, 19 April 1980, p.12.
86. AW & ST, 12 September 1983, p.32.
87. AW & ST, 14 May 1984, p.26.
88. AW & ST, 12 November 1984, p.18.
89. AW & ST, 20 August 1984, p.22.
90. AW & ST, 6 June 1983, p.28.
91. Interavia, 8, 1983, p.859.
92. Andreas C. Tsantis and Roy Pepper, Romania: The Industrialisation of an Agrarian Economy under Socialist Planning, (World Bank, Washington, D.C., 1979), p.2.
93. Ibid, p.80.
94. Ibid, p.192 and p.80. Industry as defined in Romania includes mining and the extraction of hydrocarbons.
95. Ibid, p.514.
96. Ibid, p.466.
97. Jane's 1984-85, p.184.
98. AW & ST, 13 December 1982, p.62; AW & ST, 24 January 1983, p.52.
99. Jane's 1984-85, p.187; AW & ST, 28 April

1975, p.30. Britten-Norman was subsequently taken over by Fairey Engineering which went into receivership and was in turn taken over by Swiss-based Pilatus.
100. AW & ST, 8 November 1982, p.13.
101. Malcolm R. Hill, East-West Trade, Industrial Co-operation and Technology Transfer, (Gower Publishers, Aldershot, 1983).
102. Interavia, 8. 1983, p.859.
103. Ibid, p.862.
104. AW & ST, 13 December 1982, p.62.
105. Interavia, 8, 1983, p.861.
106. AW & ST, 20 December 1982, p.39.
107. Jane's 1984-85, p.187.
108. Ibid, p.124.
109. AW & ST, 3 January 1983, p.52.
110. World Bank, World Development Report 1981, p.136.
111. Ibid, p.150.
112. Ibid, p.151.
113. In fact, Habibie initially retained his Vice-Presidency at MBB while also serving as the head of PT Nurtanio.
114. Interavia, 12, 1981, p.1236.
115. AW & ST, 19 April 1982, p.71.
116. During the 1950s and 1960s Indonesia produced a number of aircraft types including: the Sikumbang, a single-seat counter-insurgency aircraft; the Belalong 85 basic trainer; the licensed production of the Polish PZL Wilga (renamed the Gelatik); and the Kepik and Manyang rotary-wing prototypes. In contrast, Romania and Brazil possessed at least a limited indigenous design and production capability.
117. AW & ST, 22 November 1976, p.20.
118. AW & ST, 26 December 1983, p.17; Interavia, 12, 1981, p.1236.
119. FI, 3 April 1982, p.783.
120. AW & ST, 26 December 1983, p.15.
121. Interavia, 10, 1984, p.1125.
122. AW & ST, 21 February 1983, p.25; FI, 19 May 1984, p.1334.
123. AW & ST, 19 April 1982, p.68.
124. AW & ST, 16 February 1981, p.33.
125. Jane's 1984-85, p.105.
126. Interavia, 10, 1984, p.1126.
127. AW & ST, 19 April 1982, p.69; FI, 26 February 1983, p.526.
128. For example, Nurtanio signed an agreement with FIAS, the aerospace personnel training establishment linked to France's GIFAS. Under this agreement Nurtanio will send senior factory inspectors and supervisors to France for training.

129. FI, 3 April 1982, p.783; 27 February 1983, p.526.

130. William G. Tyler, Manufactured Export Expansion and Industrialisation in Brazil, (J.C.B. Mohr (Paul Sieback) Tubingen, Germany, 1976), p.32.

131. Jack Baranson, Technology and the Multinationals, (Lexington Books, Lexington, Massachusetts, 1978), p.38.

132. AW & ST, 20 September 1982, p.115.

133. AW & ST, 1 August 1984, p.31.

134. The Ipanema programme began at Embraer's main facility and was subsequently transferred to Embraer's Neiva subsidiary in 1981. More than 500 aircraft had been built by the end of 1984.

135. Interavia, 12, 1984, p.1340.

136. Alexandre de S. C. Barros, 'Brazil' in J. E. Katz (ed.), Arms Production in Developing Countries, (Lexington Books, Lexington, Mass., 1984), pp.73-87; quotation from p.79.

137. AW & ST, 7 May 1984, p.17.

138. Interavia, 7, 1981, p.707; AW & ST, 31 March 1980, p.91.

Chapter Nine

CONCLUSION

Over the course of this century the manufacture of
complete airframes has evolved from the pioneering
visions of a few entrepreneurs to become an important
component of the industrial fabric of contemporary
AICs. The importance accorded the industry stems, on
the one hand, from its economic attributes and, on
the other, from its contribution to national defence.
Indeed, it is owing to the latter reason that most
AICs – and increasingly NICs as well – have attempted
to foster an aircraft industry. Since defence falls
within the purview of traditional state responsibility, government involvement in the industry is unavoidable. Moreover, as a so-called 'high tech' sector, the aircraft industry offers potentially
sizeable benefits which are obviously brought out in
the US aerospace sector's export, employment, and R &
D performance. Thus, by virtue of the industry's
strategic importance and its economic attractiveness,
the 'targeting' of aircraft manufacture in industrial
strategies has become commonplace.
        Technological imperative is the industry's hall-
mark. Rendered possible by an interactive combination
of demand-pull and technology-push innovations, market evolution and technical development have gone
hand-in-hand. On the demand side, the industry was
compelled to respond to the requirements of military
and civil operators. In terms of the former, the
exigencies of war and international tension forced
the industry into making faster and more survivable
aircraft. In terms of the latter, the industry had to
deliver a product capable of competing with other
modes of transport and ensuring airline profitabil-
ity. On the supply side, technology-push innovations
led to new opportunities in civil passenger and cargo
transport. What is more, much of that inspiration
came from antecedent military work. While subject to
cyclical swings like other industries, the aircraft

industry differs precisely because of its extreme
dependence on military work. Consequently, the 'wave-
cycle' of international tension is more of a regulator of the industry's activity levels than is the
conventional business cycle. Coping with the down-
swings in the 'wave-cycle' is, in fact, a persistent
problem of the industry. Refuge is frequently found
in MIC arrangements or direct state control of aircraft manufacturers.

In as much as state support for the industry has
been forthcoming to counter the perils of demand
cycles, it has been equally forthcoming in underwriting R & D costs. A solid commitment to R & D is a
prerequisite for market leadership in all aeronautical fields. Furthermore, with increasingly sophisticated aircraft has come inexorably rising development
costs – to the extent, indeed, that this factor constitutes the fundamental constraint (and barrier to
entry) confronting the industry. The relative paucity
of airframe firms and the industry's concentrated
market structure is an inevitable outcome of such a
trend. In order to come to grips with this constraint, the state has been obliged to absorb the
risk-burden associated with product innovation. Capital injections have been a common instrument for
socialising risk, while, less conspicuously, state
support is frequently extended through the provision
of military R & D and procurement contracts. To be
sure, governments may go further and both nationalise
firms and compel them to undertake R & D and production on an international basis. As far as nascent
aircraft industries are concerned, the principal way
to overcoming R & D risks (and technological constraints) is to rely upon the transfer of product and
process technology from established firms; primarily
through licensed production programmes.

By way of conclusion, it is perhaps worthwhile
to speculate on the future directions of the industry. As the 1980s unfold, US aircraft manufacturers
continue to dominate the spectrum of civil and military markets: Boeing and MD in the jetliner field;
Piper, Cessna and Beech in the general aviation market; and GD, Lockheed, Grumman, Northrop, RI and
Sikorsky, among others, in military markets. In large
measure, the technological and marketing advantages
accruing to these firms derive from their ready
access to the US market – the largest single source
of demand for aircraft in the world. On the basis of
a vibrant technological environment and the extended
production runs afforded by the domestic market, US
firms are bound to retain a dominant position in
world export markets. Yet, such advantages

notwithstanding, the dominance of the US aircraft
firms in all market areas is not certain. For example, US pre-eminence in the large commercial aircraft
area has come under increasing pressure. European
nations, in particular, have made a concerted effort
since the 1960s to overturn the virtual US monopoly
on airliner production. The resultant Airbus series
is posing a serious threat to the established market
leaders, Boeing and MD. Evidence of this success is
apparent from the doubling of the European share of
the world market for short to medium-range jetliners
between 1977 and 1982. None the less, the EEC share
of the vital US market for this category of airliner
amounted to only 6.2 per cent in 1982, while in the
long-range category, the EEC share was less than one
per cent. Notwithstanding such discouraging signs,
the fact of the matter is that if European governments remain committed to supporting their aircraft
firms, the outcome can only be the further erosion of
American dominance of the world aircraft industry. It
should be stressed, however, that this challenge will
not be the exclusive preserve of the Europeans. The
Japanese, for instance, have made it clear that they
intend to enter the commercial airliner market. In a
manner comparable to the Europeans, the Japanese favour aeronautical ventures which entail international
co-production.

As well as competing directly with the Americans
in civil markets, many countries have encouraged
their aircraft enterprises to carve out market niches
through product specialisation. This strategy has
figured prominently in the development of newer aircraft industries in both the smaller AICs and the
NICs as a whole. Especially noteworthy in this
respect is the record of Brazil and the market penetration of its Embraer product, the Bandeirante. In
a similar vein, a number of countries have scored
notable successes: Canada (commuterliners), Japan
(bizjets), Israel (bizjets), the Netherlands (light
airliners) and Spain/Indonesia (light transports)
come readily to mind. The fact remains, however, that
these ventures rely, in varying degrees, on aeroengines and avionics produced by the major AICs. The
signs suggest, in fact, that technological constraints confronting fledgling aircraft industries do
not reside in the airframe sector as such, but,
rather, in systems development, production and integration.

In so far as warplanes are concerned, the technological imperative will continue to push the aircraft industry to the 'fringe' of the art. By virtue
of the correlation between technological

sophistication on the one hand, and fiscal constraints of states on the other, the military market
will become increasingly balkanised. At the upper
end of the technological scale, the US lead will continue to be challenged by the Soviet Union. For their
part, the major European countries will attempt to
maintain an indigenous warplane design and production
capability which will reside somewhere below that of
the USA. In so doing, however, the Europeans will be
forced to rely on co-operative ventures among themselves for most, if not all, of their new-generation
military aeroplanes. As for other countries, the
state-of-the-art in warplane technology is simply
beyond their technological capabilities and, besides,
is out of reach of their fiscal capacity too. They
may, however, be able to gain some compensation from
the design and production of less costly and less
technologically-intensive alternative aircraft.
Indeed, for the NICs, military procurement will
remain one of the most effective instruments for nurturing indigenous aircraft production. To be specific, military procurement can be expected to provide, first of all, a basis for either independent or
joint R & D and production programmes and, secondly,
act as a means for acquiring foreign technology to
augment national capabilities. With respect to the
former, domestic procurement requirements have
allowed neophyte aircraft industries to enter new
product areas at minimal risk. Echoing the civil market, a number of smaller aircraft industries have
attempted to fill market niches for military aircraft, especially for trainers and cheap fighters
(e.g. Brazil's Tucano and AM-X respectively). The
most important development in the military market of
late has been the marked propensity of countries to
demand compensatory offset packages as an integral
part of foreign military aircraft purchases. Moreover, this trend is likely to intensify as escalating
development costs force the major airframe firms in
the AICs to rely increasingly on export sales. The
technology transfer inherent in such offsets can only
serve to upgrade the capabilities of NIC aircraft
industries.

Whether for purposes of defence or as a supplier
of transportation equipment, the industry will continue as an important component of national industrial strategies. In any event, the future development of the industry will be predicated on the twin
concerns of fostering technological change and coming
to grips with the lavish launch costs associated with
modern aircraft. In terms of the former, the issue
appears to be as much one of industrial capabilities

as it is of political will. Tempering the political
will, of course, is the ability to marshal the con-
siderable resources necessary for aircraft programmes. Yet, the political will to establish this
industry is boosted by the prospect of acquiring
strategic benefits from the mere possession of an
aircraft manufacturing capability. States will continue to induce and maintain aircraft industries even
if that entails foregoing an element of national sovereignty in order to pursue co-production programmes.
In other words, the highly 'nationalistic' aircraft
industry is becoming, willy-nilly, a truly international business. The need to share crippling R & D
and production costs leaves firms and their government paymasters no option but to foment collaborative
aerospace ventures at both the national and international scale.

Aerofoil	Structure designed to obtain an aero-dynamic reaction.
AIC	Advanced-industrial country
AIDC	Aero Industry Development Centre.
Ailerons	Moving surfaces to control the rolling movements of aircraft, usually on wing trailing edges.
Airframe	Aircraft without engines and systems.
All-up weight	Total weight of aircraft at take-off.
ATP	Advanced Turbo Prop airliner modification of BAe 748.
Autoclave	A high-temperature, high-pressure oven.
AW & ST	Aviation Week and Space Technology periodical.
AWACS	Airborne Warning and Control Systems.
BAC	British Aircraft Corporation.
BAe	British Aerospace.
BEA	British European Airways.
BOAC	British Overseas Airways Corporation.
Bonding	The joining of parts with adhesives.
CAD/CAM	Computer-assisted design and manufac-turing.
CASA	Construcciones Aeronauticas SA (of Spain).
Centre section	The central part of the wing, often fused into the fuselage.
Cure	The process by which adhesives are hardened by chemical means.
DH	de Havilland.
DHC	de Havilland Aircraft of Canada.
DoD	Department of Defense.
EFA	European Fighter Aircraft.
Elevator	A horizontal control surface to regu-late climb and descent of aircraft.
Empennage	The aircraft tail unit.
FI	Flight International periodical.
Fin	A fixed vertical aerofoil for stabil-ising the aircraft.
Flap	A control surface designed to increase the aircraft's lift or drag.
Fuselage	The body of the aircraft.
GAZ	Gosudarstvennye Aviatsionnye Zavody or State Aircraft Factory.
GD	General Dynamics Corporation.
GE	General Electric Company (US).
HAL	Hindustan Aeronautics Ltd.
HDH	Hawker de Havilland.
HS	Hawker Siddeley.
IAI	Israel Aircraft Industries.
IHI	Ishikawajima-Harima Heavy Industries.
In-line Engine	Cylinders arranged in a row rather

	than radial or rotary pattern.
Leading Edge	Edge of an aerofoil which first comes in contact with the air in flight (opposite to the trailing edge).
LTV	Ling-Temco-Vought; aerospace component which has variously been called Chance Vought, Vought Corporation and LTV Corporation.
MBB	Messerschmitt-Bolkow-Blohm.
MD	McDonnell-Douglas Corporation.
MHI	Mitsubishi Heavy Industries.
MIC	Military-Industrial Complex.
MITI	Ministry of International Trade and Industry (Japan).
MRCA	Multi-role Combat Aircraft.
MTU	Motoren-und-Turbinen-Union München.
Nacelle	Separate enclosure on the aircraft for containing objects or crew.
NASA	National Aeronautics and Space Administration.
NC	Numerically-controlled machine.
NIC	Newly-industrialising country.
P & W	Pratt & Whitney component of UTC.
P & WC	Pratt & Whitney Aircraft of Canada.
PBN	Pilatus Britten Norman.
PZL	Pantswowe Zaklady Lotnicze or State Aircraft Factory (Poland).
R-R	Rolls-Royce.
Radial engine	Radial arrangement of cylinders around crankshaft which are stationary as opposed to those in a rotary engine.
RDT & E	Research, development, test and evaluation.
RI	Rockwell International Corporation.
Rudder	Vertical control surface for guiding the aircraft in horizontal flight.
SABCA	Société Anonyme Belge de Constructions Aéronautiques.
SNECMA	Société Nationale d'Étude et de Construction de Moteurs d'Aviation.
Spar	A spanning part of the wing.
Spoiler	An air brake.
SST	Supersonic Transport.
Stabiliser	An aerofoil used to provide stability.
STOL	Short Take-off and Landing.
Undercarriage	Landing gear and wheels.
UTC	United Technologies Corporation.
VFW	Vereinigte Flugtechnische Werke.
VTOL	Vertical Take-off and Landing.

REFERENCES

ACDA, World Military Expenditures and Arms Transfers 1972-82, (Arms Control and Disarmament Agency, Washington, DC, April 1984).

Adams, F. G. and C. A. Bollino, 'Meaning of Industrial Policy' in F. G. Adams and L. R. Klein (eds.), Industrial Policies for Growth and Competitiveness, (Lexington Books, Toronto, 1983), pp.13-20.

_____ and S. Ichimura, 'Industrial Policy in Japan' in F. G. Adams and L. R. Klein (eds.), pp.307-330.

Adams, G. The Politics of Defense Contracting: The Iron Triangle, (Transactions Books, New Brunswick, 1982).

Angelucci, E. The Rand McNally Encyclopedia of Military Aircraft 1914-1980, (Rand McNally, Chicago, 1980).

Armitage, M. J. and R. A. Mason, Air Power in the Nuclear Age, (University of Illinois Press, Urbana, 1983).

Atwood, J. L. North American Rockwell: Storehouse of High Technology, (Newcomen Society, New York, 1970).

Baranson, J. Technology and the Multinationals, (Lexington Books, Lexington, Mass., 1978).

Barros, S. C. 'Brazil' in J. E. Katz (ed.), Arms Production in Developing Countries, (Lexington Books, Lexington, Mass., 1984), pp.73-87.

Baxter, N. D. and E. P. Howrey, 'The Determinants of General Aviation Activity: A Cross-Sectional Analysis' in G. P. Howard (ed.), Airport Economic Planning, (MIT Press, Cambridge, Mass., 1974), pp.177-190.

Bowyer, M. J. F. Action Stations 6: Military Airfields of the Cotswolds and the Central Midlands, (Patrick Stephens, Cambridge, 1983).

Boyd, A. The Soviet Air Force since 1918, (MacDonald and Jane's, London, 1977).

Cao-Pinna, V. 'Regional Policy in Italy' in N. M. Hansen (ed.), Public Policy and Regional Economic Development, (Ballinger, Cambridge, Mass., 1974), pp.137-179.

Clarke, I. M. 'The Changing International Division of Labour Within ICI' in M. Taylor and N. Thrift (eds.), The Geography of Multinationals, (Croom Helm, London, 1982), pp.90-116.

Cook, C. and J. Stevenson, The Atlas of Modern Warfare, (Weidenfeld & Nicolson, London, 1978).

Corlett, J. Aviation in Ulster, (Blackstaff Press, Belfast, 1981).

Cuff, R. D. and J. L. Granastein, Ties That Bind: Canadian-American Relations in Wartime From the

Great War to the Cold War, (Hakkert, Toronto, 1977).

Cunningham, W. G. The Aircraft Industry: A Study in Industrial Location, (Morrison, Los Angeles, 1951).

Degrasse, R. W. 'Military Spending and Jobs', Challenge, vol. 26 (1983), pp.4-15.

Dorfer, I. Arms Deal: The Selling of the F-16, (Praeger, New York, 1983).

EEC, 'The European Aerospace Industry: Trading Position and Figures', EEC Commission, Staff Working Paper, Sec.(80), 1237, Brussels, 23 September 1980.

Endres, G. G. World Airline Fleets 1977, (Airline Publications & Sales, London, 1977).

Erickson, R. A. 'The Regional Impact of Growth Firms: The Case of Boeing, 1963-1968', Land Economics, vol. 50 (1974), pp.127-136.

_____ 'The Spatial Pattern of Income Generation in Lead Firm, Growth Area Linkage Systems', Economic Geography, vol. 51 (1975), pp.17-26.

Estall, R. C. and R. O. Buchanan, Industrial Activity and Economic Geography, (Hutchinson, London, 4th edition, 1980).

Evans, H. Vickers: Against the Odds 1956-1977, (Hodder and Stoughton, London, 1978).

Fabian, F. M. 'The Soviet Industrial Base' in L. D. Olvey, H. A. Leonard and B. E. Arlinghaus (eds.), Industrial Capacity and Defense Planning, (D. C. Heath, Lexington, Mass., 1983), pp.65-69.

Fearon, P. 'The Formative Years of the British Aircraft Industry, 1913-1924', Business History Review, vol. 43 (1969), pp.476-495.

_____ 'The British Airframe Industry and the State', Economic History Review, vol. 27 (1974), pp.236-251.

_____ 'The Vicissitudes of a British Aircraft Company: Handley Page Ltd Between the Wars', Business History, vol. 20 (1978), pp.63-86.

Freeman, R. Thunderbolt: A Documentary History of the Republic P-47, (MacDonald and Jane's, London, 1978).

Gansler, J. S. The Defense Industry, (MIT Press, Cambridge, Mass., 1980).

Gardner, C. British Aircraft Corporation: A History, (B. T. Batsford, London, 1981).

Gibbs-Smith, C. H. The Aeroplane: An Historical Survey of its Origins and Development, (HMSO, London, 1960).

_____ Aviation: An Historical Survey from its Origins to the End of World War II, (HMSO,

London, 1970).

Gordon, M. R. 'Are Military Contractors Part of the Problem or Part of the Solution?' in L. D. Olvey et al (eds.), Industrial Capacity and Defense Planning, (D. C. Heath, Lexington, Mass., 1983), pp.93-102.

Gorgol, J. F. The Military-Industrial Firm: A Practical Theory and Model, (Praeger, New York, 1972).

Gunston, Bill The Encyclopedia of the World's Combat Aircraft, (Salamander Books, London, 1976).
_____ Jane's Aerospace Dictionary, (Jane's, London, 1980).

Hall, G. R. and R. E. Johnson, 'Transfers of United States Aerospace Technology to Japan' in R. Vernon (ed.), The Technology Factor in International Trade, (NBER, New York, 1970), pp.305-358.

Halpenny, B. B. Action Stations 4: Military Airfields of Yorkshire, (Patrick Stephens, Cambridge, 1982).

Hartley, K. and W. S. Corcoran, 'Short-run Employment Functions and Defence Contracts in the UK Aircraft Industry', Applied Economics, vol. 7 (1975), pp.223-233.

Hayward, K. 'Politics and European Aerospace Collaboration: The A300 Airbus', Journal of Common Market Studies, vol. 14 (1976), pp.354-367.

Higham, R. 'Quantity vs Quality: The Impact of Changing Demand on the British Aircraft Industry, 1900-1960', Business History Review, vol. 42 (1968), pp.443-466.
_____ Air Power: A Concise History, (St Martin's Press, New York, 1972). Hill, M. R. East-West Trade, Industrial Co-operation and Technology Transfer, (Gower Publishers, Aldershot, 1983).

Holloway, D. 'The Soviet Union' in N. Ball and M. Leitenberg (eds.), The Structure of the Defense Industry, (St Martin's Press, New York, 1983), pp.50-80.

Hornby, W. Factories and Plant, (HMSO, London, 1958).

Jane's All the World's Aircraft, (Jane's, London, various years).

Johnston, R. J. 'Congressional Committees and the Inter-State Distribution of Military Spending', Geoforum, vol. 10 (1979), pp.151-162.

Jones, D. R. 'The Beginnings of Russian Air Power, 1907-1922' in R. Higham and J. W. Kipp (eds.), Soviet Aviation and Air Power: A Historical View, (Westview Press, Boulder, Colo., 1977), pp.15-33.

Kaldor, M. 'Technical Change in the Defence
    Industry' in K. Pavitt (ed.), <u>Technical Innova-
    tion and British Economic Performance</u>, (Macmil-
    lan, London, 1980), pp.100-121.
_____ <u>The Baroque Arsenal</u>, (Hill and Wang, New
    York, 1981).
Kanter, A. <u>Defense Politics: A Budgetary Perspec-
    tive</u>, (University of Chicago Press, Chicago,
    1975).
Kennedy, G. <u>Defence Economics</u>, (Duckworth, London,
    1983).
Koistinen, P. A. C. 'The "Industrial-Military Com-
    plex" in Historical Perspective: World War I',
    <u>Business History Review</u>, vol. 41 (1967),
    pp.378-403.
_____ 'The "Industrial-Military Complex"
    in Historical Perspective: The Inter War Years',
    <u>Journal of American History</u>, vol. 56 (1969-70),
    pp.819-839.
Kolodziej, E. A. 'France' in N. Ball and M. Leiten-
    berg (eds.), <u>The Structure of the Defense Indus-
    try</u>, (St Martin's Press, New York, 1983),
    pp.81-110.
Kucera, R. P. <u>The Aerospace Industry and the Mili-
    tary: Structural and Political Relationships</u>,
    (Sage Publications, Beverly Hills, Calif.,
    1974).
Kurth, J. R. 'The Political-Economy of Weapons Pro-
    curement: The Follow-on Imperative', <u>American
    Economic Review Papers and Proceedings</u>, vol. 62
    (1972), pp.304-311.
Lancaster, J. 'Piper Aircraft's Vero Beach Plant: An
    Analysis of Locational Determinants in Light
    Aircraft Manufacturing', <u>The Southeastern Geog-
    rapher</u>, vol. 7 (1967), pp.22-33.
Lee, A. <u>The Soviet Air Force</u>, (Harper & Brothers,
    New York, 1950).
Lewis, P. <u>The British Fighter since 1912</u>, (Putnam,
    London, 4th edition, 1979).
Lipietz, A. 'Towards Global Fordism?', <u>New Left
    Review</u>, vol. 132 (March/April 1982), pp.33-47.
Lowi, T. J. 'Towards a Politics of Economics: The
    State of Permanent Receivership' in L. N. Lind-
    berg et al (eds.), <u>Stress and Contradiction in
    Modern Capitalism: Public Policy and the Theory
    of the State</u>, (Lexington Books, Toronto, 1975),
    pp.115-124.
Mansfield, E. <u>The Economics of Technical Change</u>,
    (Longman, London, 1968).
McAndrew, W. 'The Early Days of Aircraft Acquisition
    in Canadian Military Aviation', <u>Canadian Defence
    Quarterly</u>, vol. 12 (1982), pp.35-43.

McDermott, P. and M. Taylor, <u>Industrial Organisation and Location</u>, (Cambridge University Press, Cambridge, 1982).

Meier, G. M. <u>Leading Issues in Economic Development</u>, (Oxford University Press, New York, 3rd edition, 1976).

Miller, R. and D. Sawers, <u>The Technical Development of Modern Aviation</u>, (Routledge and Kegan Paul, London, 1968).

Molson, K. M. and H. A. Taylor, <u>Canadian Aircraft since 1909</u>, (Putnam, London, 1982).

Mondey, D. (ed.), <u>The Complete Illustrated Encyclopedia of the World's Aircraft</u>, (A & W Publishers Inc., New York, 1973).

Nobbs, R. L. 'A Note on Aerospace Collaboration', <u>Journal of Common Market Studies</u>, vol. 14 (1976), pp.368-371.

Nocifora, E. 'Poles of Development and the Southern Question', <u>International Journal of Urban and Regional Research</u>, vol. 2 (1978), pp.361-378.

OECD, <u>The Industrial Policy of Japan</u>, (OECD, Paris, 1972).

_____ <u>The Impact of Newly-Industrialising Countries on Production and Trade in Manufacturing</u>, (OECD, Paris, 1979).

Okimoto, D. I. (ed.), <u>Japan's Economy: Coping with Change in the International Environment</u>, (Westview Press, Boulder, Colo., 1982).

Peck, M. J. and F. M. Scherer, <u>The Weapons Acquisition Process: An Economic Analysis</u>, (Harvard University Press, Cambridge, Mass., 1962).

Penrose, H. <u>British Aviation: The Pioneer Years</u>, (Putnam, London, 1967).

Phillips, A. <u>Technology and Market Structure</u>, (D. C. Heath, Lexington, Mass., 1971).

Plowden Report, <u>Report of the Committee of Inquiry into the Aircraft Industry</u>, (Cmnd. 2853, HMSO, London, 1965).

Price, V. C. <u>Industrial Policies in the European Community</u>, (St Martin's Press, New York, 1981).

Purcell, C. W. (ed.), <u>The Military-Industrial Complex</u>, (Harper & Row, New York, 1972).

Rae, J. B. <u>Climb to Greatness: The American Aircraft Industry, 1920-1960</u>, (MIT Press, Cambridge, Mass., 1968).

Rallo, J. 'The European Community's Industrial Policy Revisited: The Case of Aerospace', <u>Journal of Common Market Studies</u>, vol. 22 (1984), pp.245-267.

Rayner Report, <u>Government Organisation for Defence Procurement and Civil Aerospace</u>, (Cmnd. 4641, HMSO, London, 1971).

Rich, M. et al, Multinational Coproduction of
    Military Aerospace Systems, (Rand Corporation,
    Santa Monica, Calif., October 1981).
Robertson, B. British Military Aircraft Serials,
    (Patrick Stephens, Cambridge, 1979).
Roeme, M. 'Dependence and Industrialisation Strat-
    egies', World Development, vol. 9 (1981),
    pp.429-434.
Rossi, S. A. 'Italy' in N. Ball and M. Leitenberg
    (eds.), The Structure of the Defense Industry,
    (St Martin's Press, New York, 1983), pp.214-256.
Schmookler, J. Invention and Economic Growth, (Har-
    vard University Press, Cambridge, Mass., 1966).
Scott, J. D. Vickers: A History, (Weidenfeld and
    Nicolson, London, 1962).
Sealy, K. R. The Geography of Air Transport, (Hutch-
    inson, London, 1966).
Simonson, G. R. 'Missile and Creative Destruction in
    the American Aircraft Industry, 1956-61', Busi-
    ness History Review, vol. 38 (1964), pp.302-314.
Singh, P. Aircraft of the Indian Air Force, 1933-73,
    (The English Book Store, New Delhi, 1974).
SIPRI, Yearbook, (SIPRI, Stockholm, various years).
Spencer, F. A. 'A Reappraisal of Transport Aircraft
    Needs 1985-2000: Perceptions of Airline Manage-
    ment in a Changing Economic, Regulatory, and
    Technological Environment', NASA Langley
    Research Center, Hampton, Virginia, 1982.
Stone, I. F. 'Nixon and the Arms Race' in C. W. Pur-
    cell (ed.), The Military-Industrial Complex,
    (Harper & Row, New York, 1972), pp.221-235.
Straszheim, M. R. The International Airline Indus-
    try, (The Brookings Institution, Washington, DC,
    1969).
Swann, D. Competition and Industrial Policy in the
    European Community, (Methuen, London, 1983).
Taneja, N. K. Airline Traffic Forecasting: A Regres-
    sion Analysis Approach, (D. C. Heath, Lexington,
    Mass., 1978).
_____ Airlines in Transition, (D. C. Heath,
    Lexington, Mass., 1981).
Taylor, M. J. 'Industrial Linkage,"Seed-bed" Growth
    and the Location of Firms', University College
    London, Geography Occasional Paper 3, September
    1969.
Taylor, T. Defence, Technology and International
    Integration, (St Martin's Press, New York,
    1982).
Trebilcock, C. The Vickers Brothers: Armaments and
    Enterprise, 1854-1914, (Europa Publications,
    London, 1977).
Tsantis, A. C. and R. Pepper, Romania: The

Industrialisation of the Agrarian Economy under Socialist Planning, (World Bank, Washington, D. C., 1979).

Tyler, W. G. Manufactured Export Expansion and Industrialisation in Brazil, (J. C. B. Mohr, Tubingen, 1976).

Tuomi, H. and R. Vayrynen, Transnational Corporations, Armaments and Development, (Gower, Aldershot, 1982).

Vayrynen, R. 'Semiperipheral Countries in the Global Economic and Military Order' in H. Tuomi and R. Vayrynen (eds.), Militarization and Arms Production, (Croom Helm, London, 1983), pp.163-192.

Warford, J. J. Public Policy toward General Aviation, (The Brookings Institution, Washington, DC, 1971).

Whynes, D. K. The Economics of Third World Military Expenditure, (University of Texas Press, Austin, 1979).

Williams, G. et al, Crisis in Procurement: A Case Study of the TSR-2, (RUSI, Whitehall, 1969).

268

INDEX

269